DID YOU THINK THAT ALL JEWISH COOKING JUST HAD TO BE FATTENING?

Well, although chicken fat is definitely out, this modern, health-conscious cookbook offers over 200 taste-tempting recipes from around the world to help you cut your cholesterol and lose weight without sacrificing any of those traditional favorites. Replete with tables, charts, and tips for easy preparation of delicious meals, here is your passport to a kitchen full of healthy nourishment. And remember, you don't have to be Jewish to enjoy the wonderful recipes in

THE JEWISH LOW-CHOLESTEROL COOKBOOK

ROBERTA LEVITON was born in Brooklyn, New York, and graduated from New York University with a B.A. in chemistry, magna cum laude, and membership in Phi Beta Kappa and the Mathematics and Chemistry Honors Societies. She also holds an M.A. in chemistry from Radcliffe College and has done graduate work in biochemistry at New York University. Ms. Leviton has taught chemistry at Brooklyn College and DePaul University, and has worked as a newspaper reporter and contributing editor. Currently a student at the Harvard Graduate School of Design, looking forward to a career in city planning, Ms. Leviton lives in Newton Centre, Massachusetts with her husband and their two children.

THE JEWISH LOW-CHOLESTEROL COOKBOOK

by
Roberta Leviton

INTRODUCTION BY
Rabbi Meyer J. Strassfeld

A SIGNET BOOK

NEW AMERICAN LIBRARY

In memory of my father,
Ben Hammer

Contents

Preface

My first experience with heart disease was very frightening. One afternoon thirteen years ago I walked into my parents' home to see my father being carried out on a stretcher and my mother and sister quietly crying behind a door. My father was then forty-nine years old.

He survived that heart attack, stopped smoking, lost weight, and went on a low-cholesterol diet, all of which his physician had been urging him to do for years. The words "cholesterol," "saturated fat," and "unsaturated fat" began to have profound meaning for my family.

At the time, I was working as a research chemist on the relationship between the fat composition of formulas fed premature infants and the fat composition of their blood and adipose (fatty) tissue, I was impressed that within only one to two months, infant fats came to resemble formula fats.

My husband was then an intern in internal medicine. After reading about significant atherosclerosis found in young soldiers in the Korean War, we became convinced that a low-cholesterol diet was a prudent preventive health measure for people in their twenties as well as for the middle-aged. We decided to switch to a low-cholesterol diet ourselves and have followed one ever since. This book is an outgrowth of that decision.

Since we also have a kosher household, we had to conform to a double set of restrictions. Our experience has been that we can still enjoy the pleasures of good food while simultaneously keeping kosher and reducing the risk of heart attack with a low-cholesterol diet. By exploring new dishes and adapting old ones, we've had a good time gastronomically while keeping our cholesterol levels down. In this book I hope to share our experience with others.

The Jewish Low-Cholesterol Cookbook is for people who

don't care to spend all day in the kitchen. The recipes are uncomplicated. I've found them all easily realized, even with the active assistance of two toddlers.

Special thanks are in order, to my husband for innumerable consultations, to Ina Jackson for reviewing the manuscript, and to many friends and relatives for encouragement and recipes.

Introduction

This cookbook is indeed welcome, for it enables all who are concerned with cholesterol in the diet and with Kashrut to meet both needs easily and tastily. It further makes it possible to fulfill the Biblical Commandment "Take you therefore good heed unto yourself" (Deuteronomy 4:15) which is the basis for the Rabbinic interpretation of taking good care of the body and protecting our health. Maimonides in Hilchot Deot, Chapters III and IV, makes this verse the basis for all his advice and prohibitions concerning one's health.

The Laws of Kashrut (Keeping Kosher) are found in the Bible and were further expounded by the Rabbis during the past 2,000 years. Although various reasons are given for the observance of Kashrut, to the traditional Jew it is God's Commandment, and he sees it as the duty of the Jew to fulfill the Word of God.

Kashrut Terms

Kosher—properly prepared or ritually correct

Milchik—food that is or contains milk or milk derivatives

Fleischik—food that is or contains meat or meat derivatives

Pareve—food that has none of the above properties: a neutral food (fish, fruit, vegetables)

Kashrut Procedures

Do not mix milchik and fleischik food in cooking and baking. Do not interchange milchik and fleischik pots, pans, silverware, tablecloths, dishtowels, dishwashers, etc.

Do not serve milchik and fleischik foods at the same meal.

Meat and fowl must be properly slaughtered according to Jewish law. They must be purchased at a Kosher butcher shop or carry a reliable symbol if bought packaged. If it has not been made Kosher (soaked and salted) by the butcher, then it must be done by the purchaser.

Fruits and vegetables are considered pareve (neutral) and may be served with either milk or meat foods. However, if fruits and vegetables are cooked in a fleischik pot, they become fleischik, in a milchik pot, they are milchik.

Fish that has both fins and scales is considered Kosher and pareve. However, fish is not cooked together with meat.

Kashrut Symbols

The following symbols attest to the Kashrut of a product. Unless specifically indicated, one may *not* assume that such a product is pareve. Always read the ingredients.

1) Ⓤ —Union of Orthodox Jewish Congregations

2) 🄼 —Vaad Harabonim of Massachusetts

3) Ⓚ —Organized Kashruth Laboratories

4) Rabbinic Signatures

If in doubt, consult your Rabbi.

Controversies

Cheese—Most Orthodox Jewish opinions require that all hard cheeses be made under Rabbinic supervision. The non-Orthodox believe that this is not necessary since the rennet used in the processing of cheese has lost its identity in the process.

Wine—Orthodox opinion requires that all wines be made under Rabbinic supervision. The non-Orthodox do not have this requirement.

Swordfish—Most Orthodox opinions declare swordfish not Kosher. The conservative opinion considers it Kosher.

This is a brief outline of the most important Kashrut rules. With the help of this cookbook, I feel that you can conscientiously protect your own and your family's health and adhere to the age-old Kashrut traditions.

RABBI MEYER J. STRASSFELD

PART I

BASIC INFORMATION

Medical Rationale

My wife has asked that I write, from my training and experience as a physician, about research findings that pertain to the risk of coronary-artery disease, the disease that accounts for the vast majority of heart attacks. Rather than present all the data of all the studies on diet and coronary-artery disease, I prefer to provide only that information needed to make the decision, "Should I attempt to reduce my cholesterol and triglyceride blood level?" (Cholesterol is a white, waxy, fat-like substance found in animal tissues and fluids. Triglycerides are neutral fats derived from glycerine and three fatty-acid molecules.)

Coronary-artery disease kills more people than does any other disease. Thus, you are more likely to die from coronary-artery disease than from any other.

Each of the following has been implicated in the occurence of coronary-artery disease: elevated levels of blood cholesterol and triglycerides, smoking, high blood pressure, physical inactivity, environmental stresses, personality features (e.g., being competitive and time-conscious), water hardness, obesity, and family history of coronary-artery disease. Fortunately, the three most important risk factors (elevated blood-cholesterol and triglyceride levels, smoking, and high blood pressure) can be modified. Thus, two points deserve emphasis: first, coronary-artery disease does not have a single cause; second, in order to minimize your risk of coronary-artery disease, you should attempt to eliminate as many risk factors as possible.

The evidence is very impressive that people with elevated levels of cholesterol and/or triglycerides in their blood are at greater risk of coronary-artery disease than those whose levels are lower. Equally impressive is the evidence that people with elevated blood levels of these substances can reduce their risk of coronary-artery disease by lowering those levels.

There are several reasons for elevated levels of cholesterol and/or triglycerides in the blood. Most commonly, at present, such levels are viewed as diet-induced. Occasionally, the elevated levels reflect inherited metabolic traits. This possibility should be considered if one has a relative who had a heart attack before age 55. To date, all of the inherited disorders of fat metabolism can be diagnosed by blood tests. Infrequently, the elevated levels of cholesterol and triglycerides may be expressions of an underlying disease (e.g., diabetes, inadequate production of thyroid hormone, certain kidney and liver disorders).

No matter what the cause of the elevated blood-cholesterol and triglyceride levels (whether a familial metabolic disorder, consumption of a diet high in saturated fats, or a combination of these two), a diet low in cholesterol and saturated fats is an important part of a program to lower these levels.

A diet with a high content of cholesterol and saturated fats is called an atherogenic diet because it promotes atherosclerosis, the process that underlies coronary-artery disease. In atherosclerosis, fatty deposits form on the inner surface of the arteries, sometimes preventing free flow of blood.

One of the many controversies that exist in clinical medicine is concerned with who should be on a diet low in cholesterol and saturated fats. Some physicians advise that only those with elevated blood levels of cholesterol and triglycerides follow such a diet. Others, however, go so far as to advise that all children be provided diets that are not atherogenic. Two reasons are usually offered for "starting them young." First, children will learn lifelong good health habits early, and thus not have to unlearn old habits before replacing them with new ones. Second, coronary-artery atherosclerosis has been found in an appreciable portion of men who died in their late teens and early twenties as victims of automobile accidents and military activities.

Since *you* probably missed the opportunity to grow up with a non-atherogenic diet, you may wish to have your blood cholesterol and triglycerides measured before deciding whether or not to change your diet.

In the United States, the "normal" level of blood cholesterol has been viewed as somewhere between 200 and 260 mgs. per cent. If your value is 250, you may think that your blood cholesterol is not elevated. However, in rural India and Africa, where coronary-artery disease is rare, the average cholesterol levels are about 150 to 180 mgs. per cent. Studies in the United States have shown that the risk of coronary-artery disease does indeed increase progressively as the cholesterol increases above 200 mgs. per cent. Thse observations have prompted some to suggest that perhaps a blood-cholesterol level below 180 mgs. per cent is ideal. Thus, if your blood-cholesterol level is anywhere above 200 mgs. per cent, you may very well be able to reduce your risk of coronary-artery disease by following the recommendations made in this book. The greater the elevation above 200 mgs. per cent, the more you can reduce your risk by replacing your atherogenic diet with a non-atherogenic one.

A sample of the residents of Framingham, Massachusetts, has now been followed more than 20 years for the development of coronary-artery and related diseases. I am indebted to H. M. Whyte of the John Curtin School of Medical Research in Canberra, Australia, for the data in the two tables at the end of this chapter. He extrapolated from data collected after the Farmingham residents were followed for 16 years to give probabilities of heart attack during 20 years of observation. One or both of these tables may help you decide whether or not you want to reduce your blood-cholesterol level.

If you are a 35-year-old man, reducing your blood cholesterol from 310 to 210 mgs. per cent would appear to reduce your risk of coronary-artery disease (before age 55) from about 1 in 7 to about 1 in 20. As a 38-year-old man, I find such data very impressive. Even more impressive is the apparent reduction of risk when, in addition to reducing the blood cholesterol, you also control your high blood pressure and/or stop smoking. The 35-year-old man who smokes, who has high blood pressure and also elevated blood cholesterol, has a 20-year risk of coronary-artery disease that is approximately 1 in 3, which is about 6½ times greater than the risk in a man who does not smoke and has normal blood pressure and a low blood level of cholesterol.

Table II gives data for women. Compared to men of the same age, women (especially before menopause) have a considerably lower risk of coronary-artery disease. In addition, smoking adds little to their risk. The single thing that women can do to reduce their risk most effectively is to keep their blood pressure controlled. Nevertheless, women can also reduce their risk of coronary-artery disease by lowering their blood cholesterol. I recognize, however, that the most compelling reason why many young women will want to cook as my wife cooks is to reduce their risk of becoming young widows.

So far, I've dealt with the potential benefits of avoiding an atherogenic diet. What are the costs, however? The time costs should be minimal. My wife has on occasion spent a good deal of time trimming the fat from a piece of meat. After I tried to do the same thing, I decided that no piece of meat was worth a half hour spent in removing fat. As a result, we rarely have any beef now.

A diet low in cholesterol and saturated fats appears to be eminently safe. The only putative side effect that I'm aware of is an increased risk of gall stones. In 1973, one publication reported that compared to men who ate an atherogenic diet, men who followed a non-atherogenic diet had a higher risk of gall stones. These were autopsy findings, and no evidence was provided that the gall stones were in any way associated with symptoms that might be expected with gall bladder dysfunction. Two years after this provocative report, I've yet to see one confirming the increased risk of gall stones in men on a non-atherogenic diet.

Thus, the diet recommended in this book appears to be not only effective, but also eminently safe and at virtually no sacrifice of time, money, or pleasure. I personally view the cost/benefit ratio as very favorable.

A somewhat different way of looking at the situation is to determine if a change to a non-atherogenic diet is cost-effective, that is if it's worth the effort involved in changing established habits. The tables are helpful in this regard. If 1,000 men aged 35 years were to reduce their cholesterol level from 310 to 210 mgs. per cent, 84 men who would have been destined to develop clinically evident coronary-artery disease during the next 20 years would be saved from this fate. To achieve this, however, 916 men would have had to consume the same diet without apparent benefit. These data, and knowledge that all the costs of the non-atherogenic diet are negligible, lead me to consider it extremely cost-effective.

Whether or not you are convinced that a non-atherogenic diet is for you, try the recipes that follow. You may want to continue with them simply because they're enjoyable and easy.

TABLE 1

Probability (per 1,000 Men) of Developing Coronary-Artery Disease in 20 Years

| | Age | Cholesterol Level (*mg/100 ml*) | | |
		210	260	310
A. Non-smokers without	35	51	84	135
high blood pressure	45	126	169	225
	55	182	209	239
B. Non-smokers with	35	89	141	220
high blood pressure	45	206	270	352
	55	289	327	370
C. Smokers without	35	84	133	208
high blood pressure	45	196	257	335
	55	276	311	352
D. Smokers with	35	139	216	326
high blood pressure	45	307	394	495
	55	418	464	515

Reprinted from *Lancet* 1: 906, 1975.

TABLE 2
Probability (per 1,000 Women) of Developing
Coronary-Artery Disease in 20 Years

	Age	Cholesterol Level (*mg/100 ml*)		
		210	260	310
A. Non-smokers without	45	51	67	91
high blood pressure	55	94	118	149
B. Non-smokers with	45	96	124	164
high blood pressure	55	170	212	261
C. Smokers without	45	55	72	96
high blood pressure	55	99	125	157
D. Smokers with	45	101	131	172
high blood pressure	55	180	222	274

Reprinted from *Lancet* 1: 906, 1975.

Basic Principles

The aim of a low-cholesterol diet is to decrease the risk of coronary-artery disease by lowering the level of cholesterol in the blood. This aim can be accomplished by (1) reducing the dietary intake of total fat, saturated fat, and cholesterol, and (2) simultaneously increasing the dietary intake of polyunsaturated fat. Some differences between a typical American diet and a low-cholesterol diet are:

	Typical	Low-Cholesterol
Per cent calories derived from fat	40-45	30-35
Milligrams cholesterol consumed daily	650	300
Polyunsaturated/saturated fats	0.3	1 or higher

In the typical American diet, much of the total fat and saturated fat come from meat, solid shortenings, whole milk, baked goods, and whole-milk dairy products such as ice cream and cheeses. In such a diet, egg yolks are the major source of cholesterol. A description of the kinds of dietary fats follows.

Cholesterol

Cholesterol, as mentioned earlier, is a white, waxy, fat-like substance found in animal tissues and fluids. It is a precursor of certain hormones. The cholesterol in our blood has either been manufactured by our bodies primarily in the liver or absorbed from foods of animal origin. Egg yolk and organ

[9]

meats contain especially high levels of cholesterol. No cholesterol is found in plant foods.

TABLE 3

Cholesterol Content of Common Measures of Selected Foods

Food	Amount	Milligrams
Milk, skim—fluid or reconstituted dry	1 cup	5
Cottage cheese, uncreamed	½ cup	7
	1 tbsp.	12
Cream, light table	⅛ cup	20
Cottage cheese, creamed	½ cup	24
Cream, half and half	¼ cup	26
Ice cream, regular, approx. 10% fat	½ cup	27
Cheese, cheddar	1 oz.	28
Milk, whole	1 cup	34
Butter	1 tbsp.	35
Salmon	3 oz. cooked	40
Halibut, tuna	3 oz. cooked	55
Chicken, turkey—light meat	3 oz. cooked	67
Beef. Chicken, turkey—dark meat	3 oz. cooked	75
Lamb, veal	3 oz. cooked	85
Heart—beef	3 oz. cooked	230
Egg	1 yolk or 1 egg	250
Liver—beef, calf, lamb	3 oz. cooked	370
Kidney	3 oz. cooked	680
Brains	3 oz. raw	More than 1700

Source: "Cholesterol Content of Foods," R. M. Feeley, P. E. Crimer, and B. K. Watt, *Journal of the American Dietetic Association*, 61: 134, 1972.

Saturated and Unsaturated Fats

Fats are classified according to their predominant type of fatty acid, either saturated, mono-unsaturated, or polyunsaturated.

Saturated fats tend to raise blood-cholesterol levels, are usually solid at room temperature, and are usually found in

TABLE 4

Foods According to Type of Fat

Predominantly Saturated Fats	Predominantly Polyunsaturated Fats
Meat—beef, veal,* lamb, and their products, such as cold cuts	Liquid vegetable oils†— corn, cottonseed, safflower, soybean
Eggs	Margarines containing substantial amounts of the above oils in liquid form
Whole milk	
Whole-milk cheese	Fish
Cream, sweet and sour	Mayonnaise, salad dressing
Ice cream	Nuts—walnuts, filberts, pecans, almonds, peanuts
Butter	
Some margarines	Peanut butter
Hydrogenated shortenings	Products made from or with the above
Chocolate	
Coconut	
Coconut oil	*Predominantly Mono-unsaturated Fats*
Products made from or with the above, such as most cakes, pastry, cookies, gravy, sauces, and many snack foods	Olive oil
	Olives
	Avocados
	Cashew nuts

Source: "The Prudent Diet"—New York City Health Services Administration, 1972.

* Lean veal and poultry (chicken and turkey) are relatively low in total fat. Veal fat is predominantly saturated; chicken and turkey fat is more favorably distributed between polyunsaturated and saturated fat.
† Peanut oil is not polyunsaturated to the same degree as other oils.

foods of animal origin. Polyunsaturated fats tend to lower blood-cholesterol values, are generally liquid at room temperature, and are usually found in fish and vegetable oils. Mono-unsaturated fats seem neither to raise nor to lower blood-cholesterol levels.

Saturated fatty acids have as many hydrogen atoms as they can possibly hold. Mono-unsaturated fatty acids have the capacity to absorb two additional hydrogen atoms while polyunsaturated fatty acids can absorb four or more hydrogen atoms. (See appendix for chart on fatty acid composition of selected food.)

In the process of hydrogenation, liquid unsaturated fats are converted to solid saturated fats by the addition of hydrogen. This is how many margarine and solid vegetable products are made.

To summarize the basic principles guiding a low-cholesterol diet, remember that you are aiming to:

1. Limit the amount of cholesterol consumed.
2. Limit the amount of total fat consumed.
3. Limit the amount of saturated fat consumed.
4. Stress foods high in polyunsaturated fats.

Food Guide

Food Group	Eat	Don't Eat
Meat Serve moderate portions (4-6 oz. uncooked) of very lean meat trimmed of all visible fat. Use veal much more often than beef or lamb, since veal is leaner.	Veal—scallops, shoulder roast, chops, breast only occasionally Beef. Some leaner cuts are eye roast, shoulder steak, London broil, and top-of-the-rib brisket Lamb—as lean as possible Soybean ground-meat substitutes—no cholesterol, generally less than 1% fat	Marbled and fatty meats Frankfurters Cold cuts such as salami, baloney, pastrami, corned beef Organ meats such as liver, sweetbreads, kidney, heart, brain. Liver may be eaten *occasionally* because of its high vitamin and iron content Ground meat, unless it has been prepared from lean, well-trimmed meat
Poultry Serve more often than meat since it is higher in polyunsaturated and lower	Chicken Turkey Cornish hens	Duck, goose—both high in fat. Avoid skin since much of the fat is concentrated in or directly under the skin layer

Food Group	Eat	Don't Eat
in saturated fat. White meat is leaner than dark.		
Fish Serve often. Much higher in polyunsaturated and lower in saturated fat than meat.	All fresh- and salt-water fish Canned fish. Fish packed in water or cottonseed oil is preferable to that packed in olive oil or an unspecified vegetable oil	Fish roe, including caviar
Eggs	Egg whites (essentially pure protein) unlimited. Whole eggs or egg yolks—limit to 3 per week including those used in cooking.	Sauces, desserts, or baked goods high in egg yolks
Nuts, Dried Beans and Peas, Seeds	All dried beans and peas: split peas, chick peas, kidney beans, lima beans, lentils, etc., soybeans Most nuts, especially walnuts which are highest in polyunsaturated fatty acids Peanut butter, un-hydrogenated Sesame butter, tahini Sesame seeds, sunflower seeds, sprouted seeds and beans	Macadamia nuts nantly mono-unsatu-Cashews (predomirated fat) Coconuts

Food Group	Eat	Don't Eat
Cereals and Baked Goods, Starches	All cereals except those granolas containing coconut Plain breads—white, whole wheat, French, Italian, rye, pumpernickel English muffins Hard rolls Matzo Angel food cake Cakes, pancakes, waffles, cookies, pastries, breads, etc. made at home with allowed ingredients All pasta products; egg noodles less frequently than others meal Rice, barley, corn	Almost all commercial muffins, biscuits, donuts, cakes, pastries, sweet breads, pies, cookies, pancakes, waffles, etc. Commercial mixes except angel food
Vegetables and Fruits	All fruits except avocado and olive. All vegetables	Avocado, olive (use sparingly) Vegetables prepared with atherogenic ingredients such as butter or cream sauces, or deep-fat fried in saturated fat
Dairy Products	Skimmed (non-fat) milk Skimmed-milk buttermilk Skimmed-milk yogurt	Whole milk Sweet cream, half and half Sour cream Whole-milk buttermilk

Food Group	Eat	Don't Eat
	Canned evaporated skimmed milk	Whole-milk yogurt
	Cocoa made with skimmed milk	Whole-milk sherbet and ice milk
	Skimmed-milk cheeses:	Ice cream
	cottage cheese (un-creamed)	Butter
	pot cheese	Whipped cream, frozen dairy top-pings
	sapsago cheese	Canned evaporated whole milk
	Part skimmed-milk cheeses:	Whole-milk and cream cheeses—
	Use less frequently: creamed cottage cheese	Swiss, American, muenster, bleu, etc.
	farmer cheese	Most non-dairy sweet-cream and sour cream substi-tutes (usually have coconut oil or hy-drogenated fats)
	American–type process cheese slices, available with fat content as low as 8%	
	imitation process–cheese spread, avail-able with fat content as low as 1%	
	non-dairy creamers made with accept-able polyunsaturated oil	
	whipped skimmed-milk topping	
Fats and Oils	Corn oil, safflower oil, cottonseed oil, sesame-seed oil, sun-flower-seed oil, soy-bean oil	Butter
		Ordinary margarines
		Hydrogenated vege-table shortenings
		Chicken fat or chicken-fat substi-tutes
	Margarine listing one of the above *liquid* oils as its first ingredient	Meat drippings
		Coconut oil
		Olive oil (very high

Food Group	Eat	Don't Eat
	Mayonnaise Salad dressings made with acceptable oils and containing no egg yolks, whole milk products, or other atherogenic ingredients	in mono-unsaturated fat. Use infrequently.) Peanut oil (higher in mono-unsaturates and lower in polyunsaturates than the recommended oils, but may be used occasionally, such as on Passover.)
Desserts	Fresh, canned, and frozen fruits Ices Gelatin desserts Puddings made with skimmed milk Homemade cakes, pies, cookies, etc., prepared with permissible ingredients Angel food cake Homemade imitation whipped topping	Ice cream Puddings, custards made with whole milk Commercial cakes, pies, cookies, etc. except angel-food cake Whipped-cream desserts
Snacks	Raw sliced vegetables Fresh and dried fruits Homemade popcorn Permitted nuts (especially walnuts), dry-roasted or roasted in an acceptable oil Hard candy, plain mints Pretzels Crackers containing	Chocolate Candies made with chocolate, butter, cream, or coconut Potato chips Commercial popcorn

Food Group	Eat	Don't Eat
	acceptable ingredients Sunflower and pumpkin seeds Soybeans roasted in an acceptable oil	
Miscellaneous	Herbs, spices, mustard, ketchup Soft drinks, wine, beer, alcoholic beverages (no fat but high in calories) Jams and jellies Powdered cocoa (considerably less fat than solid unsweetened chocolate and can be used occasionally)	Cream soups and other creamed dishes Commercially-fried foods Most frozen or packaged dinners Sauces and gravies unless made with permitted fat or oil and skimmed stock Solid chocolate

SOURCE: Food guide adapted from American Heart Association material. Reprinted with permission.

Shopping Guide

You'll have to become an accomplished reader of food labels when you decide to go on a low-cholesterol diet. The most important thing to know about label reading is that the ingredient present in greatest quantity is listed first and that subsequent ingredients are listed in decreasing order of quantity present in the product.

Some foods now have a Nutrition Information panel which may include information on sodium, cholesterol and unsaturated-fat content. This "nutritional labeling" is compulsory only when a special nutritional or dietetic claim is made or when a nutrient is added.

Vague terms such as "low-fat" or "partially hydrogenated" should be viewed with suspicion since they may well refer to unacceptable foods. One should also be wary of "vegetable oil" or even "liquid vegetable oil" since these terms may be describing the highly saturated and prohibited coconut oil. "Vegetable shortening" usually means a saturated or hydrogenated fat. Don't hesitate to write to the manufacturers with any questions you may have about the ingredients. Some food companies are a great source of information about their products. The safest policy to follow, of course, until you have the information you want is "if in doubt, leave it out." Listed below are shopping hints for particular food items.

Fats and Oils

Margarine—Purchase only those margarines in which the ingredient listed first is one of the recommended *liquid* poly-unsaturated oils such as corn oil or safflower oil. In general, soft or tub margarines are more highly unsaturated than stick margarine. To my knowledge, Promise tub margarine is currently the most highly unsaturated margarine on the market and this is the one I use. Diet margarines contain about half the fat of regular margarines and cannot be substituted for regular margarine in cooking and baking.

Oils—Of the recommended oils, I purchase corn and safflower oils for general use and corn oil for baking. Both are available in most groceries and have very high ratios of polyunsaturated to saturated fatty acids. Some of the lower-priced mixed vegetable oils are acceptable, but I suggest writing to the food company for information on the composition of the oil before buying it. I use peanut oil only for Passover and don't use olive oil at all.

Mayonnaise—Even though mayonnaise does contain eggs, its major ingredient is vegetable oil and it has a favorable ratio of polyunsaturated/saturated fats. The cholesterol content is about 6 milligrams per tablespoon. In deciding on the use of mayonnaise, remember that a low cholesterol diet usually allows 300 milligrams of cholesterol daily.

Dairy Products

Look for dry, uncreamed cottage cheese or pot cheese. If they are not available, use this partially-creamed variety or remove the cream by rinsing the cheese in a strainer with cold running water.

Commercial yogurt is made either from whole milk or a combination of whole milk and skimmed milk. Read labels carefully to be sure to get the part-skimmed-milk variety. Better yet, make your own from entirely skimmed milk. It's very easy and lots cheaper. See the recipe section for instructions.

Check with the local dairy for the fat content of its buttermilk. Most buttermilk is low-fat and acceptable.

Be cautious when buying cheeses with the descriptive term "made from part skimmed milk." Some of these contain insignificantly less fat than whole-milk cheeses, especially if cream has been added to their curds. It's most wise to verify for yourself the actual fat content as percentage of total cheese before purchasing. For purposes of comparison, Federal standards for minimum milk fat for many familiar cheese varieties (except cottage and sapsago) range from about 20% to 33%—for example, 25.4% for Swiss, 27% for muenster, 21.8% for Parmesan. Breakstone's farmer cheese and Borden's Lite-Line process-cheese slices both contain approximately 8% fat and I use them only occasionally. My family enjoys an imitation process-cheese spread, Fisher Count Down, with only 1% fat, made by Fisher Cheese Co., Wapakoneta, Ohio 45895.

Baked Goods

Most commercial cakes, cookies, pies, muffins, and sweet breads are unacceptable, since they contain saturated-fat shortening or whole milk or eggs. However, by careful label-reading, especially in health-food stores, you should be able to find at least a few acceptable cookies and crackers. For example, Cellu Rye Spice Cookies (Chicago Dietetic Supply, Inc., La Grange, Ill. 60525) and Mi-Del 100% Whole Wheat Honey Grahams (Health Foods, Inc., Des Plains, Ill. 60018) contain no milk or eggs and have soybean oil as the shortening. Finn Crisp Rye Bread Wafers (A.V. Olsson Trading Co., Inc., Bronxville, N.Y. 10708) contain no eggs, shortening or dairy products. Also don't overlook matzo which is now made in many different flavors (even pizza) as a year-round cracker.

Pastas and Grains

Since egg noodles do have some cholesterol (50 mgs. in a 2-ounce portion), it might be prudent to use them less frequently than the other pastas and grains. The total cholesterol content of the diet should be considered, however, and also that while a low-cholesterol diet usually allows 300 milligrams of cholesterol daily, one egg yolk has 250 miligrams of cholesterol. There is now available, in fact, a cholesterol-free egg-noodle substitute, "No Yolks," made by Foulds, Inc., Libertyville, Illinois 60048.

Fish

If you can find a reliable fish store with a high turnover of fresh fish, patronize it. If not, find out the days on which your supermarket receives shipments of fresh fish. Most important, smell the fish to make sure it has no unpleasant fishy odor. Really fresh fish is odorless, or almost odorless.

Frozen Desserts

Pass up ice cream and ice milk in favor of ices, which contain no milk. Baskin Robbins and Dorothy Muriel are two companies which make flavored ices. You may also be able to find diet imitation ice cream made with skimmed milk. One such product is Thin's Inn Dietary Frozen Dessert made at Gold Star Ice Cream Co., 921 East New York Avenue, Brooklyn, N.Y. 11203.

Soybean Meat Substitutes

These ground-meat substitutes are an excellent way to save money, cut your cholesterol and saturated fat consumption and eat lower on the food chain. Most products are designed to be added to ground meat, but the Creamette Company has a product called Protein-ettes which is a complete meat replacement. If you can't find Protein-ettes in the supermarket, it can be ordered from the Creamette Company, 428 North First St., Minneapolis, Minn. 55401.

Morningstar Farms Frozen Breakfast Patties, Links and Slices are interesting new imitation-meat products which are considerably healthier than their actual meat counterparts.

They contain textured soy protein, corn oil, and partially hydrogenated soybean and cottonseed oils.

Snacks

Since most people will nosh on foods they can reach for quickly, the key to encouraging the eating of healthy snacks is to have them readily available. Keep a tray of sliced raw vegetables in the refrigerator and don't be afraid to include vegetables usually eaten cooked, such as beets, turnips, zucchini, green beans, cauliflower, and broccoli. Fresh peas make a marvelous snack.

Keep lots of fresh fruit around, too. Melon cubes, apple slices, orange sections should entice even the most serious nosher.

Dried fruits and raisins are good healthy snacks. I like the advertisement which calls raisins the natural nosh. Dried apricots are a favorite snack of my 8-year-old daughter.

Peanuts are acceptable, but with their large amount of mono-unsaturated fats, have no cholesterol-lowering effect. Dry roasted nuts are preferable to those roasted in oil, unless you can determine that the oil used for roasting is a healthy one. Cashews have more saturated fat than most other nuts and should generally be avoided.

Potato chips are usually made with hydrogenated vegetable oil and should not be used. Check with the individual companies about the composition of the oil in commercial snack foods made with vegetable oil.

By careful label reading at health food stores, you may be able to find candy bars or other snacks suitable for a low-cholesterol diet.

One example is "MOO Munchies," made by Superior Products Co., 15614 New Century Drive, Gardena, Calif., 90248. These are made with the acceptable soybean oil and contain less than a milligram of cholesterol in a one-ounce package.

Miscellaneous Food Items

Thin-type chocolate syrup and chocolate pudding and hot-cocoa mixes contain little fat and are acceptable occasionally as long as they're used with skimmed milk. For baking and cooking, plain breakfast cocoa is preferable to solid unsweetened chocolate since cocoa has about half the saturated fat content of solid chocolate. For information on how to substitute cocoa for solid chocolate, see the section on adapting recipes.

Adapting Recipes

Many recipes can be easily adapted to meet low-cholesterol requirements with minimal flavor change. Don't be afraid to experiment with adapting some of your own favorite dishes. Remember that even crepês suzettes were once just an experiment.

I frequently use the following substitutions when adapting recipes:

High Cholesterol	Low Cholesterol
1. Sour cream	Skimmed-milk yogurt, mock sour cream
2. Sweet cream	Skimmed evaporated milk or enriched skimmed milk made with twice the recommended amount of powdered milk
3. Beef or lamb stew meat	Veal stew meat
4. Ground beef or lamb	Ground veal, soybean ground-meat substitute
5. Unsweetened chocolate, one square	3 tbsp. cocoa plus 1 tbsp. margarine
6. 1 whole egg	2 egg whites
7. Cream sauce thickened with egg yolk	Cream sauce made with skimmed milk and thickened with flour or cornstarch
8. Butter	Polyunsaturated margarine, or slightly smaller volume of corn oil, butter extract added if desired for flavor
9. Olive oil	Safflower or corn oil
10. Whipped cream	Whipped topping

Meals Away from Home

A low-cholesterol diet need not be abandoned when one has to dine outside the home since most restaurants offer at least several acceptable choices for each meal.

Dining in other people's homes presents a more sensitive situation than restaurant dining since one wants to avoid embarrassing one's host or hostess. Toward this end, as guests we sometimes will accept small portions of foods we generally don't eat, rationalizing these occasional lapses with the knowledge that we watch our diets quite carefully at home. Use your own judgment.

Here are some suggestions for meals which must be eaten away from home:

Breakfast

Grapefruit, melon, stewed fruit or fruit juice
Toast, English muffin or bagel with preserves or jelly. Ask that the item ordered not be buttered
Smoked fish
Dry cereal if skimmed milk is available
Hot cereal if you can determine that it was made with water or skimmed milk and that no butter, margarine or cream was added.

Lunch

If possible, become a brown-bagger, that is, bring your own lunch. Cottage cheese, yogurt, salad, gelatin, sardines, soup, chowder, and leftover fish or chicken can be taken in small thermos containers. I often plan my dinners to have these leftovers to be taken along for lunch. Sandwiches can be made of sliced chicken or turkey, tuna fish, salmon, chicken salad. Fresh fruit and homemade cookies or cake can be taken for dessert. In restaurants, the following possibilities usually exist:

Low-fat yogurt or low-fat cottage cheese

Sandwiches—Sliced chicken or turkey, tuna fish, salmon, chicken salad. Ask that mayonnaise be spread on the bread instead of butter or margarine

Soup—Clear consommé or vegetable soup

Salad—Vegetable or fruit with an acceptable dressing

Fish—Smoked fish or herring in wine sauce (not in cream sauce)

Dessert—Fruit, gelatin, ices, angel food cake

Dinner

Appetizer—Melon, grapefruit, fruit juice, fruit cup, tomato juice, smoked fish or herring in wine sauce

Soup—Clear consommé or vegetable soup

Main Course—Fish prepared without butter or cream sauce, broiled or baked chicken, Cornish hen or turkey, veal

Salad—Vegetable or fruit with an acceptable dressing

Vegetables—All except deep-fried or with a butter or cream sauce

Dessert—Stewed fruit, fruit cup, baked apple, angel food cake, ices

Meals for Children

We've tried to stress a low-cholesterol eating pattern for our own children, now ages 8 and 11. We encourage them to drink skimmed milk instead of whole milk, have ice milk, ices or sherbet instead of ice cream, have few eggs and little meat but much fish and chicken, and choose fresh fruits for snacks.

For school lunches, our children take sandwiches of unhydrogenated peanut butter, salmon, tuna fish, and sliced chicken or turkey. We've been able to order skimmed milk in containers for them from their public school food-services department.

Choosing low-cholesterol foods which will arouse enthusiasm in children need not be a problem. Since most children will usually joyfully eat anything connected with spaghetti, you might want to try including chunks of canned tuna, cooked fish or cooked chicken in the sauce. Cottage-cheese noodle puddings also seem to go over very well with children. My next-door neighbor keeps patties of ground fish in her freezer for her teenage sons to fry instead of hamburger patties when they're hungry. My own son enjoys the Morningstar Farms imitation meat products and cooks them himself.

In warm weather, I make frozen-fruit-juice popsicles in specially designed plastic molds available from Tupperware and other companies. My children adore these popsicles which can be made particularly interesting with food coloring or varied by using skimmed milk flavored with chocolate syrup.

Since children are the greatest innovators alive, we might look to them for food suggestions for a low-cholesterol diet. Our neighbor's youngest son has introduced us to the combination of cottage cheese and applesauce, and my daughter prepares a fantastic ice-milk mélange.

Difficult as it may be, try to avoid encouraging overeating in children. It can lead to their developing excessive appetites to plague them in adulthood.

In general, our goal with respect to our children's eating habits should be to set healthy life-long eating patterns for them. Probably the best way to achieve this is by setting good examples ourselves.

Jewish Tradition on Health and Diet

Trying to protect one's health through a low-cholesterol diet fits readily into the pattern of Jewish tradition. According to the *Code of Jewish Law* (*Shulchan Aruch*, Chapter 32: "Rules Concerning Physical Well-Being"), it is God's will that man's body be kept healthy and strong. The *Code* continues that it is man's duty to avoid anything which may harm his body and to try to form habits that will help him to become healthy. Choosing a healthy diet could be a current-day means of following this counsel.

The *Shulchan Aruch* says, further, that to preserve one's physical well-being, one should adopt the happy mean and eat neither too little nor too much. Also, one should eat only when one has a natural desire for food which occurs when the stomach is empty and not an indulgent desire which is a desire for a particular kind of food. The dieters among us might want to heed these statements.

In Deuteronomy, IV, 9, Moses cautions the people of Israel, "Only take heed of thyself." He repeats the admonition in Deuteronomy, IV, 15, "Take ye therefore good heed unto yourselves." These verses have been interpreted by the Sages as an obligation to take good care of one's body and to avoid any act or partake of any food which may endanger one's life. If one accepts the premise that atherogenic foods are life-endangering, then a low-cholesterol diet is a logical means of following the advice given us.

In Biblical and Talmudic times, the main contributions of Jewish medicine were in the areas of prevention of disease and the care of community health, especially through hygienic regulations. A low-cholesterol diet at this time could possibly be viewed as a continuation of Jewish concern with preventive medicine. The Talmudic view on the value of human life and the importance of health is expressed by: "The saving of life (pikku'ah nefesh) takes precedence over Sabbath" (Yoma 85a).

The Jewish custom of eating special food at the various holidays need not be abandoned on a low-cholesterol diet. We can still enjoy kreplach, taiglach, gefilte fish, tzimmes, potato latkes, hamantaschen, matzo balls, blintzes, cheesecake along with the warm connotations they provide for us. I've included recipes for all of these traditional dishes and more.

Weight Reduction

The days are over when being zaftig (plump) meant being healthy. Now we know that the overweight person has a higher risk of heart disease as well as other diseases.

While a low-cholesterol diet is not necessarily a weight-reduction diet, you may find that trimming all visible fat from meat before cooking, skimming fat from cooked dishes, using only skimmed milk and skimmed-milk cheeses, substituting yogurt for sour cream, and eliminating fat-rich desserts will help keep your weight down to a healthy level.

Remember, though, that calories do count. To lose weight you must either consume fewer calories or use up more calories or both. Even though fad diets may take off pounds temporarily, the only sure way to remain slim is to make eating moderately a permanent part of your way of life.

Here are a few suggestions to help dieters:

1. Keep washed, cut, raw vegetables available in the refrigerator for quick between-meal snacks.
2. Ask for tomato juice when offered a cocktail.
3. Try varied diced-fruit combinations for dessert.
4. Eat lots of salad.
5. Don't eat standing up. This in itself may eliminate many snacks.
6. Moderately increase your physical activity.
7. Buy a new article of clothing one size smaller than you now wear.

Reluctant Low-Cholesterol
Dieters

Once a person has had a heart attack, he or she is usually sufficiently frightened to be willing to alter certain eating habits. Motivating a person to change dietary pattern as a means of preventing initial disease is often much more difficult.

If some members of your family are reluctant to try a low-cholesterol diet, suggest their reading pages 3–8 (Medical Rationale) and American Heart Association pamphlets which can easily be obtained from your local chapter. Remind reluctant dieters that Dr. Paul Dudley White's maxim was "Death from a heart attack before the age of 80 is not God's will, it is man's will." He practiced what he preached and lived to be 87.

If you're still meeting resistance, don't be afraid to be sneaky. Home-baked products made with egg whites or Egg Beaters are unlikely to be detected as any different from those made with whole eggs. Introduce changes slowly and possibly imperceptibly. Go from whole milk to low-fat milk rather than directly to skimmed milk at first, and from creamed cottage cheese to partially creamed cottage cheese. Switch from butter to a stick polyunsaturated margarine and then later to a tub margarine. Gradually decrease the number of meat meals per week and the size of the meat portions while increasing the amount of salad and vegetables served.

Try very hard to get truly fresh fish. Often someone who claims to hate fish has never had the opportunity to enjoy good fish.

Set an example of healthy eating habits yourself.
Good luck!

REFERENCES

1. "Your Heart Has Nine Lives" by Alton Blakeslee and Jeremiah Stamler, M. D. Prentice-Hall, New York.
2. "The Prudent Diet"—Bureau of Nutrition, New York City Health Services Administration, New York, New York 10013
3. American Heart Association booklets "You and Your Heart," "The Way To A Man's Heart," "Eat Well But Wisely," "Planning Fat-Controlled Meals for 1200 and 1800 Calories"

PART II

RECIPES

APPETIZERS

You'll be pleased to find a choice of many permissible appetizers which are both tempting to eat and easy to prepare. You can even make a "mock" sour cream which can be used in your own sour-cream dip recipes.

For really quickie appetizers, serve herring or smoked fish on crackers with slices of cucumber, onion or tomato.

Nuts are acceptable on a low-cholesterol diet, with the exceptions of cashews, macadamia nuts, and coconuts. Remember that walnuts are highest in polyunsaturates and that dry-roasted nuts are preferable to those roasted in oil. Roasted soybeans which contain fewer calories than nuts are also readily available. My favorite nosh is popcorn, popped in corn oil. This has the additional virtue of being the cheapest appetizer I can think of.

Your guests who are watching their weight (and nowadays who isn't?) may appreciate a bowl of fresh green peas and a platter of sliced fresh vegetables which can include carrots, celery, broccoli, beets, turnips, scallions, cauliflower, cherry tomatoes, and radishes.

In the fall, roasted chestnuts and roasted pumpkin seeds make novel and healthy appetizers.

Interesting appetizers from the Israeli cuisine are fallafel which are spicy fried balls of ground chickpeas or fava beans. Fallafel mixes by Telma (an Israeli product) or Sahadi are available in many supermarkets. Water is all you have to add to either mix.

Canned rice-stuffed grape leaves can also be found in most supermarkets. Wash these off well under running water since they're packed in olive oil. Sprinkle with fresh lemon juice and serve with toothpicks.

Hot Appetizers

As a general rule, allow 3 pieces of hot appetizer per person.

POPCORN

¼ cup corn oil
⅓ cup dried corn kernels
salt

margarine
⅛ teaspoon liquid butter flavoring (optional)

1. Heat the oil in a 3 to 3½-quart pot until a kernel begins to sizzle when it is dropped in.
2. Immediately add the rest of the corn kernels and put the cover on the pot. Keep over high heat, shaking the pot several times, until no more popping is heard. Remove at once from the heat and empty into a large bowl.
3. Flavor with salt and melted margarine. Add butter flavoring to margarine if desired.

About 3 quarts popcorn

ROASTED CHESTNUTS

1. With a sharp knife, make 2 intersecting ½-inch slits on the chestnut. Opinions seem to vary about whether these slits are best made on the rounded or flat side of the chestnut, but we've had success with both.
2. Roast the chestnuts in a 400° oven for 20-25 minutes. Serve, warning your guests that the chestnuts are really hot.

TOASTED PUMPKIN SEEDS

In case you ever have occasion to open a pumpkin, be sure to try this recipe instead of throwing the seeds out.

1. Wash the pumpkin seeds well under running water and drain in a colander.
2. Spread the seeds on a baking pan and sprinkle with salt while they are still damp. Bake at 350° about 20 minutes or until the seeds are light brown.

ANCHOVY TOASTS

An amazingly easy and delicious appetizer. Perfect for when you have to get dinner ready in a hurry. Reduce or expand the recipe as needed, using 1 minced anchovy per tablespoon of margarine.

4 anchovies, finely minced
4 tablespoons margarine

5-6 slices white bread (depending on the size) with crusts trimmed off

1. Cream the minced anchovies and margarine together. Spread on the slices of bread. Cut each slice into 4 triangles.
2. Place on a baking sheet and bake in a 350° oven about 12 minutes or until gold and crisp.

20-24 slices

BAKED STUFFED MUSHROOMS

These can be made ahead, frozen and reheated. They're simple to make and delicious to eat.

1 pound (about 16) medium mushrooms
1 tablespoon oil
2 tablespoons sherry

¼ teaspoon salt
dash pepper
1 tablespoons bread crumbs

1. Wash the mushrooms well and separate the stems from the caps.
2. Chop the stems finely and sauté them in oil for about 5 minutes or until they are soft. (A wooden chopping bowl is very handy for chopping the stems.)
3. Add the sherry and continue cooking a few minutes.
4. Mix in the seasonings and bread crumbs and stuff the mushroom caps.
5. Bake in a greased pan at 350° for 25 minutes.

16 stuffed mushrooms

VEGETABLE KISHKE

I like this even better than the real thing. Surprise your friends with it before a dairy meal and see if they can tell the difference. It can be prepared months ahead and frozen until needed. On serving day, just heat it up.

8 ounces wheat crackers
2 carrots, coarsely chopped
6 celery stalks, coarsely chopped

1 medium onion, quartered
4 tablespoons margarine, melted
2 teaspoons salt

1. Pulverize the crackers in portions in a blender. This yields 2¼ cups of fine crumbs. Set the crumbs aside.
2. Finely chop the vegetables in the blender. I chop the carrots first with water which I drain off after chopping. Then I chop the celery and onion in 2 or 3 batches, adding some of the melted margarine to each batch. With a more powerful blender you may be able to chop the carrots right in with the other vegetables.
3. Mix the cracker crumbs, finely chopped vegetables, margarine and salt all together in a large bowl.
4. Oil 3 pieces of aluminum foil 8 inches by 12 inches. Form the vegetable-cracker mixture into 3 rolls about 1½ inches by 9 inches on the foil sheets. Roll up the sheets and fold the edges to seal. Freeze overnight or until hard.
5. Unpeel the foil and place the frozen rolls on heavily greased baking sheets or pans. Bake at 350° for 1 hour. Cut into ¾-to 1-inch slices.

30-36 slices

MUSHROOM ROLL-UPS

I'm continually amazed at how quickly this appetizer disappears from the serving platter. The filling can be prepared several days ahead of time. The final assembly takes little time and can be done shortly before serving.

½ pound fresh mushrooms
2 tablespoons corn oil
1 tablespoon sherry
½ teaspoon salt
dash pepper

1 tablespoon dry bread crumbs
12 thin slices bread margarine
1-2 tablespoons melted margarine

1. Chop the mushrooms finely in a wooden chopping bowl.
2. Heat the oil in a frying pan and sauté the mushrooms for about 5 minutes or until they are soft.
3. Add the sherry and continue cooking a few minutes. Mix in the seasonings and bread crumbs. If necessary, add additional bread crumbs to absorb any excess liquid.
4. Trim the crusts from the bread slices. Flatten each slice as thin as possible with a rolling pin.
5. Spread each bread slice lightly with margarine. Spread one tablespoon of the mushroom mixture over each slice. Roll up as if making a jelly roll. Place seam-side down on oiled baking sheets or baking pans. Brush with melted margarine.
6. Bake at 425° for 8-10 minutes or until lightly browned. Cut each slice of bread into 2 pieces and serve.

24 pieces

HOT COTTAGE-CHEESE PASTRIES

These are light, flaky and delicious. They're perfect for Shavuot or any dairy meal.

2 cups flour
½ teaspoon salt
½ cup plus 2 tablespoons corn oil

6 tablespoons cold fruit juice or cold water

Filling

1 cup dry cottage or pot cheese
1 egg white
2 teaspoons sugar

¼ teaspoon cinnamon
2 tablespoons halved raisins (optional)

Glaze (Optional)

1 egg yolk

3 tablespoons water

1. Stir all the filling ingredients together and set aside.
2. Stir the flour and salt together with a spoon until they are thoroughly mixed.
3. Beat the oil and juice or water together with a fork or wire whisk and pour all at once into the flour. Stir the liquid and dry ingredients together with a fork and then knead them a few times into a dough.
4. Roll the dough out in small batches on a floured surface (I use a kitchen counter top) until it is very thin. Cut into circles with a 3-inch round cutter.
5. Place a teaspoon of filling in the center of each round. Fold the round in half and pinch the edges together. Gently shape the semicircle into a crescent.
6. If a shiny surface is desired, brush the tops of the pastries with the egg yolk and water mixtures.
7. Bake 15-20 minutes or until golden brown in a 400° oven.

30 pastries

HOT FISH CANAPÉS

This is a kosher version of Chinese shrimp toast.

1 pound ground fish (scrod, cod, haddock, or any white fish)
1 egg white
¼ cup finely chopped scallions or celery
2 tablespoons finely chopped parsley
1 tablespoon cornstarch
1 teaspoon salt
dash white pepper
8 slices day-old thin-sliced white bread, each slice cut into 4 squares or 4 triangles
corn or safflower oil for frying

1. Combine the first 7 ingredients, stirring until well mixed.
2. Spread the fish mixture on the bread triangles.
3. Heat enough oil in a frying pan so that the depth of oil is at least ½ inch.
4. Fry the triangles, fish side down, in the hot oil for 2 minutes or until the edges are brown. Turn over and fry for another minute. Remove the triangles with a slotted spoon or slotted spatula and drain on paper towels. Serve immediately or re-heat for 5 minutes in a 350° oven.

32 appetizers

INDIAN POTATO FRITTERS

You might call this an Indian version of potato latkes. This recipe makes enough for a very large party, so halve it for a smaller crowd or plan to freeze some. Reheat frozen about 15 minutes in a 350° oven.

¾ cup diced onion	2 teaspoons salt
1½ cups peeled ½-inch potato cubes	1½ teaspoons cumin
	1½ teaspoons coriander
¼ cup water	1 teaspoon baking soda
¾ cup flour	corn oil for frying
¾ cup cornstarch	

1. Put the onion, potato and water into a blender and blend at chop speed just until all the potato and onion has gone through the blades.
2. Stir the dry ingredients together until well mixed. Stir in the potato-onion mixture and blend well.
3. Pour oil to a level of at least ¼ inch in a frying pan and warm over medium heat. Drop the batter by teaspoonfuls into the hot oil and fry on each side until golden brown, adding more oil as needed. If you prefer larger fritters, drop the batter by tablespoonfuls. Drain on 2 thicknesses of paper towels. Reheat in a 350° oven 5-8 minutes.

60-70 small fritters

FILO-PASTRY HORS D'OEUVRES

Filo dough is a paper-thin, silk-like dough made of flour and water and used extensively in the Middle East. Sheets of filo dough about 12 by 16 inches can be bought in one-pound packages fresh or frozen in Greek or Armenian groceries and many supermarkets. Frozen dough will keep for 6 months or even longer. It should be defrosted slowly in the refrigerator.

Use only a few filo sheets at a time since they dry very rapidly and crumble upon exposure to air. Filo sheets can be folded into many different shapes, but the triangle is the most popular.

Pastry

4 sheets of filo dough
3 tablespoons melted margarine

Cheese Filling

1 cup dry cottage cheese
½ egg white
¼ teaspoon salt
½ teaspoon dried mint flakes (measure and then powder between fingers)

½ teaspoon dried dill or
1 tablespoon fresh dill
2 tablespoons chopped fresh parsley or chopped scallions

1. Cut the filo sheets into strips about 4 inches wide and 6 to 8 inches long (about 6 per sheet). Work with only one strip at a time and keep the others fresh meanwhile by covering them with a damp dish towel.
2. Fold the edges of the strip toward the center so that the strip becomes 2 inches wide. Brush the entire length with melted margarine using a pastry brush.
3. Put ¾ teaspoon of the filling near one end of the strip. Fold one corner of the strip over the filling to form a small triangle, enclosing the filling. Continue folding the triangle over until the whole strip is folded.
4. Brush the top of the triangle with melted margarine. The triangles may be frozen at this point.
5. Place the triangles on a greased baking sheet and bake at 350°for 15-20 minutes or until they are golden brown. Frozen triangles may be baked without defrosting for 20-30 minutes.

2 dozen

Cold Appetizers

TAHINI

Tahini or ground hulled sesame seed is the basis for several unusual and flavorful Israeli and Middle Eastern spreads. It can be found in jars or cans in most supermarkets and health food stores.

Tahini separates, like peanut butter, into a thick, solid bottom layer covered by a thin layer of oil. Stir the oil and solid material into a smooth paste before measuring. This may take a while, but remember that once the tahini is well mixed the rest of the preparation is very quick.

¾ cup tahini
¼ cup water
¼ cup fresh lemon juice
1 clove garlic, crushed

½ teaspoon salt
2 tablespoons chopped fresh parsely

1. Combine all the ingredients except the parsley in a bowl and blend well with a spoon.
2. Garnish with the parsley. Serve with sesame-seed crackers or triangles of pita or Syrian bread.

EGGPLANT TAHINI—BABA GANOUSH

The smoky flavor of the eggplant is one you won't forget.

1 medium eggplant—about
  1 pound
6 tablespoons tahini
6 tablespoons water
1 clove garlic, crushed

3 tablespoons fresh lemon
  juice
½ teaspoon salt
2 tablespoons chopped
  parsley

1. Grill the eggplant over a gas flame or under a gas or electric broiler, turning occasionally, until the skin is black and blistery. The inside will be very soft. Peel off the charred skin and scoop out the pulp. Squeeze the pulp to remove bitter juices.
2. Combine the eggplant pulp with the remaining ingredients except for the parsley and blend well.
3. Garnish with the chopped parsley and serve with sesame crackers or triangles of pita or Syrian bread.

CHICK PEA TAHINI—HUMMUS

1 20-ounce can cooked
  chick peas
2 tablespoons chick pea
  packing liquid
½ cup fresh lemon juice

2 cloves garlic, coarsely
  minced
¾ teaspoon salt
½ cup sesame tahini
chopped parsley or paprika
  for garnish

1. Drain the chick peas but save the liquid. Put the chick peas, 2 tablespoons packing liquid, lemon juice, garlic and salt

in a blender container and purée. Add a small additional amount of packing liquid if necessary to facilitate blending.
2. Add the sesame tahini and blend it into the chick pea mixture. Serve with pita bread, crackers, and raw vegetables.

MRS. WISEMAN'S CHOPPED HERRING

All commercial chopped herring I've seen contains cholesterol-rich hard-boiled egg yolk. This recipe gives you a delicious and healthy herring salad minus egg yolk, of course. If boning a herring doesn't appeal to you, substitute a small jar of herring pieces for the whole fish and start with step 3.

1 herring
1 tart apple (not McIntosh)
1 medium mild onion (Bermuda, if possible)
1 slice rye bread with crusts trimmed off, soaked in

3-4 tablespoons red wine vinegar
1 hard-boiled egg white, chopped or cut in thin slivers, for garnish (optional)
salt, pepper, sugar, if desired

1. Soak the herring overnight in cold water in a glass or porcelain bowl.
2. Remove the head, tail, skin and bones. Cut into 1-inch pieces. Squeeze fish pieces to remove water.
3. Cut the apple and onion into chunks. Put the apple, onion, fish and rye bread into a chopping bowl and chop until very fine.
4. Season with salt, pepper or sugar if desired. Chill. Garnish with egg white if desired. Serve as an appetizer with crackers or as a luncheon salad.

MARINATED SALMON WITH MUSTARD DILL SAUCE (GRAVLAKS)

This Swedish dish makes an absolutely superb appetizer or luncheon dish. The recipe can be enlarged and made with larger pieces of salmon fillets if you're expecting many people. It can be served on rye or pumpernickel party-size bread slices or crackers if you want to avoid dishes for a separate course.

2 equal-sized salmon fillets, about ½-pound each
1 tablespoon salt
1 tablespoon sugar

2 teaspoons coarsely ground peppercorns
5 whole large sprigs of fresh dill (about ⅓ of a bunch)

Mustard Dill Sauce

3 tablespoons Dijon or other strong dark mustard
2 teaspoons sugar
3 tablespoons vinegar
dash pepper

½ teaspoon salt
½ cup oil
6 tablespoons chopped fresh dill

1. Place the salmon fillets skin side down on a large piece of aluminum foil. Mix the salt, sugar, and peppercorns together and sprinkle evenly over the pink flesh of each fillet.
2. Wash the dill and shake or pat it dry. Place the dill over one of the fillets. Cover the dill with the other salmon fillet, skin side up. Fold the aluminum foil up and around the fish.
3. Place the foil-wrapped fish on a plate or pan and cover with another plate or pan. Place several heavy food cans on top of all. Refrigerate 2-3 days, turning the salmon every 12 hours.
4. Remove the dill and scrape away the seasonings. Place the salmon skin side down on a carving board and slice it thinly like lox.

5. Prepare the sauce by mixing the mustard, sugar, vinegar, salt and pepper together in a small, deep bowl. Gradually beat in the oil with a whisk until a mayonnaise-like consistency is reached. Stir in the chopped dill. This can be prepared early in the day for use that evening, but it may separate if allowed to stand overnight or longer.

CURRIED CHICKEN SPREAD

This is one of the tastiest ways I know of to use up leftover cooked chicken. It's also excellent as a sandwich spread.

2 cups (½ pound) slivered cooked chicken
¾ teaspoon curry powder
½ teaspoon salt

4-5 tablespoons mayonnaise
dash pepper
2 tablespoons chopped parsley

1. Chop the chicken very finely in a wooden chopping bowl.
2. Blend in the curry powder, salt, pepper and mayonnaise.
3. Garnish with the chopped parsley if desired, and serve in a small bowl surrounded by crackers and celery stalks.

CHOPPED CHICKEN WITH PINEAPPLE

This may sound like an unlikely combination to you, but if you try it your curiosity will be well rewarded.

2 cups (½ pound) slivered cooked chicken
½ cup crushed pineapple drained

2-3 tablespoons mayonnaise
3 tablespoons chopped celery

1. Chop the chicken very fine in a wooden chopping bowl.
2. Blend in the other ingredients. Serve with crackers and celery stalks.

MOCK SOUR CREAM—I

This has the texture and consistency of real sour cream. It can be used as the basis for dips calling for sour cream.

12 ounces pot cheese or dry
cottage cheese

¼ cup lemon juice
⅞ cup skimmed milk

Blend all the ingredients together in an electric blender until very smooth.

MOCK SOUR CREAM—II

Blend equal volumes of dry cottage cheese and skimmed-milk buttermilk in an electric blender until very smooth. Flavor with a small amount of lemon juice.

ANCHOVY-SOUR CREAM DIP

This is my favorite "sour cream" dip. Drain off as much of the anchovy packing oil as possible.

| 2 cups mock sour cream | 1-2 cloves garlic, crushed |
| 2 tins anchovies, finely minced | 2 tablespoons minced fresh chives (optional) |

Stir all the ingredients together until they are well mixed. Serve with raw vegetables—cauliflower, beets, turnips, broccoli, mushrooms, etc.

TUNA DUNK

An extremely versatile and unusual dip. Try it also on cooked vegetables or cold sliced veal or turkey.

1 can tuna fish	½ cup corn oil
6 anchovies	2 tablespoons chopped parsley garnish (optional)
6 tablespoons lemon juice	

Put the tuna, anchovies, lemon juice and corn oil into a blender and blend until very, very smooth. Garnish with parsley, if desired. Serve with an assortment of raw vegetables.

LOX SPREAD

This is an excellent use for those inexpensive "lox bits" or "lox pieces" which are sometimes available. A 2-ounce can of anchovies can be substituted for the lox, but remember to drain off as much of the olive oil as possible.

| 2 ounces finely minced lox | 8 ounces farmer cheese |
| ¼ cup low-fat or skimmed-milk yogurt | |

Mix the ingredients together well and serve in a bowl with a spreading utensil. Garnish with chopped parsley, if desired. Serve with celery stalks, crackers, or party-size slices of rye or pumpernickel bread.

MARINATED MUSHROOMS OR ARTICHOKES

½ pound fresh small mushrooms or
1 14-ounce can artichoke hearts, drained

½ cup Good Seasons or Seven Seas Italian Salad Dressing

1. Wash the mushrooms and cut a ⅛-inch slice off the stem end.
2. Pour the salad dressing over the mushrooms or the artichokes and refrigerate overnight, stirring several times. Serve cold with toothpicks.

LOW-CALORIE EGGPLANT APPETIZER

This is perfect for your dieting friends to have with tomato juice. If you're not worried about calories, interesting variations can be made by adding 3 tablespoons of tomato paste and/or ¼ cup toasted sesame seeds.

1 1-pound eggplant
1½ tablespoons fresh lemon juice
1 clove garlic, crushed

1 tablespoon minced onion
¾ teaspoon salt
dash pepper
chopped parsley for garnish

1. Bake the eggplant for 1 hour or until it collapses when pricked with a fork.

2. Scoop out the inside and mash with a fork.
3. Mix in the seasonings and refrigerate.
4. Garnish with parsley and serve cold with sesame crackers and short lengths of celery stalks.

RYE OR PUMPERNICKEL ROUNDS

These canapés let you exercise your artistic instincts. They wind up looking too good to eat. I've left the exact amounts of fillings and garnishes up to you, since they vary directly with the size of rye and pumpernickel breads in your neighborhood.

Fillings

tuna, canned
salmon, canned
cooked chicken, chopped
cooked fish, mashed
mayonnaise

Garnishes

chopped hard-boiled egg whites (mixed with mayonnaise, if desired, for easier handling)
chopped parsley
pimento, chopped or in strips
anchovies
capers

pickle relish or thin strips of pickle
radishes, chopped or sliced
carrots, grated or in thin strips
red and green peppers, in thin slivers
scallions, chopped or in strips

1. Slice the rye or pumpernickel breads horizontally into as thin rounds as you can manage. Very often the bakery can do this for you.
2. Combine the desired filling with mayonnaise and spread over the entire circle of bread.
3. Now comes the fun. Decorate the rounds with whatever

garnishes you have handy or your imagination can conjure up. I usually put a ½-inch border of chopped garnish around the outside and have thin slivers of another garnish radiating from the center.

4. Cut the rounds into sixths or eighths and serve, leaving the canapés in their circular shape for your guests to admire before eating.

ROASTED SOYBEANS

Higher in protein and lower in calories and cost than peanuts.

¾ cup dry soybeans
1½ cups water
salt

garlic powder or onion powder (optional)

1. Wash the soybeans and soak them in water overnight. Drain well.
2. Spread the soybeans on a lightly greased cookie sheet. Sprinkle with salt and garlic powder or onion powder if desired.
3. Bake at 375° for 20-25 minutes or until golden brown. Shake the pan several times during the baking period.

about 1¼ cups

SOUPS

Increasing your repertory of soups is a wise move when embarking on a low-cholesterol diet. Soup, salad, and bread or crackers make an excellent, healthy lunch. At dinnertime, a first course of an interesting soup will more than compensate for the reduction in portion size of chicken or meat. If you're not familiar with cold soups, be sure to try a few. They're a delightful way to start off a warm-weather meal.

In adapting your own soup recipes, refrigerate meat or chicken broths before serving so that you can remove the top layer of fat. In dairy soups, substitute evaporated skimmed milk or regular skimmed milk enriched with dry skimmed-milk powder for cream and substitute polyunsaturated margarine for butter. A small amount of liquid butter extract can be added for butter flavor.

I usually prepare soup in large batches and freeze it in quart amounts. This way I can serve my family chicken soup and kreplach every Shabbat during the cold months without having to start from scratch each week. Kreplach can be frozen successfully either in the soup or separately. Remember that soups containing potatoes generally do *not* freeze well. To defrost soup quickly, place the jar or freezer container into a large pot of room-temperature water and change the water when it becomes cold.

The supermarket offers a variety of permissible soups. These include some powdered fruit-soup mixes, some powdered instant broths (i.e. Romanoff's MBT vegetable broth), and some dried-bean soup mixes (i.e. Goodman's split-pea soup mix), all of which contain no fat at all. In many kosher canned soups, the only fat ingredient listed is "vegetable oil." I advise writing to the individual food companies for further information on the composition of the oil. As always when buying commercial food products, read the labels carefully.

Hot Soups

ASPARAGUS-POTATO SOUP

An excellent spring variation on vichyssoise.

1 pound asparagus
1 pound potatoes (3 medium), peeled and diced
1 small onion, sliced
3 sprigs parsley

3 cups water
1½ teaspoon salt
1 bouillon cube or 1 tsp. powdered chicken soup mix

1. Snap off and discard the lower tough parts of the asparagus stalks. Wash well and cut into 2 to 3-inch lengths.
2. Put all the ingredients into a pot and bring to a boil. Simmer covered about 15 minutes or until the potatoes and asparagus are tender.
3. Puree in a blender. Serve hot or cold.

6-8 servings

CREAM OF ASPARAGUS SOUP

1 pound fresh asparagus, cut
  in 2- to 3-inch lengths
1 scallion, chopped, or 2
  slices onion
1 sprig parsley
1 cup water
¾ teaspoon salt
1 bouillon cube (pareve) or
  1 teaspoon pareve pow-
  dered instant soup

3 tablespoons flour
3 tablespoons oil
1½ cups skimmed milk
lemon juice, chopped dill, or
  chopped mint (optional)

1. Snap off the lower tough parts of the stalks. Wash well
   and cut into 2- to 3-inch lengths.
2. Put the asparagus, scallion or onion, parsley, water, and
   bouillon cube into a pot and bring to a boil. Simmer covered until the asparagus is tender, about 10-15 minutes.
3. Purée in an electric blender.
4. Stir the flour into the oil over low heat in a medium
   saucepan. Stir the milk in slowly until the sauce has thickened and is almost at the boiling point.
5. Stir in the purée and bring just to the boiling point again.
   Add lemon juice, chopped dill, or chopped mint if desired
   and serve hot.

4 servings

BLACK BEAN SOUP

1 pound (2½ cups) black beans
1 cup chopped onion
1 clove garlic, minced
2 tablespoons oil
3 stalks celery, cut into 3-inch lengths
2 quarts of water
2 bay leaves
2 teaspoons salt
¼ teaspoon pepper
2 tablespoons sherry (optional)
2 tablespoons lemon juice (optional)

1. Soak the beans overnight in water. Drain in a colander and rinse with cold water.
2. In a 5-quart pot, sauté the onion and garlic in oil until tender, about 5-10 minutes.
3. Add the water, beans, celery, bay leaves and seasonings. Bring to a boil and simmer, covered, for 3 hours.
4. Remove the bay leaves and purée in the blender.
5. If desired, stir in the lemon juice and/or sherry. Serve hot.

8-10 servings

BEEF AND BARLEY SOUP

This soup is a favorite of my son's.

1 pound very lean beef chuck or stew beef, cut into 2-inch chunks, well trimmed of fat
6 cups water
6-8 peppercorns
1 small or medium onion
1½-2 teaspoons salt
2 carrots, chopped
1 medium onion, chopped
2 stalks celery, chopped
½ cup barley

1. The day before serving, place the beef, water, peppercorns, onion and salt in a pot and bring to a boil. I put the peppercorns in a metal tea strainer or wrap them in cheesecloth to facilitate removal later on. Simmer covered about 1½ hours.
2. Remove the beef with a slotted spoon and set it aside. Remove the onion and peppercorns and discard them. Refrigerate the beef and stock separately overnight.
3. The next day skim the congealed fat off the top of the stock. Place the stock, beef, vegetables and barley in a large pot. Bring to a boil and simmer covered about 40 minutes or until the meat is tender and the barley cooked. Add more water if the soup is thicker than you prefer. Add salt and pepper if desired.

8 servings

BEEF BORSCHT

This recipe makes a thick borscht. Add more water if you prefer it thinner. To stretch the soup, you could add a drained can of small whole white potatoes.

2½ pounds very lean beef chuck, well trimmed of fat, and cut into 1½-inch cubes
2½ cups water
1 medium onion
1 teaspoon salt
1 bay leaf
8-10 peppercorns

4 cups sliced cabbage (about ¾ pound)
1 pound fresh beets, peeled and finely shredded
1 1-pound, 12-ounce can tomatoes, undrained
1-2 medium onions, thinly sliced
¼ teaspoon pepper
1 tablespoon lemon juice

1. The day before serving, bring the chuck, water, onion, salt, peppercorns, and bay leaf to a boil and simmer covered for 1½ hours. I find it convenient to tie the pepper-

corns and bayleaf in cheese cloth or to put them in a metal tea strainer.

2. Remove the beef with a slotted spoon and set it aside. Remove the onion, peppercorns, and bayleaf and discard them.

3. Transfer the stock to an upright jar or refrigerator container. Refrigerate the beef and the stock separately overnight.

4. The next day, remove the fat layer from the top of the broth with a spoon. Put the beef and broth in a 5-quart pot. Add the cabbage, beets, tomatoes and onions. Bring to a boil and simmer covered 1-1½ hours or until all ingredients are tender.

5. Adjust the seasonings with salt, pepper and lemon juice.

8 servings

CARROT SOUP

1 pound carrots, thinly sliced	½ teaspoon sugar
	1 quart water
1 small onion, chopped	2 teaspoons salt
2 medium potatoes, peeled and diced	2 teaspoons powdered chicken soup or 2
2 tablespoons oil	chicken-bouillon cubes

1. Sauté the carrots, onion and potatoes in oil in a large saucepan over low heat 15 minutes.

2. Add the water and seasonings. Bring to a boil and simmer covered until the vegetables are tender, 15-20 minutes.

3. Purée the vegetables and liquid in an electric blender and return the purée to the pot.

4. Add 1-2 cups of water, depending on the thickness of the soup desired. Serve hot, garnished with chopped parsley, chives, or dill.

8 servings

CREAM OF CAULIFLOWER SOUP

This soup is very delicately flavored and especially easy to make.

1 small or ½ large head of cauliflower	dash white pepper
2½ cups water	⅔ cup powdered skimmed milk
1 teaspoon salt	

1. Separate the cauliflower into flowerets and discard the stalk and leaves.
2. Put the flowerets in a medium saucepan with the water and salt. Bring to a boil and simmer covered 10 minutes or until the flowerets are tender.
3. Drain the cauliflower, saving the cooking liquid. Purée the cauliflower with half of the cooking liquid in an electric blender.
4. Dissolve the powdered milk in the remaining cooking liquid.
5. Bring the purée to a boil.
6. Add the milk and bring just to the boil again.
7. Adjust the seasonings. Serve hot, garnished with chopped parsley, ground nutmeg, or paprika.

4 servings

CHICKEN SOUP

What would a Jewish cookbook be without a recipe for chicken soup? I like to double or triple this recipe and freeze it in quart jars. I often use chicken thighs which sometimes can be obtained frozen in bulk at a price lower than that for fresh chicken. The cooked chicken can be removed from the bones and saved for chicken salad, or chow mein, or casseroles. The cooked vegetables are very good served in the hot soup. Be sure to try with kreplach and matzo balls.

4 pounds chicken parts	2 sprigs fresh dill if available
2 carrots cut in thirds	or ½ teaspoon dill seeds
1-2 parsnips cut in thirds	3 sprigs parsley
1 celery stalk with leaves,	3 cloves, 6 peppercorns
cut in thirds	1-2 teaspoons salt
1 large onion cut in half or	7 cups water or water to
2 leeks if available	cover

1. Place the chicken, carrots, parsnips, celery, onion or leeks, water and salt in a pot.
2. Wrap the dill or dill seeds, parsley, cloves and peppercorns in cheesecloth or put them in a large tea strainer and add to the pot.
3. Bring to a boil and simmer covered 2½-3 hours.
4. Remove the chicken and vegetables with a slotted spoon.
5. Refrigerate the soup overnight. With a spoon, carefully remove top layer of congealed fat. Serve hot.

About 2 quarts

VARIATIONS ON BASIC CHICKEN SOUP

Chicken-Watercress Soup

To each serving of chicken soup add 1 teaspoon sherry and 2 tablespoons chopped watercress. This is an excellent first course for a meal with an oriental theme. It is also a good choice to serve to dieters.

Chicken-Mushroom Broth

Float a few slices of raw mushroom and fresh bean curd in each bowl of soup and it will become a perfect beginning for a Japanese-style meal.

LENTIL SOUP—I

This makes a huge amount but it freezes well and can be served as a main dish.

1 pound lentils (2½ cups)
3 quarts of water
1 1-pound can of tomatoes, undrained
1 large onion, sliced
3 carrots, coarsely chopped
3 stalks celery, coarsely chopped
2 sprigs parsley
1 bay leaf
2-3 teaspoons salt or to taste
pepper to taste

1. Spread the lentils, 1 cup at a time, in a single layer on a large baking sheet. Carefully pick over the lentils and remove any foreign particles. Wash the lentils well in a colander under running water.
2. Place all the ingredients in a very large pot. Bring to a boil and simmer covered for 2 hours.
3. Purée in an electric blender and reheat to serve.

About 4 quarts

LENTIL SOUP—II

An easy and delicious Middle Eastern version of lentil soup suggested by Denise Telio.

2 cups lentils
1 onion, sliced
1 stalk celery cut in 3-inch lengths
6 cups water

¾ teaspoon salt
¼ teaspoon garlic powder
¾ teaspoon cumin
½ cup fresh lemon juice

1. Spread the lentils out, one cup at a time, on a large baking pan. Carefully pick over the lentils and remove any foreign particles. Wash well with running water in a colander.
2. Place the lentils, onion, celery, water and salt in a large pot. Bring to a boil and simmer covered 1½ hours.
3. Purée the lentils with the cooking liquid and vegetables in an electric blender.
4. Heat the purée; stir in the garlic powder, cumin and lemon juice and serve.

8 servings

LIMA BEAN SOUP

Delicious on a cold winter day. Nourishing, cheap, easy, pareve. What more could one want from a soup?

1½ cups dried lima beans
2 tablespoons oil
1 cup diced onion
1 cup diced carrots
2 cloves garlic, minced

1 parsnip, diced
4 sprigs parsley, chopped
6 cups water
1-1½ teaspoons salt

1. Soak the lima beans overnight in 3 cups of water. Drain.
2. Heat the oil in a large pot (at least 3-quart size) and sauté the onion, carrots, and garlic over medium heat until the onions are soft, about 10 minutes.
3. Add the rest of the ingredients. Bring to a boil; skim off any foam. Cover and simmer over low heat for 2 hours. Adjust seasonings.

8-10 servings

Variations:

1. Add 3 tablespoons barley during the last 30 minutes of cooking.
2. Mix a few tablespoons of tomato paste with a cup of water before cooking.

MUSHROOM SOUP

I often double this recipe, freeze the puréed stock in quart containers, and add the milk just before serving. This is an elegant beginning to any dairy meal.

1 pound mushrooms, quartered
⅔ cup onion, chopped
⅔ cup celery, chopped
3 tablespoons oil or margarine
1 sprig parsley
4 cups water
2 pareve bouillon cubes or 2 teaspoons pareve instant soup

2 teaspoons salt
1½ cups evaporated skimmed milk or 1 cup powdered skimmed milk plus enough water to make 1½ cups milk

1. Sauté the mushrooms, onion, and celery in oil in a medium saucepan over low heat 10-15 minutes.
2. Add the parsley, water, bouillon cubes and salt. Bring to a boil and simmer covered 15 minutes.
3. Purée the vegetables and liquid in an electric blender. About 6 cups of purée result. This is a good point at which to freeze the soup.
4. Bring the purée to a boil and add the milk. Bring just to the boiling point again and serve. Sprinkle with nutmeg if desired, or add 1 teaspoon of sherry for each serving.

For a thicker soup, after step 3 prepare a cream sauce from 3 tablespoons oil or margarine, 4 tablespoons flour, and 1½ cups evaporated skimmed milk. Gradually stir in the mushroom purée. Bring just to the boiling point. Season and serve.

6-8 servings

SPLIT PEA SOUP

Sometimes on a cold, wintry day, you want an easy soup that's something special. I can't think of one better than this split pea soup.

2 cups green split peas	1 parsnip, diced*
1 cup chopped onions	4 sprigs parsley, chopped*
1 cup chopped carrots	6 cups water
2 cloves garlic, minced	1½ teaspoons salt

1. Look over the split peas for foreign particles and then wash in a colander.
2. Heat the oil in a large pot and sauté the onions, carrots, and garlic until the onions are tender.
3. Add the remaining ingredients and bring to a boil. Skim off any foam. Cover and simmer about 1½ hours or until the peas are soft.
4. Purée in blender or put through strainer if a smooth texture is desired.

*Note: If the soup is to be puréed, don't bother chopping the parsley or the parsnip.

8-10 servings

TOMATO-ONION SOUP

This is an interesting variation on the familiar onion soup.

3 cups chopped onion
  (2 large)
3 tablespoons oil
½ cup crushed fine noodles
  (pressed down with your
  knuckles in a 2-cup measuring cup)

1 6-ounce can tomato paste
4 cups water
2 teaspoons powdered in-
  stant chicken-soup mix
1 teaspoon salt
dash pepper

1. Sauté the onions over medium heat in the oil until they
   are light brown.
2. Add the noodles and continue cooking, stirring frequently, until the noodles are light brown and the onions
   are a darker brown.
3. Add the rest of the ingredients, bring to a boil, and simmer covered for 15 minutes.

4-6 servings

POTAGE CRESSON (CREAM OF WATERCRESS SOUP)

This is a very elegant soup with a subtle taste. Be sure to note that it contains potatoes and should not be frozen.

½ cup chopped onion
1 tablespoon oil or margarine
2 cups chopped watercress
1 pound (3 medium) potatoes, peeled and cubed
5 cups water
3 teaspoons pareve instant soup mix (chicken flavored) or 3 pareve bouillon cubes

1¼ teaspoons salt
dash white pepper or to taste
¾ cup evaporated skimmed milk or ½ cup powdered skimmed milk plus enough water to make ¾ cup liquid

1. Sauté the onion over low heat in a 3-quart saucepan until the onion is soft, about 5-10 minutes.
2. Add the watercress and sauté a few minutes longer.
3. Add the potatoes, water, bouillon cubes, salt and pepper. Bring to a boil and simmer covered over low heat until the potatoes are soft, about 15 minutes.
4. Purée in an electric blender. Makes about 6½ cups of purée.
5. Just before serving, bring the purée to a boil. Stir in the milk, bring to the boiling point again, and serve. If more richness is desired, swirl in a few tablespoons of margarine.

8 servings

ZUCCHINI SOUP

Peggy Wacks introduced me to this easy, flavorful soup which is equally good hot or cold. Be sure to try it both ways.

1 pound zucchini, cut in chunks
3 cups water
2 chicken-bouillon cubes or 2 teaspoons powdered instant chicken soup

1 medium onion, sliced
¼ teaspoon orégano
¼ teaspoon rosemary
¾ teaspoon salt
dash pepper

1. Put all the ingredients into a saucepan and bring to a boil. Cover and simmer 15-20 minutes.
2. Blend in an electric blender until smooth. Reheat or chill.

6 servings

KREPLACH

When I asked my great-aunt Pessel to tell me how she made her marvelous kreplach, she told me that I shouldn't bother with them. I strongly disagreed, and if you try these you'll know why.

2 cups flour
1½ teaspoons salt
3 egg whites plus enough water to measure ½ cup

1 recipe chicken or meat filling

1. Stir the salt and flour together.
2. Beat the egg whites and water lightly with a fork and pour the mixture over the flour. Mix well and knead into a stiff dough. If necessary, add a small amount of water to remove all the flour from the sides of the bowl.
3. Divide the dough in half. Roll each half on a lightly floured surface into a 9 × 12 inch rectangle. Be prepared to roll hard since this is a stiff dough. Cut the dough into twelve 3-inch squares.
4. Place a tablespoon of filling on each square. Fold the dough over to form a triangle and pinch the edges together firmly. Moisten the edges with water if needed to get them to stick together.
5. Place in a large pot of boiling salted water and cook covered for 20 minutes. Drain and serve in soup.

24 kreplach

Chicken Filling for Kreplach

½ pound cooked chicken (about 2 cups shredded cooked chicken)
3 tablespoons oil

1½ cups chopped onion
1½ teaspoons salt
dash pepper

1. Sauté the onion in the oil until tender, about 10-15 minutes.
2. Finely chop the chicken and onion mixture together in a wooden chopping bowl. Season with salt and pepper.

Beef Filling for Kreplach

¾ pound very lean chuck, trimmed of all visible fat
3 cups water
1 small onion

3 tablespoons oil
1½ cups chopped onion
1½ teaspoons salt
dash pepper

1. Bring the chuck, water, and small onion to a boil and simmer covered for 1½ hours or until the meat is tender. Remove the meat and onion with a slotted spoon. Discard the onion. I generally refrigerate the stock overnight, remove the top layer of fat, and save the stock for soup.

2. Sauté the chopped onion in oil until tender, about 10-15 minutes.
3. Chop the beef and onion mixture together in a wooden chopping bowl until fine. Season with salt and pepper.

MATZO BALLS

Devising a recipe for a light flavorful matzo ball without chicken fat or egg yolk was probably the most difficult cooking problem I faced in preparing this book. The idea of using baking powder came to me one July day. Despite the heat, I tried it immediately and, to my delight, it worked.

½ cup matzo meal
1 teaspoon baking powder
½ teaspoon salt
¾ teaspoon powdered instant chicken soup

dash onion powder
3 egg whites
1 tablespoon water
2 tablespoons chopped parsley

1. Stir the dry ingredients together.
2. Beat the egg whites, water and parsley (if desired) with a fork and pour over the dry ingredients. Mix well and refrigerate at least ½ hour.
3. Form into 8 1½-inch balls and drop into a large pot of boiling salted water.
4. Reduce heat and simmer covered for 30 minutes. Do not remove the lid during the cooking period. Remove with a slotted spoon and serve in soup.

8 matzo balls

Cold Soups

BLUEBERRY SOUP

When blueberries are plentiful, surprise your family or guests with this special treat.

1 pint berries
2 cups water
2 tablespoons sugar
¼ teaspoon cinnamon
⅛ teaspoon cloves

1 tablespoon lemon juice
1 teaspoon grated lemon
rind
yogurt

1. Bring the berries, water, sugar, cinnamon and cloves to a boil and simmer covered 15 minutes.
2. Push the berries through a strainer or food mill and discard the skins.
3. Refrigerate the soup. When cool, add the lemon juice and lemon rind. Serve chilled, with yogurt.

3-4 servings

COLD BORSCHT

This is a delight to the eyes as well as to the taste buds. Served with yogurt it's a perfect choice for a summer lunch.

1 pound fresh beets (about 4 medium)
3 cups water
1 teaspoon salt

2 tablespoons sugar
4 teaspoons lemon juice
yogurt

1. Cut the beets off from their stems. Reserve the leafy part of the stem for use as a green vegetable and chop the remaining length of stem into ½-inch pieces. Peel the beets and cut any very large ones in half. Bring the beets, chopped stems, water and salt to a boil and simmer covered until the beets are tender, about 40-50 minutes.
2. Shred the cooked beets on a coarse grater and return to the liquid.
3. Flavor with sugar and lemon juice. Serve chilled with yogurt.

5-6 servings

CHERRY SOUP

1 1-pound can water packed, pitted sour red cherries (with liquid)
¼ cup sugar
2 teaspoons cornstarch

¼ teaspoon cinnamon
1 teaspoon grated orange rind
½ cup orange juice

1. Put all ingredients except for a few cherries into an electric blender and blend until the cherries are puréed.
2. Pour into a saucepan; heat, stirring constantly, until the mixture comes to a boil and thickens.
3. Chill and serve garnished with a few whole cherries.

3-4 servings

CHILLED CRANBERRY SOUP

I make this in the summer with the box of cranberries which has been sitting in my freezer since Thanksgiving.

1 pound raw cranberries
3 cups orange juice
3 whole cloves or 3 whole allspice
¼ cup sugar

1 teaspoon grated orange rind
½ teaspoon grated lemon rind

1. Bring the berries, orange juice, cloves or allspice, and sugar to a boil and simmer covered until the skins of the berries pop open (about 5 minutes).
2. Push the pulp and liquid through a strainer or food mill. Discard the skins.
3. Stir in the orange and lemon rinds and chill.

4-5 servings

PLUM SOUP

This is a very elegant way to start any summer meal. Variations could include stirring in yogurt or red wine. I enjoy it just the way it is.

1 pound ripe red plums, halved and pitted
2½ cups water
2 tablespoons sugar
1 small stick cinnamon
1 tablespoon fresh lemon juice

1. Bring all ingredients except lemon juice to a boil and simmer covered until the plums are soft, about 10-15 minutes.
2. Discard the cinnamon. Press the remaining ingredients through a strainer or food mill. Discard the skins.
3. Stir in lemon juice and chill.

4 servings

RHUBARB SOUP

This is a lovely pink soup which could hardly be easier to make.

1 pound rhubarb, cut in 1-inch pieces (about 3 cups)
3 cups pineapple juice
1 10-ounce package of frozen sliced strawberries, defrosted

1. Bring the rhubarb and pineapple juice to a boil and simmer covered until the rhubarb is soft, about 15 minutes. Let cool and chill.
2. Stir in the strawberries. Serve alone or with yogurt.

4-6 servings

STRAWBERRY-PINEAPPLE SOUP

I begin salivating whenever I think of this soup. Besides being delicious, it has the additional virtue of being the fastest soup I know of to prepare. For a variation, substitute white wine for part of the pineapple juice.

2 cups fresh strawberries
2 cups pineapple juice
¼ cup sugar

½ teaspoon grated lemon rind

1. Blend all the ingredients in an electric blender until smooth. Chill.

4-5 servings

SALADS AND
SALAD DRESSINGS

Nutritious and low in fat, salads are an important component of any low-cholesterol meal. Interesting salads can also be a major source of gastronomic satisfaction whether served as an appetizer, side dish, or main dish. Try the recipes that follow, but also let your imagination soar and create some of your own.

Most bottled commercial salad dressings list vegetable oil as one of their ingredients without specifying which vegetable oil. If your favorite salad dressing falls into this category, I suggest writing to the food company for information about the dressing's fat composition. Commercial dressings I use are Seven Seas French and Russian dressings, which are made with the acceptable soybean oil and Good Seasons Italian salad dressing mix made with corn or safflower oil.

If you're accustomed to salad dressings containing olive oil, which has no cholesterol-lowering effect, try substituting corn or safflower oil for a portion of the olive oil.

Although commercial mayonnaise contains egg yolk, it also contains a large amount of liquid vegetable oil with polyunsaturates and is permissible on a low-cholesterol diet. Hellman's mayonnaise has a polyunsaturated/saturated (P/S) ratio of 2.8. Kraft's Imitation Mayonnaise has a P/S ratio of 3.0 and fewer than half the calories of regular mayonnaise.

Dieters may also enjoy a dressing of lemon juice and fresh herbs, or a yogurt dressing, or some of the commercial low-calorie dressings.

If you hesitate to prepare gelatin salads because of unmolding difficulties, try the plastic Tupperware molds, or lightly oiling your metal molds.

For many years one of my favorite time-saving tricks has been to prepare enough green salad for several days and store it in a Tupperware container. I've found that the salad stays perfectly fresh this way. Dressing, of course, should be added just before serving.

Side Dish Salads

ASPARAGUS VINAIGRETTE

If you like asparagus, be sure to try it this way for a delightful spring salad. Use the dressing described here or your own favorite French dressing.

1½ pounds fresh asparagus
3 tablespoons fresh lemon juice
5 tablespoons corn oil
½ teaspoon salt
dash pepper (optional)
dash garlic powder (optional)
¼ teaspoon tarragon
¼ teaspoon orégano or dill weed

1. Snap off and discard the lower, tough portions of the asparagus stalks. Wash well.
2. Place in boiling salted water and cook uncovered until the stalks can be easily pricked with a fork but are still firm

(about 8-10 minutes). Drain at once and place in an attractive shallow dish.

3. Beat the lemon juice, oil, salt and spices together with a fork or a small whisk. Pour over the asparagus, covering each stalk with dressing. Let cool and refrigerate until ready to serve.

6 servings

THREE-BEAN SALAD

This is excellent for a party since it serves many and is very easy to make. As a variation, substitute chickpeas for one of the other beans.

1 1-pound can green beans, sliced	1 green pepper sliced very thin
1 1-pound can yellow beans, sliced	⅓ cup sugar
1 1-pound can red kidney beans	1 teaspoon salt
	½ teaspoon pepper
1 red onion sliced very thin	½ cup vinegar
	½ cup oil

1. Drain the beans in a colander. Rinse well with cold water and drain again.
2. Beat together the sugar, salt, pepper, oil and vinegar with a fork or wisk.
3. Put the beans, onion and green pepper into a large bowl. Pour the dressing over them and mix.
4. Let stand several hours or overnight, stirring several times.

10 servings

WHITE KIDNEY BEAN SALAD
(CANNELLINI)

I always keep a can of these beans on stock for those times when I'm out of most fresh salad ingredients. Chopped celery or chopped carrots could be substituted for the green pepper if that's what you happen to have around. Very similar to Three Bean Salad.

1 1-pound can cannellini
1 small to medium green pepper
1 very small onion
2 tablespoons red wine vinegar

2 tablespoons oil
¼ teaspoon salt
dash pepper
1 teaspoon sugar

1. Drain the beans in a colander. Wash well with cold water and drain completely.
2. Slice the pepper and onion very thinly. Put in a bowl with the beans.
3. Beat the oil, vinegar, and seasonings together with a fork or small wisk. Pour over the vegetables and stir with a large spoon until the dressing is well distributed. Chill at least 2 hours and serve.

3-4 servings

BEAN SPROUT SALAD

Fresh bean sprouts can be bought in Chinese groceries, health food stores, and some supermarkets. If you enjoy watching things grow, you can also sprout them at home from mung beans. Sprouts are vitamin-rich, yet have only 40 calories per cup. Here's an especially tasty, healthy and unusual salad.

1 pound bean sprouts
4 tablespoons soy sauce
2 tablespoons vinegar
4 teaspoons sugar

3 tablespoons sesame seeds (optional)
chopped scallions (optional)

1. Spread the sesame seeds out on a flat pan and toast them in a 350° oven until they are golden brown—about 10 minutes.
2. Dissolve the sugar in the soy sauce and vinegar.
3. Toss all the ingredients together and serve cold.

6-8 servings

BROCCOLI AND ONION SALAD

This is simple to prepare, very attractive, and very good.

1 bunch fresh broccoli or 2 packages frozen broccoli
1 medium red Spanish onion, cut into very thin slices

½ cup basic French dressing or Good Seasons Italian Dressing

1. If using fresh broccoli, remove the leaves and cut off the tough part of the stalk. Cut any very large stalks in half. Cook, uncovered, in boiling salted water until just tender—about 10 minutes. Drain. If using frozen broccoli, cook according to package directions.
2. Place the warm broccoli in a shallow dish (I use a Pyrex pie plate with a scalloped rim). Cover with the sliced onion and pour the dressing over the vegetables. Chill and serve.

6-8 servings

HERBED CARROTS

Any herb mixture can be substituted for the parsley and dill, but fresh herbs are best.

1 pound (about 6 medium) carrots, cut in ¼-inch slices
2 cups boiling water
½ teaspoon salt
3 tablespoons oil
1½ tablespoons red wine vinegar

½ teaspoon salt
dash pepper
2 tablespoons chopped fresh parsley
2 tablespoons chopped fresh dill

1. Cook the carrots in the boiling salted water until tender—about 10 minutes. Drain.
2. Beat the oil, vinegar, salt and pepper together and pour over the carrots.
3. Add the parsley and dill. Chill before serving.

4-6 servings

CARROT AND RAISIN SALAD

3 cups coarsely grated carrots (about 4 medium)
¼-½ cup raisins (or chopped dates)
¼ cup chopped walnuts
¼ cup orange juice

½ cup mayonnaise
1 tablespoon grated orange rind
1 teaspoon confectioner's sugar (optional)

1. Stir the carrots, raisins and walnuts together.

2. Beat the orange juice, mayonnaise, orange rind and sugar (if desired) together with a wisk or fork. Toss with the carrot mixture.

4-6 servings

RAW CAULIFLOWER SALAD

This crunchy salad will bring requests for second helpings from pleasantly surprised guests.

1 small cauliflower (about 1½ pounds)
6 radishes, sliced
¼ cup red Spanish onion, chopped

3 tablespoons chili sauce
¼ cup mayonnaise
1 teaspoon chopped fresh dill or ½ teaspoon dried dill

1. Divide the cauliflower into flowerettes and cut into ¾- to 1-inch pieces. A 1½-pound cauliflower will yield about 5-6 cups of pieces.
2. Put the cauliflower, radishes and onion in a bowl. Stir the chili sauce, mayonnaise and dill together. Add to the vegetables and toss until thoroughly mixed. Garnish with chopped parsley if desired.

6 servings

CHERRY PIE-FILLING FRUIT SALAD

This is sweet and could also be used as a dessert. It's likely to appeal to children, especially if you add a handful of miniature marshmallows.

1 can cherry-pie filling
1 #2 can pineapple chunks, drained
2 bananas, sliced

2 cups blueberries, seedle grapes or halved pitted cherries

Stir all ingredients together and serve chilled.

8-10 servings

COLE SLAW

The flavor seems to improve with several hours standing, so don't hesitate to prepare this salad a bit in advance.

2 pounds cabbage, thinly sliced, about 10-11 cups
¾ cup mayonnaise
3 tablespoons vinegar

3 tablespoons sugar
1 teaspoon salt
½ teaspoon pepper

1. Stir the mayonnaise, vinegar, sugar, salt and pepper together. Mix with cabbage in a very large bowl.

10-12 servings

CRANBERRY-PINEAPPLE SALAD

This was the first gelatin salad I ventured to try as a bride and novice cook. It's still one of my favorites.

1 3-ounce box red Jello
1 cup boiling water
1 16-ounce can whole cranberries
1 cup crushed pineapple, undrained

¼ cup chopped celery (optional)
¼ cup chopped walnuts (optional)

1. Dissolve Jello in boiling water.
2. Stir the cranberries into the hot liquid and mix well to break up any clumps of cranberry gel. Chill in the refrigerator until slightly thickened.
3. Stir in the crushed pineapple and other ingredients (if desired). Pour into a small (4- or 5-cup) mold.
4. Return to the refrigerator and chill until firm.

6 servings

CUCUMBERS WITH DILL

Any leftover dressing from this salad is delicious with sliced tomatoes.

6 cups thinly sliced cucumbers	¼ teaspoon salt
	¾ teaspoon dill
1 cup water	¼ cup mayonnaise
1 cup white vinegar	

1. Place the cucumber slices, water and vinegar in a bowl and refrigerate several hours or overnight.
2. Drain the cucumber slices. Mix the salt, dill and mayonnaise together and stir into the cucumbers.

6-8 servings

GRAPEFRUIT GELATIN SALAD

A tart, refreshing summer salad.

1 envelope unflavored gelatin
½ cup water
2 tablespoons sugar
1 16-ounce can grapefruit sections
fruit juice

¼ cup white wine
1 tablespoon fresh lemon juice
1 cup diced raw vegetables—cauliflower, green pepper, carrot, etc.

1. In a small saucepan, sprinkle the gelatin over the water and allow to stand for 5 minutes. Bring the water slowly to a boil, stirring until the gelatin is dissolved.
2. Drain the can of grapefruit sections, saving the syrup. Add enough fruit juice to the syrup to make one cup of liquid.
3. Add the fruit juice-syrup mixture, white wine and lemon juice to the gelatin mixture. Refrigerate until just beginning to thicken.
4. Cut the grapefruit sections into ½ inch pieces and add with the diced vegetables to the gelatin. Pour into a 4- or 5-cup mold and chill until firm.

4-6 servings

GREEN SALAD

A tossed green salad enhances almost any meal. For special interest, use several different greens selected from the many varities of lettuce (Bibb, Boston, chickory, escarole, iceberg, romaine, red leaf, salad bowl, etc.), spinach, watercress, or any other green leafy vegetable.

2 quarts salad greens, torn into bite-sized pieces	2½ tablespoons vinegar
½ cup French dressing, or 5 tablespoons oil	½ teaspoon salt
	¼ teaspoon pepper

1. Wash the greens well and drain in a colander. Dry them with an absorbent towel and tear into bite-sized pieces.
2. Place the greens in a large bowl. Beat or shake the French dressing and toss gently with the greens just before serving. To prevent wilting of the greens, it is sometimes suggested to toss first with the oil and then with the beaten vinegar, salt and pepper mixture.

6-8 servings

Salad Additions

For variety, add any of the following to a green salad:

anchovies
artichoke hearts
carrots
cauliflower
celery
chickpeas (garbanzo beans)
croutons
hard-boiled egg whites
fruits—orange or grapefruit sections, apples, pears, pineapple chunks, grapes, etc.

herbs
mushrooms
onions
peppers
radishes
red cabbage
scallions
tomatoes
zucchini

HAMAN SALAD

Great fun for a children's party. Arrange on lettuce:

1 canned apricot	head
½ canned pear (hollow side down)	neck and body
carrot and celery sticks	arms and legs
banana strips	arms and legs
raisins, slivered almonds, carrot slivers	eyes, nose, mouth, buttons
parsley, green pepper strips	hair

LENTIL SALAD

A nourishing and interesting salad.

2 cups lentils	1 teaspoon salt
1 stalk celery	1 small or ½ large red Spanish onion, chopped
1 small onion	
4 cups water	½ green pepper, chopped

Dressing

5 tablespoons oil	¾ teaspoon salt
3 tablespoons vinegar	¼ teaspoon pepper

1. Pour the dry lentils, one cup at a time, on a large baking sheet and pick over carefully to remove any foreign particles. Then wash well in a colander.

2. Put the lentils, celery, onion, salt and water into a pot. Bring to a boil and simmer covered until the lentils are tender but not mushy, about 30-40 minutes. Drain in a colander, remove the onion and celery, and transfer the lentils to a bowl.
3. Beat the oil, vinegar, salt and pepper together with a fork or wisk and pour the dressing over the warm lentils.
4. Allow the lentils to cool to room temperature and stir in the green pepper and red onion. Serve chilled.

6-8 servings

DENISE'S MIDDLE-EASTERN SALAD

This refreshing salad is especially attractive served from a clear glass bowl.

2 cucumbers, peeled and cut into ½-inch chunks
2 green peppers, diced
8-10 radishes, sliced
1 bunch scallions, chopped
¾ cup parsley, chopped

4 medium tomatoes cut into ½-inch chunks
½ cup oil
¼ cup fresh lemon juice
¾ teaspoon salt
¼ teaspoon pepper

1. Beat the lemon juice, salt and pepper together with a fork or wisk. Gradually beat in the oil.
2. Toss with the vegetables just before serving.

6 servings

POTATO SALAD

This salad is even better the day after it's made when all the flavors have blended. The white wine or vermouth can be omitted but an intriguing taste will be lost.

3 pounds medium-sized cooking potatoes	¼ teaspoon pepper
6 tablespoons white vermouth or dry white wine	4 tablespoons mayonnaise
5 tablespoons oil	4 tablespoons chopped fresh parsley
2½ tablespoons red wine vinegar	4 tablespoons chopped Spanish onion or scallions
¾ teaspoon salt	4 tablespoons chopped celery (optional)

1. Cook the unpeeled potatoes in boiling salted water 20-30 minutes or until tender but still firm. Be sure not to overcook.
2. Drain, peel and cut the potatoes into ¾ inch cubes while still warm.
3. Sprinkle the white wine over the potatoes and let stand 10 minutes.
4. Beat the oil, vinegar, salt and pepper together with a wisk or fork. Pour over the potatoes and toss gently (using a wooden spoon for tossing helps keep the potato cubes intact). Allow the potatoes to cool to room temperature. The salad may also be refrigerated overnight at this point.
5. Drain off any unabsorbed oil by tilting the bowl with one hand and holding the potatoes back with the other. Add mayonnaise, onion or scallions, celery, and parsley and mix gently.

8 servings

RUSSIAN SALAD

This is a very good way to use up leftover vegetables. The proportions of the individual vegetables can be varied to suit whatever you have available.

1 cup diced cooked carrots or beets

1 cup cooked peas or diced cooked string beans

1½ cup diced cooked potatoes

1½ cup diced tomatoes

½ cup French dressing

3 tablespoons chopped onion or scallions

1 teaspoon chopped dill (optional)

3 tablespoons mayonnaise

2 tablespoons chopped parsley

1. Marinate the cooked vegetables in the French dressing for at least one hour and drain off any excess dressing.
2. Add the tomatoes, onion, dill (if desired), and mayonnaise to the cooked vegetables and toss well. Garnish with chopped parsley.

8 servings

SPINACH AND ORANGE SALAD

This is my favorite dinner-party salad. It invariably brings compliments.

10 ounces fresh spinach

3 oranges, peeled and sectioned

1 medium red Spanish onion, cut in very thin slices

½ cup French dressing (see salad dressings) or Good Seasons Italian Dressing

1. Thoroughly wash the spinach and drain in a colander. Dry in a towel and tear into bite-size pieces.
2. Place the spinach, orange sections and onion slices in a salad bowl. Just before serving, toss with the dressing.

6 servings

TABOULLI OR CRACKED-WHEAT SALAD

Refreshing, colorful, tangy salad, especially good in the summertime.

2 cups bulgur or cracked wheat
4 cups water
1 bunch scallions, chopped
1 bunch parsley, chopped
1-2 green peppers, chopped
3-4 medium tomatoes, chopped

1 teaspoon salt
¼ teaspoon pepper
3 tablespoons safflower oil
¼ cup fresh lemon juice
2 sprigs mint, chopped, or ½ teaspoon dried mint flakes, crumbled (optional)

1. Soak the bulgur in the water for about one hour. Drain in a strainer or in a colander lined with cheesecloth. Press out excess water.
2. Mix the bulgur well with all the other ingredients and serve chilled.

12 servings

ZUCCHINI VINAIGRETTE

2 pounds small zucchini, cut into ¼-inch slices
¾ cup basic French dressing
1 clove garlic, crushed

½ cup chopped red Spanish onion
1 teaspoon orégano or basil
¼ cup chopped parsley

1. Drop the zucchini into a large pot of boiling salted water and cook for 2 minutes only. Immediately drain in a colander and run cold water over the zucchini to stop the cooking.

2. Put the zucchini in a bowl and add the onion, oregano and parsley.
3. Beat the crushed garlic into the French dressing and pour the dressing over the zucchini mixture.
4. Toss well and chill.

8 servings

Main Dish Salads

MIMI'S TUNA-CHICK PEA SALAD

This superb salad was adapted from a French recipe and is a perfect summer luncheon dish.

2 1-pound cans chick peas
1 medium onion, chopped
1-2 stalks celery, chopped
6-8 radishes, sliced
1 7-ounce can tuna, flaked
1 3-ounce can flat anchovies, minced
¼ cup chopped parsley
2 medium tomatoes, chopped
3 hard-boiled eggs
2 tablespoons red wine vinegar
4 tablespoons corn oil
½ teaspoon salt
¼ teaspoon pepper

1. Drain the chick peas in a colander. Rinse with cold water and drain well.
2. Put the chick peas in a large bowl with the onion, celery, radishes, tuna, anchovies, parsley and tomatoes.
3. Cut the hard-boiled eggs in half. Scoop out and discard the yolks. Cut the egg whites into thin strips and add to the other ingredients.
4. Beat the oil, vinegar, salt and pepper together with a fork or wisk and pour over the salad. Toss well and serve over lettuce.

4-6 servings

TUNA-TOMATO-MACARONI SALAD

An excellent one-dish summer meal.

8 ounces elbow macaroni
2 cups diced tomato in ½-inch cubes
1 cup diced cucumber in ½-inch cubes
½ cup diced celery or green pepper
½ cup diced scallions or red onions

¼ cup minced fresh parsley
1 7-ounce can tuna fish, drained and flaked
½ cup mayonnaise
1 package dry Italian salad dressing mix

1. Cook the elbow macaroni according to package directions. Drain. Rinse thoroughly with cold water and drain well again.
2. Transfer the macaroni into a large bowl. Add the vegetables and tuna fish.
3. Stir the mayonnaise and Italian salad dressing mix together and spoon over the other ingredients.
4. Toss well and serve chilled.

4-6 servings

CHICKEN SALAD

A simple, speedy meal from leftover boiled chicken.

2 cups (½ pound) diced cooked chicken
1 cup diced celery
3-4 tablespoons mayonnaise

½ teaspoon salt
dash pepper
1-2 tablespoons capers (optional)

1. Stir all the ingredients together. Garnish with parsley sprigs and sliced tomatoes and cucumbers.

2-3 servings

HAWAIIAN CHICKEN SALAD

A delicious version of chicken salad which you'll want to serve often, especially in the summertime.

2 cups (½ pound) diced cooked chicken
1 cup diced celery
1 cup well-drained pineapple tidbits

1 cup halved seedless grapes
¼ cup mayonnaise
¼ cup toasted slivered almonds

1. Stir all ingredients together. Serve over crisp lettuce.

2-3 servings

HERRING-POTATO SALAD

The beets tint the potatoes pink to produce an exotic-looking salad with a delightful mélange of flavors.

2 pounds potatoes
1-pound jar beets, drained and diced
¾ cup diced red onion
2 medium unpeeled apples, diced

8-ounce jar herring fillets in wine sauce, drained and cut into ¾- to 1-inch pieces
¼ cup oil
¼ cup vinegar
¾ teaspoon salt
dash pepper

1. Cook the potatoes unpeeled in boiling salted water 20-30 minutes or until tender but still firm. Peel and cut the potatoes into ¾-inch cubes.
2. Beat the oil, vinegar, salt and pepper together and pour over the potatoes. Toss gently.
3. Toss the remaining ingredients with the potatoes. Serve cold.

4 servings

MACARONI-CHICKEN SALAD

Tuna can be substituted for chicken in this easy, tasty main-dish salad.

½ pound elbow macaroni
½ pound diced cooked
   chicken (2 cups)
1 green pepper, diced
1 cup diced red onion
¼ cup chopped parsley
½ cup mayonnaise

½ cup chili sauce
½ teaspoon salt
1 teaspoon dried dill or 2
   teaspoons chopped fresh
   dill
1 tablespoon horseradish
   (optional)

1. Cook the macaroni according to package directions. Drain. Rinse thoroughly with cold water and drain again.
2. Transfer macaroni to a large bowl. Add chicken, green pepper, onion, and parsley.
3. Stir together the mayonnaise, chili sauce, salt, dill and horseradish (if desired). Spoon over the other ingredients and toss until completely mixed. Serve chilled.

4-6 servings

SALAD NIÇOISE

To feel really Parisian, serve this with French bread and chilled white wine.

1 7-ounce can tuna fish,
   drained and broken into
   chunks
2 2-ounce cans anchovy fillets or 1 can anchovy fillets plus 2 tablespoons
   capers
1 hard boiled egg
1 cup diced tomatoes

¾ cup diced cucumbers or
   cooked diced green beans
⅓ cup diced green pepper
⅓ cup diced red onion
2 tablespoons chopped
   parsley
2 tablespoons oil
2 tablespoons vinegar
¼ teaspoon salt
dash pepper

1. Drain the anchovies on paper toweling. Cut each into quarters.
2. Cut the egg in half. Scoop out and discard the yolk. Cut the egg white into thin slivers.

3. Toss the tuna, anchovies (capers), and egg white with the vegetables.
4. Beat the oil and vinegar. Pour over the salad and toss gently. Serve over a bed of lettuce.

3 servings

CHICKEN-CRANBERRY GEL

The flavor of the gelatin is mild and doesn't overpower the solid ingredients in this attractive main-dish salad.

2 envelopes unflavored gelatin
3½ cups cranberry juice
⅛ teaspoon salt
2 tablespoons fresh lemon juice

2 cups diced cooked chicken (½ pound)
⅔ cup diced celery
⅓ cup toasted slivered almonds

1. Sprinkle the gelatin over 1 cup cranberry juice in a small saucepan. Allow to stand for 5 minutes. Slowly bring to a boil, stirring until the gelatin is dissolved.
2. Combine the gelatin mixture with the remaining cranberry juice, salt, and lemon juice. Refrigerate until slightly jelled.
3. Stir in the chicken, celery, and almonds. Pour into a mold and refrigerate until firm. Serve on a bed of lettuce.

4 servings

BLUEBERRY-RASPBERRY MOLD

As delightful to look at as it is to eat, especially on a warm summer day. It can also be served without the cottage cheese, as a dessert.

3 3-ounce packages raspberry gelatin
3 cups boiling water
1½ cups cold water

1 15-ounce can blueberries in syrup
1 cup low-fat yogurt
1 pound dry or low-fat cottage cheese

1. Dissolve gelatin in boiling water. Add cold water and blueberry syrup. Refrigerate until just beginning to gel.
2. Fold in yogurt and blueberries. Pour into a 7- or 8-cup ring mold and refrigerate until set.
3. Unmold and fill center with cottage cheese. If desired, decorate the outer edge of the mold with melon balls or grape clusters.

4-6 servings

Salad Dressings

FRENCH DRESSING

Endless variations are possible on basic French dressing. Use
your imagination to create your own.

¾ teaspoon salt   ¼ cup red wine vinegar (or
¼ teaspoon pepper   fresh lemon juice)
                                 ½ cup safflower or corn oil

1. Beat the salt, pepper and vinegar together with a fork or
   wisk, until the salt dissolves.
2. Beat in the oil gradually. Beat again or shake in a covered
   jar just before using.

¾ cup

Variations:

Garlic—Beat one crushed garlic clove with the vinegar

Mustard—Beat ½-1 teaspoon dry or Dijon mustard with the
vinegar

Curry—Beat ½ teaspoon curry powder with the vinegar

Anchovy—Beat 3-4 finely chopped anchovies with the vinegar

Herb—Add 3 tablespoons finely chopped fresh herbs to the
basic dressing

Caper—Add 2 teaspoons capers to the basic dressing

Italian—Beat ¼ teaspoon basil and 1 mashed garlic clove with
the vinegar

TEXAN POPPY SEED DRESSING

I was first introduced to this sweet dressing by a hospitable friend from Texas. Try it over any green salad.

⅔ cup oil
¼ cup red wine vinegar
1 tablespoon poppy seeds

½ teaspoon dry mustard
½ teaspoon salt
¼ cup sugar

1. Beat together with a fork or wisk the vinegar, poppy seeds, mustard, salt and sugar until the salt and sugar dissolve.
2. Gradually beat in the oil. Beat in a bowl or shake in a covered jar before serving.

About 1 cup

HONEY-LEMON DRESSING

I like to serve this dressing on a green salad with a Shavuot meal of blintzes, yogurt and sweetened berries.

½ teaspoon salt
½ teaspoon grated lemon rind
2 tablespoons honey

2 tablespoons red wine vinegar
2 tablespoons fresh lemon juice
½ cup oil

1. Beat together the salt, grated lemon rind, honey, vinegar and lemon juice.
2. Gradually beat in the oil. Keep refrigerated. Beat again or shake in a covered jar before serving.

Almost 1 cup

THOUSAND ISLAND DRESSING

⅔ cup mayonnaise
⅓ cup chili sauce
1-2 tablespoons of any of
   the following:

chopped onion
chopped celery
chopped green pepper
chopped radish

Mix all ingredients together and refrigerate.

1 cup

ANCHOVY SALAD DRESSING

This is an excellent way to use up any extra anchovies you
may have from another recipe.

¼ cup mayonnaise
¼ cup yogurt

4-8 finely minced anchovies

Mix together well and chill.

½ cup

LOW-CALORIE YOGURT DRESSING

This mild dressing is excellent over any combination of fruits.

1 cup yogurt
1 teaspoon grated lemon
   rind

1 packet artificial sweetener
   (equivalent to 2 teaspoons
   sugar)

Blend all ingredients well.

1 cup dressing

CRANBERRY-APRICOT RELISH

An interesting variation on plain cranberry sauce.

1 pound raw cranberries
1½ cups dried apricots, diced
1½ cups water

1 cup sugar
2 teaspoons grated orange rind

1. Put the cranberries, apricots, sugar and water into a large saucepan. Bring to the boiling point and simmer covered until all the cranberries have popped—about 10 or 15 minutes. Stir in the grated orange rind. Chill.

8 servings

CRANBERRY-ORANGE RELISH

This tasty relish can be made ahead and frozen. I prefer the smaller amount of sugar which yields a tart relish and saves on calories.

1 pound fresh cranberries
2 oranges

1-2 cups sugar

1. Grate the rind of the oranges and set aside.
2. Peel and section the oranges.
3. Chop the cranberries and orange sections together in small batches in an electric blender. Frozen berries can be chopped without defrosting.
4. Stir in the sugar and grated rind. Refrigerate and serve chilled.

6-8 servings

CRANBERRY-SHERRY RELISH

3 cups fresh cranberries
1 cup water
½ cup sugar
4 teaspoons cornstarch

¼ cup water
2 tablespoons sherry
2 teaspoons grated orange rind

1. Bring 1 cup water, cranberries and sugar to a boil. Cook until the berries pop, about 10 minutes.
2. Mix the cornstarch and ¼ cup water together and stir into the hot berries. Cook a few minutes until clear and thickened.
3. Stir in the sherry and grated orange rind. Serve hot or cold.

4-6 servings

VEGETABLES

Eating more vegetables is an excellent way to keep both cholesterol and calories down. Vegetables should be stressed on a low-cholesterol diet because they contain no cholesterol and have small amounts of saturated fat.

Unfortunately, many people dislike or at best are neutral toward vegetables because they've only had them served unimaginatively and overcooked, even in restaurants. I hope that the recipes in this chapter will convince you that vegetables can be an enjoyable as well as a healthy part of the diet.

Most cooked green vegetables can easily be made into something a little special with a lemon juice-margarine sauce or a topping of walnuts or almonds browned in margarine. Be sure to try these on asparagus, green beans, broccoli and Brussels sprouts. Tossing cooked peas with melted mint jelly or melted margarine plus crumbled dried mint is a simple way to make them more tempting.

ARTICHOKES

Artichokes are fun to serve—hot or cold as a first course, salad or side dish. Allow one per person. Many recipes call for cutting ½ inch off the top of the artichoke and trimming the sharp points off the outer leaves with a scissors. I generally omit both steps and have never been bothered by the points on the artichoke leaves.

| 4 artichokes | ¼ cup melted margarine |
| boiling salted water | ¼ cup fresh lemon juice |

1. Trim the stem to about ½ inch from the base. Remove any discolored leaves.
2. Drop into a large pot of boiling salted water. Simmer covered for about 45 minutes or until a leaf can be pulled out easily and the base can be pricked with a fork. Remove and drain upside down.
3. Serve hot with melted margarine or a margarine and lemon juice sauce. Serve cold with a flavored mayonnaise or French dressing.
4. To eat an artichoke, pull off each leaf, dip the bottom into the sauce, and scrape off the tender edible portion by pulling it through your teeth. Discard the leaves as you go along. Eventually you will come to a hairy central portion called the choke which should be scraped out with a teaspoon and discarded. Underneath the choke is the artichoke heart which is eaten with a knife and fork, each bite dipped in the sauce.

4 servings

SAUTÉED ASPARAGUS

I serve this simple and delicious dish at least once a week in the springtime.

1 pound fresh asparagus	⅛ teaspoon garlic powder
2 tablespoons oil	(optional)
½ teaspoon salt	

1. Snap off and discard the lower, tough portions of the stalks. Cut the asparagus on the diagonal into 1½-inch pieces.
2. Heat the oil in a large frying pan which has a cover. Add the asparagus. Sprinkle with salt and garlic powder (if desired).

3. Sauté the asparagus over medium heat covered, stirring several times until the asparagus is cooked but still crisp. This should take about 5-8 minutes.

4 servings

BAKED HERBED ASPARAGUS

1 pound fresh asparagus
2 tablespoons chopped)
  fresh parsley)
1 teaspoon chopped fresh)   or your favorite herbs
  dill)
2 tablespoons oil
½ teaspoon salt
dash pepper
dash garlic powder

1. Snap off and discard the lower tough portions of the stalks.
2. Pour the oil into an 8-inch-square baking dish and tilt the dish to cover the bottom with oil. Place the asparagus spears in the dish and roll them around to coat them with oil.
3. Sprinkle with salt, pepper and herbs. Bake covered at 375° for 20-25 minutes.

4 servings

GREEN BEANS

Green beans seem to be an almost universally liked vegetable. Since they also compliment most main dishes, they're a good safe choice for company. Here are 3 interesting variations on plain boiled green beans.

1 pound fresh green beans	2 quarts water

1. Snap off the ends of the beans and break into 2- to 3-inch lengths.
2. Bring the water to a boil. Add the beans, return to boiling, and cook uncovered for 7-8 minutes or until tender but still crisp. Drain in a colander and pour cold water over the beans to stop the cooking. This step can be done early in the day or even the day before. Use the cooked beans in the following recipes.

GREEN BEANS WITH ANCHOVIES

If you like anchovies, you'll love green beans prepared this way.

1 pound green beans, boiled as above	1 clove garlic, crushed
2 tablespoons oil	½ of 3-ounce tin anchovies, finely minced

1. Warm the oil and sauté the garlic over medium heat for a few minutes. Add the anchovies and stir briefly.
2. Add the beans. Cover and cook only until the beans are heated through, about 3-5 minutes.

4-6 servings

GREEN BEANS WITH GARLIC AND PIMENTO

This dish adds color and flavor to your meal.

1 pound fresh green beans,
  boiled as above
2 tablespoons oil
1 large or 2 small cloves
  garlic, crushed

½ teaspoon salt
3-4 tablespoons chopped
  pimento

1. Warm the oil and sauté the garlic over medium heat.
2. Stir in the green beans, salt and pimento. Cover and cook only until the beans are heated through, about 3-5 minutes.

4-6 servings

GREEN BEANS WITH MUSHROOMS

1 pound fresh green beans,
  boiled as above
2 tablespoons oil

½ pound mushrooms, sliced
¾ teaspoon salt

1. Warm the oil over medium heat in a frying pan or wide saucepan. Add the mushrooms and cook, stirring, until the mushrooms are almost done, 5-7 minutes.
2. Stir in the beans and salt. Cover and cook only until the beans are heated through, about 3-5 minutes.

6 servings

HERBED GREEN BEANS

1 pound fresh green beans
3 tablespoons oil or margarine
1 small or medium onion, chopped

1 clove garlic, minced
⅓ cup celery, chopped
½ teaspoon orégano
¼ teaspoon rosemary
¾ teaspoon salt

1. Snap off the ends of the beans and break into 2- to 3-inch pieces.
2. Sauté the onion, garlic and celery for 10 minutes in the oil or margarine.
3. Stir in the beans, herbs and salt. Cover and cook over low heat until the beans are tender, about 15-18 minutes. Stir several times during the cooking.

4-6 servings

BEAN CURD WITH MUSHROOMS AND SCALLIONS

Bean curd, also called tofu or soy cheese, is made from soy milk which in turn is derived from soybeans. Fresh bean curd is soft and will keep for several days in water in the refrigerator. Bean curd itself has a very mild flavor and blends well with other ingredients. It can be bought in oriental groceries.

½ cup water or chicken broth
½ teaspoon salt
1 tablespoon soy sauce
2 teaspoons cornstarch
3 tablespoons oil

3 scallions, cut in ½-inch pieces
¼ pound mushrooms, sliced
1 clove garlic, minced
1 bean-curd cake, cut once horizontally and then cut in ½-inch cubes

1. Mix the water, salt, soy sauce and cornstarch together and set aside.
2. Heat the oil in a large frying pan or wok. Add the scallions, mushrooms and garlic; sauté about 5 minutes.
3. Push the vegetables to one side of the pan and add the bean curd. Gently turn the bean-curd cubes for a few minutes until they are heated through. Stir in the vegetables.
4. Pour the soy-sauce mixture into the pan and heat just a minute or two until the sauce is clear and thickened.

2 servings

ORANGE-GLAZED BEETS

1 pound fresh beets
2 tablespoons margarine

2 tablespoons frozen orange juice concentrate

1. Scrub the beets well and cook them unpeeled in boiling salted water until tender—about 45 minutes to 1 hour depending on the size of the beets.
2. Peel and cut into slices about ¼ inch thick.
3. Melt the margarine and stir in the orange juice concentrate. Stir in the sliced beets and cook until heated through.

4-6 servings

ORIENTAL BROCCOLI

This dish is certain to please broccoli fans and may even gain converts to this often neglected vegetable.

2 tablespoons oil
1 medium onion, chopped
1 10-ounce package frozen broccoli, defrosted
½ cup water or chicken bouillon

2 tablespoons soy sauce
½ teaspoon sugar
dash garlic powder
1 tablespoon cornstarch
1 teaspoon gin (optional)

1. Cut the broccoli into ½ inch diagonal slices.
2. Sauté the onion in the oil for about 5 minutes. Add the broccoli and stir gently for 2 minutes.
3. Stir the remaining ingredients together. Add to the pan and cook until sauce is clear and thickened.

2-3 servings

SWEET AND SOUR RED CABBAGE

4 cups sliced red cabbage
1 tart apple, unpeeled, sliced
few slices onion
dash salt

1 tablespoon vinegar
1 tablespoon sugar
¼ cup water

1. Place all ingredients in a saucepan. Bring to a boil and simmer covered over low heat for 1 hour.

3-4 servings

CARROT KUGEL

My friend Shirley, who gave me this recipe, says that it has gone around the world. Try it once and you'll know why. My children can't think of a better way to have carrots.

1¼ cup flour
¾ teaspoon salt
1½ teaspoon baking powder
1 teaspoon baking soda
1 teaspoon cinnamon
¼ teaspoon ginger
¼ teaspoon nutmeg
¼ teaspoon cloves

¾ cup oil
½ cup brown sugar
2 egg whites
1 tablespoon water
1 tablespoon lemon juice
1½ cups grated carrots
(about 4 medium-sized carrots)

1. Stir together all the dry ingredients except the sugar.
2. Beat the oil, brown sugar and egg whites. Stir in the flour mixture.
3. Stir in the water, lemon juice and grated carrots. Carrots can be grated in water on high speed in an electric blender. Drain before incorporating into the batter.
4. Bake at 350° in a greased 8-inch baking dish for 45 minutes.

6-8 servings

CARROT TZIMMES

Serve this to make any Jewish holiday or Shabbat even more festive.

1 pound carrots, scraped and cut in ¼-inch slices
1½ cups pitted prunes or apricots or a combination of both
1½ cups water
1 6-ounce can orange juice concentrate, defrosted
2 tablespoons honey

1. Cook the carrots in boiling, salted water until tender, about 15-20 minutes. Drain and place in a 1½-quart casserole or saucepan.
2. While the carrots are cooking, bring the dried fruit and water to a boil in a small saucepan and simmer covered for 15-20 minutes. Drain and save the cooking liquid. Add the cooked fruit to the carrots.
3. Mix together the orange juice concentrate, honey and 2 tablespoons of the reserved fruit-cooking liquid. Pour the mixture over the carrots and fruit.
4. Heat over a low flame covered for 10 minutes, stirring gently a few times, or warm in a 350° oven for 15 minutes.

6-8 servings

ORANGE HONEY CARROTS

This is a very quick way to make canned carrots into an interesting dish. Don't be ashamed to serve it to company because it's so easy.

1 1-pound can sliced carrots, drained
2 tablespoons orange juice concentrate
1 tablespoon honey
1 tablespoon margarine (if desired)

1. Heat the orange juice concentrate and margarine (if desired) and honey in a small pan. Add the carrots and heat through.

3-4 servings

ORIENTAL CAULIFLOWER

This is an excellent way to lend interest to a meal with a simple main dish.

2 tablespoons soy sauce
2 tablespoons water
1 tablespoon cornstarch
1 small or ½ medium cauliflower (about 1 pound)

2 tablespoons oil
3 scallions, chopped
¼ pound mushrooms, sliced
⅞ cup chicken broth
¾ teaspoon salt

1. Stir the soy sauce, water and cornstarch together and set aside.
2. Separate the cauliflower into flowerets. Cut the flowerets into ¼-inch slices. Cut any large slices in half to make bite-sized pieces.
3. Heat the oil and sauté the scallions and mushrooms about 5 minutes. If the dish is not to be served immediately, stop at this point and continue just before serving.
4. Add the cauliflower and sauté a minute or two. Add the broth and salt. Bring to a boil and simmer covered about 3 minutes or just until the cauliflower can be pricked with a fork. This step is the key to the entire dish. The cauliflower must not be overcooked.
5. Stir in the cornstarch mixture and cook until the sauce thickens, just a minute or two.

3-4 servings

BAKED EGGPLANT SLICES

1½-pound eggplant   ¾ teaspoon salt
¼ cup oil   ⅛ teaspoon pepper
2 cloves garlic, crushed   ½ teaspoon orégano

1. Trim off the ends of the eggplant and cut crosswise into ½-inch slices. Sprinkle the slices well with salt and let stand in a colander for at least ½ hour. Press out as much liquid as possible to remove a bitter taste.
2. Beat the oil, garlic, and seasonings together with a fork. Brush each side of the eggplant slices with the oil mixture.
3. Place the slices in a single layer on a well-greased cookie sheet or shallow pan. Bake at 400° for 20 minutes or until tender.

6 servings

RATATOUILLE

When you look at the ingredients, you'll know why I like to say that ratatouille can also be called "what to do after you take down the succah." Ratatouille is equally good hot or cold. By adding canned tuna fish, it can be made into a complete one-dish meal.

2 tablespoons oil
2 medium onions, sliced
2 cloves garlic, crushed or minced
1-pound eggplant (1 medium eggplant) unpeeled, cut into 1 to 1½-inch cubes
salt

1½ pounds zucchini cut into 1 to 1½-inch cubes
1 large green pepper, chopped
1 15-ounce can tomato purée
¾ teaspoon orégano
½ teaspoon basil
¾-1 teaspoon salt

1. Sprinkle the eggplant cubes well with salt and let stand in a colander for at least ½ hour. Press out the liquid which contains bitter juices.
2. Sauté the onions and garlic over medium heat about 10 minutes in a very large pot.
3. Add all remaining ingredients, bring to a boil, and simmer covered until the eggplant and zucchini are tender but not mushy, about 40 minutes. Stir frequently during the cooking.

8 servings

LEMON-FLAVORED LEEKS

Leeks, a mild-flavored onion often used in soups, make an interesting side dish when cooked alone as a vegetable. Allow enough preparation time for very careful washing of the leeks.

6 leeks (1½ pounds)
boiling salted water
2 tablespoons margarine

2 tablespoons fresh lemon juice

1. Cut off the roots of the leeks and all but 1 inch of the green leaves. Save the leaves for use in soups. Wash the leeks very carefully, removing any traces of soil between the layers. Cut into ¾-inch lengths.

2. Cook the leeks in boiling salted water until tender, about 8-10 minutes. Drain.
3. Melt the margarine and add the lemon juice. Warm for a minute or two and pour over the cooked leeks.

4 servings

SAUTÉED GREEN PEPPERS

This is one of the simplest and best ways to prepare green peppers. For variety, sauté sliced onion or sliced mushrooms with the pepper strips.

2 tablespoons oil
6 medium green peppers, cut in ⅓-inch strips

1 large or 2 small cloves garlic, crushed
½ teaspoon salt
dash pepper

1. Heat the oil in a large frying pan. Add the garlic, pepper slices, salt and pepper. Sauté over medium heat for 5 minutes.
2. Cover and cook a few minutes longer until pepper strips can be pricked with a fork.

6-8 servings

ITALIAN ROAST PEPPERS

Allow 1 pepper for each person and multiply the recipe appropriately. Be prepared for a marvelous aroma while the peppers are baking.

1 medium green pepper, halved and seeded
1 teaspoon margarine
1 teaspoon red wine vinegar

12 dried rosemary leaves
salt
dash pepper

1. Place the pepper halves cut side up on a greased baking pan or dish. Add ½ teaspoon margarine, ½ teaspoon red wine vinegar and 6 dried rosemary leaves to each pepper half. Sprinkle with salt and pepper.
2. Bake at 350° about 40 minutes or until tender.

1 serving

POTATO KUGEL

For Passover, the baking powder can be omitted.

2 pounds potatoes, peeled and grated
1 small or medium onion, grated
4 egg whites

4 tablespoons matzo meal
1 teaspoon salt
1 teaspoon baking powder
dash pepper

1. Drain the grated potatoes. Mix well with all the other ingredients.
2. Bake in a greased 8-inch square pan at 350° for 35 minutes or until firm.

8 servings

POTATO LATKES

In this recipe, the potatoes and onion are grated in a blender. If you don't have a blender or if you can use a hand grater without winding up with bloody fingers, do the grating by hand. If the batter seems too liquid, add more matzo meal or blot off excess water with a paper towel.

3 pounds potatoes, peeled and cut into ½-inch cubes
1 medium onion, quartered
4 egg whites
1½ teaspoon salt
1 teaspoon baking powder
¼ teaspoon pepper
2 tablespoons flour
3 tablespoons matzo meal
corn oil

1. Blend the potatoes and onion in 4 batches. For each batch, first put 1 egg white into the blender container. Then add 2-2½ cups potato cubes and ¼ onion. Cover and blend on chop or high speed just until all the potatoes and the onion go through the blades. Be sure not to overblend.
2. Stir the remaining ingredients into the combined batches of grated potatoes.
3. Warm a few tablespoons oil in a 10-inch frying pan over medium heat. Using a large spoon, pour batter for 4 pancakes into the pan. Fry until brown on both sides, adding more oil as needed.

Note: If you're pressed for time, consider the Carmel Kosher Potato Pancake Mix. Just use 3 egg whites or commercial egg substitute for the 2 eggs required.

36 3- 4-inch pancakes

NEW POTATOES WITH DILL

New potatoes are very small potatoes with reddish skins. Their appearance in the supermarket along with asparagus is a sure sign of spring. Since the skins are attractive and flavorful, peeling isn't necessary.

1 pound new potatoes
3 tablespoons margarine
3 tablespoons fresh lemon
juice

1 teaspoon chopped fresh dill
or ½ teaspoon dried dill

1. Cook the new potatoes in boiling salted water until they're tender, about 20 minutes.
2. Melt the margarine in a small saucepan, stir in the lemon juice and dill. Pour the sauce over the drained cooked potatoes and serve.

4 servings

SWEET POTATOES AND APPLES

3 pounds sweet potatoes,
peeled, cooked, and
mashed
3 tablespoons lemon juice
4 tablespoons orange juice
¼ teaspoon salt

4 medium apples, peeled and
thinly sliced
¾ cup brown sugar, firmly
packed
1 teaspoon cinnamon

1. Beat the lemon juice, orange juice, and salt into the sweet potatoes.
2. Stir the cinnamon and brown sugar together.
3. Spoon ⅓ of the potatoes into a well-greased 2½-quart casserole. Cover with ⅓ of the apples and sprinkle with ⅓ of the sugar-cinnamon mixture.
4. Repeat the layering twice.
5. Bake covered at 350° for 60-70 minutes or until the top apple layer is tender.

8-10 servings

SWEET POTATOES AND PINEAPPLE

A light fruity-flavored sweet potato casserole.

2 pounds sweet potatoes, peeled, cooked, and mashed

¼ cup brown sugar, firmly packed

1 cup undrained crushed pineapple

1½ tablespoons orange juice or rum

¾ teaspoon grated orange rind

½ teaspoon cinnamon

⅛ teaspoon salt

1. Combine all the ingredients and mix well.
2. Bake covered in a 1½-quart greased casserole at 350° for 30 minutes.

6 servings

SPINACH, SWISS CHARD, OR BEET GREENS WITH GARLIC

Swiss chard is a leafy dark green vegetable which looks and tastes very much like spinach. My gardening friends tell me that it's extremely easy to grow.

Fresh beets are generally sold with their tops or beet greens on. You can make yourself proud of your thrifty ways by cooking the beet greens as well as the beets.

10 ounces fresh spinach, swiss chard, or beet greens

2 tablespoons oil or margarine

1 clove garlic, minced

¼ teaspoon salt

dash pepper

1. Wash the leaves well, trim the stems and shake off excess water. Tear into 2- or 3-inch pieces.
2. Warm the oil or margarine over medium heat in a large pan and cook the minced garlic a minute or two. Add the vegetables, salt, and pepper. Cook, stirring, just until the leaves wilt, about 3-5 minutes.

2-3 servings

GRATED TURNIPS

This tangy dish may convince people who never eat turnips to add turnips to their vegetable repertoire.

2 tablespoons oil
1 medium onion, chopped
1 clove garlic, chopped

1 pound fresh turnips, grated on a medium grater
½ teaspoon salt

1. Sauté the onions in the oil over medium heat until tender, about 10 minutes.
2. Add the garlic and sauté another few minutes.
3. Add the turnips and salt. Cover and cook over low heat, stirring occasionally, for 15-20 minutes.

6 servings

SAUTÉED ZUCCHINI

This is quick, easy, and very good. Any leftovers are delicious served cold with a few tablespoons of wine vinegar poured over them.

1 pound zucchini cut in
¼-inch slices or ½-inch
cubes
2 tablespoons oil

½ teaspoon salt
½ teaspoon orégano
⅛ teaspoon garlic powder
dash pepper

1. Heat the oil in a large frying pan. Add the zucchini and seasonings. Sauté uncovered for a few minutes. Then cook covered for about 8 minutes or until the zucchini is tender but not mushy.

4 servings

ZUCCHINI WITH APRICOTS

This delightful combination was suggested to me by my friend, Denise Telio, who teaches Middle-Eastern cooking.

2 pounds small zucchini, cut
in ¼-inch slices
3 tablespoons oil
1 teaspoon salt
1 cup small dried apricots

1 cup water
1 tablespoon brown sugar
2 tablespoons lemon juice
1 tablespoon cornstarch
2 tablespoons water

1. Put the apricots and water in a small saucepan. Bring to a boil. Cover and simmer until the apricots are tender but not mushy, about 20 minutes. Mix in the sugar and lemon juice. Set aside.
2. Heat the oil in a large pot or frying pan and sauté the zucchini over medium heat, stirring often, for 5 minutes. Sprinkle with salt.
3. Pour the apricot mixture, undrained, on top of the zucchini. Cover and cook until the zucchini are tender but still crisp, about 5 minutes.
4. Mix the cornstarch and 2 tablespoons of water together and stir into the pan. Heat another minute or two until the sauce thickens.

8 servings

LEMON ZUCCHINI

1 pound small zucchini
2 tablespoons margarine
2 tablespoons lemon juice

½ teaspoon grated lemon rind
chopped parsley or chopped dill (optional)

1. Scrub the zucchini and cut crosswise into ¼-inch slices. Cook uncovered in boiling salted water 3-4 minutes or until the zucchini is cooked but still crisp. Drain immediately.
2. Heat the margarine, lemon juice and lemon rind, stirring well until the margarine is melted. Pour over the zucchini. Sprinkle with parsley or dill if desired.

4 servings

ZUCCHINI WITH TOMATOES
(CAMPFIRE ZUCCHINI)

If you or your friends have a vegetable garden, you'll understand why a cook can never have too many recipes for zucchini. Our friends, the Gilles family, made this zucchini dish for us on a camping trip.

2 tablespoons oil
1 medium onion, chopped
1 clove garlic, minced
1 pound zucchini cut in ¼-inch slices or ½-inch cubes

2-3 medium fresh tomatoes, chopped, or one 8-ounce can tomato sauce
¾ teaspoon orégano or basil
½ teaspoon salt
dash pepper

1. Warm the oil over medium heat and sauté the onions and garlic until the onion is wilted, about 5-10 minutes.
2. Add the rest of the ingredients and continue cooking covered until the zucchini is tender, about 10-15 minutes.

4 servings

GRAINS AND PASTAS

Grains and pastas are perfectly acceptable for a low-cholesterol diet. Although not especially low in calories,* they can be prepared hundreds of different ways and can lend a great deal of interest to meals.

Of the different kinds of rice available, I generally prefer long grain rice because the grains remain separate after cooking. Short grain rice gives a cooked product in which the grains stick together and is a good choice for rice pudding. Converted rice retains more nutrients than other white rice. Brown rice with its bran coat retains the most nutrients of all and requires longer cooking time than white rice.

To give a yellow color and a mild flavor to rice, add ½ teaspoon crumbled saffron or powdered turmeric to the cooking liquid. Some prepared pilaf mixes are acceptable and, of course, extremely easy.

Since pasta seems to have universal appeal to children, try adding tuna or cooked chicken to the sauce for a simple, one-dish family meal. I like to combine a pasta with cottage cheese for a main-dish casserole.

Egg noodles contain 50 milligrams of cholesterol in a 2-ounce portion and might be used less often than the other pastas. For purposes of comparison, one egg yolk has 250 milligrams of cholesterol and a low-cholesterol diet usually allows 300 milligrams of cholesterol daily.

For an interesting change from rice or pasta, try kasha

---

*Calories in 1 cup of cooked product:
rice-225 egg noodles-200
spaghetti or macaroni-155
U.S. Department of Agriculture Home and Garden Bulletin No. 72 "Nutritive Value of Foods"

(buckwheat groats), polenta or mamaliga (corn meal), bulgur (cracked wheat), barley, or couscous.

See the chapter on Meatless Main Dishes.

RICE AND NOODLE CASSEROLE

This is a superb company dish. It makes a lot and looks harder to prepare than it actually is.

2 cups very fine noodles
3 tablespoons corn oil
1 cup Uncle Ben's converted rice

3 cups chicken broth or 3 cups water plus 1 tablespoon chicken soup concentrate
1¼ teaspoons salt

1. After measuring the noodles, crush them into small pieces with your knuckles. Warm the corn oil over low heat. Add the noodles and cook them, stirring constantly until they're medium brown. Watch the noodles carefully since they burn quite easily.
2. Stir in the remaining ingredients. Bring to a boil and simmer covered over low heat for 25 minutes or until all of the liquid is absorbed.

6 servings

Variation:

Substitute ⅓ cup Orzo rice-shaped macaroni for the noodles. Brown the macaroni without crushing first.

SPICED ORANGE RICE

Such an easy way to make rice into a special dish! The cinnamon gives it a sweet flavor.

2 tablespoons oil	2½ cups orange juice
1 medium onion, diced	1 teaspoon salt
1 cup Uncle Ben's Converted Rice	⅛ teaspoon ginger
	⅛ teaspoon cinnamon

1. Heat the oil in a medium saucepan and sauté the onion until wilted. Add the rice and stir briefly to coat all the grains with oil.
2. Stir in the orange juice and seasonings. Bring to a boil and simmer covered over low heat for 25 minutes.

6 servings

MUSHROOM PILAF

For even more flavor, substitute ½ cup white wine for ½ cup chicken broth in this recipe.

2 tablespoons oil	1 cup Uncle Ben's Converted Rice
½ pound mushrooms, chopped	2½ cups chicken broth (or 2½ cups water and 2½ teaspoons powdered instant chicken soup)
1 medium onion, finely chopped	
1 clove garlic, minced or crushed	1 teaspoon salt

1. Sauté the mushrooms, onion and garlic in the oil for 10 minutes or until the onions are soft.

2. Stir in the rice, chicken broth, and salt. Bring to a boil and simmer covered for 25 minutes or until all the water is absorbed.

6 servings

MEGADARRAH (RICE WITH LENTILS)

The recipe for this Middle-Eastern rice dish comes from Denise Telio who was born and raised in Egypt.

⅓ cup uncooked lentils
1 cup water
½ small onion
3 2-inch pieces of celery
2 tablespoons oil
½-¾ cup sliced onion
½ cup chopped onion

½ cup Uncle Ben's converted rice
½ teaspoon cumin
½ teaspoon salt
2 tablespoons margarine (optional)
low-fat yogurt

1. Pick over and wash the lentils. Place the lentils, ½ small onion and celery in a saucepan. Bring to a boil, lower the heat, and simmer covered for 15 minutes. Drain and save the cooking liquid. Discard the onion and celery.
2. Heat the oil in a medium-sized pot and sauté ½-¾ cup sliced onion until deep brown. Remove the onion and set aside, leaving as much oil in the pan as possible.
3. Add more oil to the pot if necessary and sauté the ½ cup chopped onion until golden brown. Add the reserved lentils, rice, cumin, and salt. Add enough water to the reserved lentil-cooking liquid to make 1 cup of liquid. Stir into the other ingredients.
4. Bring to a boil and simmer covered over very low heat for at least 30 minutes or until the rice is tender and all of the water has been absorbed. Top with reserved fried onion and serve with a separate bowl of plain yogurt. Even better if allowed to rest for a while before served.

4-6 servings

RICE WITH PINE NUTS

3 tablespoons oil
1 medium or large onion, chopped
1 garlic clove, minced or chopped
1 cup Uncle Ben's Converted Rice

2½ cups water or chicken stock
6 tablespoons tomato paste
1 teaspoon salt
¼ teaspoon allspice
¼ cup pine nuts

1. Sauté the onion and garlic in 1 tablespoon oil until the onion is wilted.
2. Add the rice, water or stock, tomato paste, salt and allspice. Stir well to blend the tomato paste into the liquid. Bring to a boil, lower the heat, and simmer covered for 25 minutes.
3. While the rice is cooking, fry the pine nuts in the remaining 2 tablespoons of oil until they are golden brown. Stir frequently to prevent burning.
4. Stir the pine nuts into the cooked rice.

6 servings

RICE PUDDING

Easy and delicious.

1 cup raw rice cooked according to package directions
2 tablespoons sugar
½ teaspoon vanilla
½ teaspoon cinnamon

1 teaspoon lemon juice
3 egg whites
¾ cup skimmed milk
¼ cup melted margarine
½ cup raisins or chopped dates (optional)

1. Mix all ingredients together and pour into a greased 8-inch square baking dish or a greased 1½-quart casserole.
2. Bake covered at 350° for 1 hour or until the top is firm and a knife inserted comes out dry. If a crisp top is desired, bake another 5 minutes uncovered.

6 servings

BARLEY AND VEGETABLES

6 cups boiling water
1½ teaspoons salt
1 cup medium pearl barley
2 tablespoons oil
1 medium or large onion, chopped

1 large or 2 small cloves garlic, minced or crushed
½ pound mushrooms, sliced or chopped, or
1½ cups finely chopped celery
salt and pepper

1. Stir the salt and barley into the boiling water. Cover and simmer 45-60 minutes or until tender. Drain.
2. While the barley is cooking, sauté the onion and garlic in

the oil until the onion is translucent. Add the mushrooms or celery and sauté another 5-10 minutes or until the vegetables are soft.

3. Stir the hot drained barley and the sautéed vegetables together. Season with salt and pepper.

6 servings

COUSCOUS

Couscous, a staple of North African dishes, is made from wheat grain and resembles semolina. I use it very frequently because of its extremely short cooking time. Sautéed onions or mushrooms can be added for variety.

2 cups water   1 cup couscous
1 teaspoon salt

1. Bring the water and salt to a boil. Stir in the couscous and cook uncovered about 3 minutes or until most of the water is absorbed.
2. Remove from the heat. Cover and let stand about 7 minutes or until all of the water is absorbed.

4-6 servings

BULGUR PILAF

Bulgur or cracked wheat retains almost all of the nutrients in the whole wheat kernel. It has a pleasing nut-like flavor and is definitely worth trying if you've never had it. It can be found in the foreign-food section of most large supermarkets or in Armenian or Middle Eastern food stores.

2 tablespoons oil
2 medium onions, chopped
2 cloves garlic, crushed or minced

1 cup bulgur
2 cups water or chicken broth
1 teaspoon salt

1. Sauté the onion and garlic in the oil for about 10 minutes or until the onion is translucent.
2. Add the bulgur, water or broth, and salt. Bring to a boil, lower the heat, and simmer covered for 20-25 minutes or until all of the liquid is absorbed.

4-6 servings

KASHA VARNISHKAS
(KASHA WITH BOW TIES)

2 tablespoons oil
1 medium or large onion, chopped
1 cup kasha (buckwheat groats)

2 egg whites
2 cups water
1 teaspoon salt
2 cups (4 ounces) bow ties

1. Sauté the chopped onion in the oil until light brown. Set aside.
2. Mix the kasha and egg whites. Heat in a large pan, stirring constantly until the kernels become dry and separate. Add the water and salt. Bring to a boil and simmer covered over low heat until the water is absorbed, about 10-15 minutes.
3. While the kasha is cooking, cook the bow ties according to package directions. Drain. Stir the hot bow ties and sautéed onions into the hot cooked kasha.

6-8 servings

MUSHROOM KUGEL

I am indebted to Barbara Epstein for allowing me to adapt her delicious family recipe for this book.

3 tablespoons oil or margarine
1½-2 cups finely chopped sweet Spanish onion
½ pound chopped fresh mushrooms
1 teaspoon salt
8 ounces fine noodles
3 egg whites

1. Sauté the onion in the oil or margarine until the onion becomes soft. Add the mushrooms and sauté lightly about 5 minutes. Season the onions and mushrooms with 1 teaspoon salt.
2. Cook the noodles in boiling salted water according to package directions. Drain well.
3. Combine the cooked noodles, mushroom-onion mixture, and egg whites. Add more salt if desired.
4. Place in a greased 9-inch square pan and bake uncovered at 350° for 30 minutes. This gives a kugel with a crisp top. If a softer kugel is preferred, bake covered.

6-8 servings

PEACH OR APRICOT KUGEL

I've never met anyone who doesn't like kugel. It's a good choice for anyone except a very serious dieter. Here's an especially easy recipe.

12 ounces broad noodles, cooked
3 tablespoons oil or melted margarine
1 12-ounce jar of peach or apricot jam
½ teaspoon almond extract
¼ cup orange juice
3 egg whites
¾ cup raisins
½ cup chopped walnuts
brown sugar (if desired)

1. Toss the cooked noodles with the oil or margarine. Combine with the remaining ingredients.
2. Place the noodle mixture into a 2½-quart greased casserole or a 9- by 13-inch greased baking dish. Sprinkle with brown sugar, if desired.
3. Bake at 350° covered for 20 minutes and then uncovered for 10 minutes longer.

8-10 servings

MEATLESS MAIN DISHES

There are many reasons for reducing meat consumption aside from prevention of atherosclerosis. Increasing numbers of people are eating lower on the food chain because of the world food crisis, concern about an association between bowel cancer and beef consumption, and a desire to reduce food bills.

In response to the world food shortage, the Synagogue Council of America has made the following recommendation: "We urge American Jews to observe one or more meatless days on weekends, and to reserve meat meals for Sabbaths and Festivals."* I generally follow this recommendation in my menu planning.

Uncreamed cottage cheese is an excellent protein source for meatless main dishes. It contains considerably more protein per calorie than meat, poultry, or fish and has almost no cholesterol or fat.

Soybeans are another excellent protein source and at about 50 cents per pound they're probably the least expensive source of usable protein. Besides being high in protein, soybeans are the only vegetable which contains all amino acids (protein building blocks) needed for human growth. They have no cholesterol and their fat is high in polyunsaturated fatty acids. Soybean cookery is clearly an area we all should explore.

Soy grits are lightly toasted soybeans which have been cracked into 8 or 10 pieces. They require considerably less cooking time than soybeans and are very good in casseroles or loaves.

* *Resolution on World Hunger* adopted by the Plenum of the Synagogue Council of America on January 8, 1975.

Textured soybean products or textured vegetable-protein products as they're often called are made from specially processed soy flour. These products are designed to simulate the flavor, appearance, and texture of meat and generally appear in the supermarket as ground-meat extenders. They have no cholesterol and only very small amounts of fat. I find one of these products, "Protein-ettes," especially useful because it can be cooked alone without any ground meat. If you have difficulty obtaining Protein-ettes, it can be purchased directly from the Creamette Company, Minneapolis, Minnesota 55401. I've included several recipes using this product.

For a quick and easy meatless main dish, I always keep handy a package of Osem Vegetarian Cholent Casserole imported from Israel (Nakid Ltd., Tel Aviv). Various prepared mixes for vegetarian patties can be found in most health food stores.

SOYBEANS IN BARBECUE SAUCE

If you've never had soybeans, you'll be pleased to find that they have an enjoyable nut-like taste which blends well with many different types of seasonings. Soybeans do not become mushy and lose their shape with long cooking as other beans do. They just become tender.

1 cup dry soybeans
1 teaspoon salt
2½ cups water
⅓ cup chopped onion
⅓ cup chopped green pepper
⅓ cup chopped celery

2 teaspoons molasses
2 tablespoons tomato sauce or ketchup
2 tablespoons brown sugar, firmly packed

1. Wash the soybeans under running water in a colander and drain. Add the soybeans and salt to the 2½ cups water and soak overnight. Bring to a boil and simmer covered for about 2½ hours or until the soybeans are tender. Check

several times during cooking and add more water if necessary.
2. Drain the soybeans and save ¾ cup of the cooking liquid. Add water if necessary to give ¾ cup liquid.
3. Combine the soybeans, ¾ cup of cooking liquid, and all the other ingredients in a 1½-quart flameproof casserole. Taste the liquid and add salt if desired. Bring to a boil and bake covered at 350° for about 1 hour.

CURRIED SOYBEANS

1 cup dry soybeans
1 teaspoon salt
2½ cups water
1 tablespoon oil
1 medium onion, chopped

1 medium unpeeled apple, chopped
1 teaspoon curry powder
¼ teaspoon cinnamon

1. Wash the soybeans under running water in a colander and drain. Add the soybeans and salt to the 2½ cups water and soak overnight. Bring to a boil and simmer covered for about 2½ hours or until the soybeans are tender. Check the soybeans several times during cooking and add more water, if necessary.
2. Drain the soybeans and save ¾ cup of the cooking liquid. Add water if necessary to give ¾ cup liquid.
3. In a 1½-quart flameproof casserole, sauté the onion in oil until it becomes translucent. Add the drained soybeans, ¾ cup cooking liquid, chopped apple, curry powder, and cinnamon. Taste the liquid and add salt, if desired.
4. Bring to a boil and bake covered at 350° for about 1 hour.

3 servings

SOYBEANS CACCIATORE

1 cup dry soybeans
1 teaspoon salt
2½ cups water
2 tablespoons oil
1 cup chopped onion
¼ cup diced green pepper

1 clove garlic, minced or crushed
1 1-pound can tomatoes or stewed tomatoes
½ teaspoon basil
¼ teaspoon orégano

1. Wash the soybeans under running water in a colander and drain. Add the soybeans and salt to the 2½ cups water and soak overnight. Bring to a boil and simmer covered for about 2½ hours or until the soybeans are tender. Check the soybeans several times during cooking and add more water, if necessary.
2. Drain the soybeans.
3. In a 1½- or 2-quart flameproof casserole, sauté the onion, green pepper and garlic until the onion is translucent. Add the drained beans, tomatoes, basil and orégano. Taste and add salt if desired.
4. Bring to a boil and bake covered at 350° for about 1 hour. Very good served with rice.

3-4 servings

ORIENTAL STYLE SOYBEANS

1 cup dry soybeans
1 teaspoon salt
2½ cups water
3 scallions, chopped

2 tablespoons soy sauce
2 teaspoons finely minced candied ginger or ½ teaspoon powdered ginger

1. Wash the soybeans under running water in a colander and drain. Add the soybeans and salt to the 2½ cups water and soak overnight. Bring to a boil and simmer covered for about 2½ hours or until tender. Check several times during cooking and add more water, if necessary.
2. Drain the soybeans and save ¾ cup of the cooking liquid. Add water if necessary to give ¾ cup liquid.
3. Combine the soybeans, ¾ cup cooking liquid, scallions, soy sauce, and ginger in a 1½-quart flameproof casserole.
4. Bring to a boil and bake covered at 350° for about 1 hour. Serve with rice, if desired.

3 servings

MUSHROOM-SOY GRITS LOAF

Very flavorful and much less fat than a meat loaf.

1 cup soy grits	½ pound fresh mushrooms, chopped
2 cups water	
1½ teaspoons salt	3 egg whites
2 tablespoons oil	Cream Sauce (Optional).
1 small onion, chopped	See Cream Sauce for
1 clove garlic, minced	Poached Fish.

1. Bring the water, soy grits, and 1 teaspoon salt to a boil and simmer covered for 30-45 minutes.* Drain well.
2. While the soy grits are cooking, heat the oil and sauté the onion and garlic for about 7-10 minutes. Add the mushrooms and sauté 5 minutes longer.
3. Combine the drained soy grits, mushroom mixture, remaining ½ teaspoon salt, and egg whites. Blend well and spoon into a greased 9- by 5-inch loaf pan. Bake uncov-

*Different products labeled "soy grits" may vary in their cooking time. Check the soy grits several times during the cooking period. If all of the water has been absorbed, stop cooking and go on to the next step.

ered at 350° for 25 minutes. Especially good served with a mushroom cream sauce.

3-4 servings

SPINACH-SOY GRITS LOAF

The herbs and the cruchy texture of the soy grits make this a very interesting dish. Please read note under recipe for Mushroom-Soy Grits Loaf.

1 cup soy grits	½ teaspoon orégano
2 cups water	¼ teaspoon rosemary
1½ teaspoons salt	3 egg whites
1 10-ounce package frozen spinach	

1. Bring the water, soy grits, and 1 teaspoon salt to a boil and simmer covered for 30-45 minutes. Drain well.
2. While the soy grits are cooking, prepare the spinach according to package directions. Drain in a colander or strainer and press out excess water with a wooden spoon.
3. Combine the drained soy grits, spinach, oregano, rosemary, remaining ½ teaspoon salt, and egg whites. Blend well and spoon into a greased 9- by 5-inch loaf pan. Bake uncovered at 350° for 25 minutes. Serve accompanied by a cream sauce, if desired.

3-4 servings

MUSHROOM CUTLETS

Delicious vegetable patties.

2 medium potatoes (about
  ¾-1 pound)
2 tablespoons oil
1 cup finely chopped onion
1 clove garlic, minced or
  crushed
¾ pound mushrooms, finely
  chopped

1 egg white
1 teaspoon salt
dash pepper
6 tablespoons bread crumbs
bread crumbs for coating
  patties
oil for frying patties

1. Peel and dice the potatoes. Cook in boiling salted water.
   Drain and mash. This gives about 2 cups of mashed potatoes.
2. While the potatoes are cooking, sauté the onion and garlic
   in the oil until the onion is soft. Add the mushrooms and
   sauté another 5-10 minutes or until the mushrooms are
   soft.
3. Combine the mashed potatoes, sautéed vegetables, egg
   white, salt, pepper, and 6 tablespoons bread cumbs. Mix
   well. Add more bread crumbs if necessary to make the
   mixture firm enough to be formed into patties. Shape into
   12 3-inch patties.
4. Dip the patties into bread crumbs to coat them on both
   sides.
5. Fry in hot oil until golden brown.

4 servings

APPLESAUCE-COTTAGE CHEESE-NOODLE PUDDING

This noodle pudding plus a green salad makes an easy complete dairy meal. It's a sure hit with children and one of our favorite family dishes.

12 ounces noodles, cooked and drained
3 tablespoons margarine
1 pound dry or low-fat cottage cheese
1 cup applesauce
½ cup brown sugar
1½ teaspoons cinnamon
½ teaspoon salt
4 egg whites
raisins or chopped dates (optional)
chopped walnuts (optional)

1. Toss the hot cooked noodles with the margarine. Stir in the remaining ingredients.
2. Pour into a greased 2½-quart casserole or 9- by 13-inch greased baking dish* and bake covered at 350° for 30 minutes. If a crisp top is desired, uncover for the last 10 minutes of baking.

6-8 servings

*I frequently use two 1- or 1½-quart casseroles and freeze one of them unbaked. On an especially busy day, I remove the casserole from the freezer early in the morning, defrost it at room temperature, and then bake it for supper.

PINEAPPLE-COTTAGE CHEESE-NOODLE PUDDING

8 ounces noodles, cooked and drained
2 tablespoons margarine
12 ounces dry or low-fat cottage cheese

10 ounces or 1¼ cup un-drained crushed pineapple
½ cup brown sugar
½ teaspoon salt
1 teaspoon cinnamon
3 egg whites

1. Toss the hot cooked noodles with the margarine. Combine with the remaining ingredients.
2. Bake covered in a greased 8-inch square baking dish or a greased 1½-quart casserole at 350° for 30 minutes. If a crisp top is desired, uncover for the last 10 minutes of baking.

4-6 servings

PARSLEY-DILL-COTTAGE CHEESE CASSEROLE

8 ounces noodles or maca-roni, cooked and drained
2 tablespoons margarine
12 ounces dry or low-fat cottage cheese
¾ cup low-fat yogurt
3 egg whites

¾ teaspoon salt
1 tablespoon chopped fresh dill or 1 teaspoon dried dill
¼ cup chopped fresh parsley
¼ cup chopped fresh chives or scallions

1. Toss the hot cooked macaroni or noodles with the margarine. Stir in the remaining ingredients.
2. Bake covered in a greased 8-inch square baking dish or a greased 1½-quart casserole at 350° for 30 minutes.

4-6 servings

MACARONI WITH SPINACH AND COTTAGE CHEESE

I often bring this dish when I'm asked to contribute a casserole for a pot luck supper. It's tasty, filling, healthy and inexpensive.

2 10-ounce packages frozen chopped spinach
1 pound dry or low-fat cottage cheese
4 egg whites
4 cups tomato sauce (homemade or canned)

salt and pepper to taste
½-1 teaspoon orégano or to taste
½-1 teaspoon basil or to taste
1 pound macaroni—elbow or any other tube-shaped macaroni

1. Cook the frozen chopped spinach according to package directions and drain well in a colander or strainer. Press out as much water as possible.
2. Combine the spinach with the cottage cheese, egg whites, tomato sauce and seasonings.
3. Cook the macaroni until almost done and drain in a colander. Combine with the cottage cheese–tomato sauce mixture.
4. Pour into a greased 9- by 13-inch baking dish and bake covered at 350° for 30 minutes.

8 servings

MAMALIGA (CORN MEAL)

This is a Rumanian dish but the applesauce is a Leviton addition designed to attract children.

Pack any leftover cooked corn meal into a bread pan or other small rectangular container and refrigerate. Cut the hardened corn meal into ¼-inch slices and serve for breakfast fried in oil or margarine and topped with syrup, honey, or applesauce.

2 cups corn meal	margarine
1 cup cold water	cottage cheese
4 cups boiling water	applesauce
1½ teaspoon salt	

1. Mix the corn meal and cold water. Slowly pour the corn meal mixture into the boiling salted water, constantly stirring. Cook covered over low heat for 20 minutes. Stir frequently.
2. Serve hot and let individuals help themselves to margarine, cottage cheese and applesauce, all of which can be mixed in with the cooked corn meal.

4-6 servings

BLINTZES

Once you acquire the knack of preparing blintzes, you'll want to make them all year round and not just for Shavuot. I use the same batter for crêpes and blintzes. See the Dessert

Crêpe recipe for more information on preparation and storage of the pancakes.

1 cup flour	3 egg whites
2 tablespoons sugar	1¼ cups milk
½ teaspoon salt	2 tablespoons oil
1 teaspoon grated orange rind (Optional but very good)	

Filling

1 pound dry or low-fat cottage cheese	3-4 tablespoons sugar
1-2 egg whites	¼-½ teaspoon cinnamon

1. Stir the flour, sugar and salt together. Beat the orange rind, egg whites, milk and oil together lightly and stir into the flour mixture. Beat with an electric beater at low to medium speed until smooth.
2. To prepare the blintz pancakes, use a 7-inch crêpe pan if you have one or else a 9-inch Teflon frying pan, which is what I use. Brush the pan lightly with 1 tablespoon oil. Warm over medium heat. Pour in 2-3 tablespoons batter. Quickly tilt the pan to spread the batter thinly in all directions. Fry until the underside of the pancake is light brown and the top surface is cooked. Remove and place browned side up on a large plate. Add a very small amount of oil to the pan and continue cooking in this way until all the batter is used up. Stack the cooked pancakes on top of each other. The pancakes may be refrigerated for several days covered with plastic wrap or may even be frozen wrapped in foil.
3. Stir the filling ingredients together. Use 2 egg whites with dry cottage cheese and 1 egg white with low-fat cottage cheese. Put about 2 tablespoons of filling on the *browned* side of each pancake, 1 or 2 inches from the top of the pancake. Fold the 1- or 2-inch strip over the filling. Fold the sides of the pancake in toward the center and roll up the pancake to completely cover the filling. The blintzes may be refrigerated or frozen at this point.
4. Fry the blintzes in oil over medium heat until browned on

each side. Serve with thawed frozen berries, applesauce, low-fat yogurt or Mock Sour Cream.

12-14 blintzes

SPEEDY BLINTZES

These "blintzes" are actually a cross between regular blintzes and French toast. They remind me of the ones my mother used to make when I was a child, and taste almost as good. They're an excellent idea for a quick, nourishing supper.

Filling

1 pound dry or low-fat cottage cheese (2 cups)
1 egg white

¼ cup sugar
½ teaspoon cinnamon

14-15 large (4-inch by 4½-inch) slices of bread
(allow for more slices if smaller sized ones are used)

4 egg whites
2 cups milk
½ teaspoon cinnamon
oil for frying

1. Mix all the filling ingredients together.
2. Spread each slice of bread with about 3 tablespoons of filling. Top with another bread slice. Continue until all the filling is used up. Cut the sandwiches in half if desired.
3. Beat the 4 egg whites, milk, and cinnamon together in a flat baking dish about 8 inches by 8 inches in size. Soak the "blintzes" in the milk mixture for a few minutes on each side.
4. Warm 2 tablespoons of oil in a frying pan over medium heat. Fry the "blintzes" until golden brown on each side. Add more oil as needed. Serve with any of the usual accompaniments for blintzes or French toast.

about 6 servings

EGGPLANT WITH COTTAGE CHEESE

This is a healthy and tasty one-dish casserole meal. It can be stretched further by putting in a few layers of cooked noodles or ziti. If this is done, use a larger casserole and more tomato sauce.

1 medium eggplant (about 1 pound)
salt
1-2 egg whites
dry bread crumbs
oil

1 pound dry or low-fat cottage cheese
2 cups tomato sauce, canned or home-made
orégano (optional)

1. Peel the eggplant and cut it horizontally into ½-inch slices. Sprinkle with salt and let stand in a colander for at least ½ hour. Press out as much liquid as possible, to remove the bitter juices from the eggplant.
2. Dip the eggplant slices in the egg white and then in crumbs. Heat a few tablespoons of oil in a frying pan and fry the eggplant on both sides until crispy brown.
3. In a 2-quart greased casserole, put layers of sauce, eggplant, and cottage cheese beginning and ending with sauce. If desired, sprinkle each sauce layer with orégano. Bake covered at 350° for 35 minutes.

4 servings

COTTAGE CHEESE-MUSHROOM LOAF

A delicious dairy main dish. Chopping the mushrooms takes only a few minutes with a wooden chopping bowl and hand chopper.

3 tablespoons corn oil
1 medium or large onion, chopped
1 pound mushrooms, finely chopped
2 cloves garlic, crushed or minced

1 pound dry or low-fat cottage cheese
3 egg whites
1 teaspoon salt
1 teaspoon orégano or basil
dash pepper
½ cup bread crumbs, preferably fresh

1. Sauté the onion in the oil in a large frying pan over medium heat for 5 minutes.
2. Add the chopped mushrooms and garlic and sauté 10 minutes longer.
3. Stir the cottage cheese into the mushroom mixture. Add the remaining ingredients and mix until well blended.
4. Spoon into a well-greased 9- by 5-inch baking pan. Bake at 375° for 50-55 minutes or until set and firm.

4-6 servings

COTTAGE CHEESE PINWHEELS

Especially good served with applesauce or thawed frozen berries.

Dough

2 cups flour
2 teaspoons baking powder
½ teaspoon salt
2 tablespoons sugar

½ cup margarine
⅓ cup low-fat yogurt
½ teaspoon vanilla

Filling

1 cup dry or low-fat cottage cheese

2 tablespoons sugar
½ teaspoon cinnamon

1. Stir the flour, baking powder, and salt together.

2. Cream the margarine and sugar. Beat in the yogurt and vanilla.
3. Blend the flour mixture into the margarine mixture to form a dough. Divide the dough in half. On a lightly floured surface, roll each half into a rectangle about 8 by 11 inches.
4. Combine the filling ingredients.
5. Spoon ½ of the filling in a narrow strip about 1½ inches from the edges of the dough along the long side of the rectangle.
6. Starting at the edge of the dough near the filling, roll up as for a jelly roll. Press the ends together firmly and place seam side down on a greased cookie sheet.
7. Bake at 350° for 20 minutes or until golden brown. Cut into 1- to 2- inch slices.

6 servings

COTTAGE CHEESE PANCAKES

¾ cup flour
1¼ teaspoons baking powder
¼ teaspoon salt
½ teaspoon cinnamon
2 tablespoons sugar

2 egg whites
1 tablespoon oil
½ cup skimmed milk
½ cup dry or low-fat cottage cheese

1. Mix the flour, baking powder, salt, cinnamon and sugar together.
2. Beat the egg whites, oil, and milk together. Pour into the flour mixture and mix until completely blended. Stir in the cottage cheese.
3. Fry in hot oil until golden brown on both sides.

8 or 10 3- to 4-inch pancakes

COTTAGE CHEESE-APPLESAUCE PANCAKES

An excellent dairy meal for a Chanukah evening.

1 cup flour
1½ teaspoons baking powder
½ teaspoon salt
¾ teaspoon cinnamon
2 tablespoons sugar

1 cup applesauce
2 egg whites
1 cup dry or low-fat cottage cheese
2 tablespoons skimmed milk

1. Stir the flour, baking powder, salt, cinnamon, and sugar together.
2. Beat the applesauce, egg whites, cottage cheese, and milk together. Add the dry ingredients and stir until completely blended.
3. Fry in hot oil until golden brown on both sides. Serve with applesauce.

about 14 3- or 4-inch pancakes

SPINACH-COTTAGE CHEESE PIE

An elegant supper or luncheon dish. The low-cholesterol answer to quiche.

1 pre-baked 8- or 9-inch pie shell
1 10-ounce package frozen spinach
1 small or medium onion, chopped

2 tablespoons margarine
½ teaspoon salt
dash pepper
8 ounces (1 cup) dry or low-fat cottage cheese
3 egg whites

1. Cook the spinach according to package directions. Drain in a strainer or colander and firmly press out as much liquid as possible with the back of a spoon. Set aside.
2. Sauté the onion in the margarine until golden.
3. In a large bowl, combine the spinach, onion, and remaining ingredients. Mix thoroughly and pour into the prebaked pie shell.
4. Bake at 350° for about 45 minutes or until the filling is set and firm in the center of the pie.

4-6 servings

SPANAKOPITA (SPINACH CHEESE PIE)

This Greek dish makes an elegant and healthy appetizer or main course.

Filling

2 tablespoons oil or margarine

1 large bunch scallions, chopped

1 large bunch parsley, chopped

2 10-ounce packages frozen chopped spinach

12 ounces dry or low fat cottage cheese

3 egg whites

1½ teaspoons salt

¼ teaspoon pepper

1 pound filo dough

½ cup melted margarine

1. Warm the 2 tablespoons of oil or margarine over medium heat and sauté the scallions for about 5 minutes. Add the chopped parsley and sauté for another few minutes. Cool.
2. Cook the spinach as directed on the package. Drain in a colander or strainer and press out as much water as possible.
3. Add the drained spinach, cottage cheese, egg whites, salt, and pepper to the scallions and parsley. Mix well.
4. Grease a 9- by 13-inch baking dish with oil or margarine. Place a sheet of filo dough into the baking dish and press

it up against the sides of the dish and into the corners. Brush with melted margarine. Layer half the sheets of filo dough in the same way and brush each with margarine. To save time, some of the filo sheets may be folded in half and layered in that manner.

5. Spread the spinach-cheese mixture evenly over the pastry. Cover with the remaining filo sheets and brush each with margarine. Brush the top sheet with margarine.

6. Bake uncovered at 350° in the center of the oven for about 45 minutes or until the top of the pie is golden brown. Cut into squares and serve hot.

6 main-dish servings
12 first-course servings

PIZZA

My daughter would rather eat pizza than almost anything else. I like this recipe because the dough has to rise only 20 minutes.

1 cup warm water
1 package dry yeast
1 teaspoon sugar
1 teaspoon salt
2½-3 cups flour

1½ cups tomato sauce seasoned with orégano or basil
4 ounces shredded part-skimmed-milk mozzarella cheese

1. Stir the yeast into the warm water in a medium bowl and let stand for 5 minutes.
2. Stir in the sugar and salt.
3. Stir in 2½ cups flour, cover with a dish towel and let rise about 20 minutes.
4. Stir down the dough. Mix in enough flour to make a soft but not sticky dough. I usually require 4-6 tablespoons of flour. Knead the dough for a minute or two in the bowl until smooth. Divide into 2 balls. On a lightly floured surface, roll out each ball into a large circle. Place each round on a lightly greased 10- to 11-inch pizza pan and pat

the dough out to the edges of the pan. If you don't have pizza pans, roll the entire dough out into a large rectangle and pat the dough into a 10½-inch by 15½-inch by 1-inch lightly greased pan.

5. Spoon the sauce over the dough up to ½ inch from the edge of the dough. Sprinkle with the cheese. Bake at 425° for 20 minutes.

5-6 main dish servings

Variations:

"Sausage Pizza"—Add ¼-inch slices of Morningstar Farms Breakfast Links before baking. The links can be sliced frozen.
Mushroom Pizza—Reduce the amount of cheese used or omit it entirely. Add ½-1 pound of lightly sautéed mushrooms seasoned with salt, garlic powder, and orégano. This is the way I prepare pizza for my husband and myself.

AMERICAN CHOP SUEY

A sure winner with children. This version substitutes a soy protein product for the customary ground beef.

3 tablespoons oil
2 cups chopped onion
1 green pepper, chopped
2 garlic cloves, crushed or minced
3 cups tomato sauce

1 teaspoon orégano
1 3-ounce package beef-flavored Creamettes Protein-ettes
1 pound elbow macaroni

1. Sauté the onion, pepper and garlic in the oil for 10-15 minutes.
2. Add the tomato sauce and orégano and simmer 5 minutes.
3. While the tomato sauce is simmering, cook the Protein-ettes and macaroni according to package directions. Drain well. Mix with the hot tomato sauce and serve.

8-10 servings

LASAGNE

A quick and easy lasagne recipe chock full of protein for unsuspecting children.

1 pound lasagne noodles
1 3-ounce package beef-flavored Creamettes Protein-ettes, cooked and drained
5 cups tomato sauce
1 teaspoon orégano

1½ pounds low-fat cottage cheese
2-3 ounces part-skimmed-milk mozzarella cheese for topping (optional)

1. Cook the lasagne noodles in boiling salted water according to package directions. Add 1-2 tablespoons of oil to the water to prevent the noodles from sticking together.
2. Stir the cooked Protein-ettes and orégano into the tomato sauce.
3. Grease a 9- by 13-inch baking dish. Spoon a thin layer of the sauce over the bottom of the dish. Cover with a single layer of noodles, then a layer of cottage cheese and finally a layer of sauce. Continue layering the noodles, cheese and sauce until all the noodles are used up (4-5 layers). Finish with a layer of sauce and top with mozzarella cheese if desired. Cover loosely with aluminum foil and bake at 350° for 30 minutes.

8-10 servings

MACARONI AND CHEESE

Originally prepared to taste for my son and now enjoyed by the whole family.

3 tablespoons margarine	dash salt
3 tablespoons flour	3 cups cooked macaroni
1 cup skimmed milk	
1 8-ounce tub imitation cheese spread*—cheddar flavor	

1. Melt the margarine in a saucepan. Stir in the flour. Very gradually add the milk while constantly stirring with a wisk. Heat until simmering and thickened.
2. Add the cheese spread in small pieces. Heat until the cheese melts. Mix well. Stir in the salt.
3. Stir in the macaroni. Pour into a well-oiled baking dish and bake uncovered at 350° for 20 minutes.

3 servings

YOGURT

Homemade yogurt, prepared with skimmed milk, contains less fat than any of the commercial brands. It's also very inexpensive and not at all difficult to make. The basic principle is to create favorable (i.e., warm) conditions for growth of lactic acid bacteria. These bacteria feed on the milk sugar, lactose, and produce lactic acid which denatures milk protein and gives yogurt its thick quality. If you don't care to try the method below, you might want to consider buying one of the electric yogurt makers.

Homemade yogurt is not quite as thick as the store-bought variety, but the taste is fine. Yogurt is very good served with all fruits and berries, with dry cottage cheese, or with thawed, undiluted frozen fruit juices stirred through it.

| 3¼ cups water | ¼ cup yogurt (source of lactic-acid bacteria) |
| 1½ cups dry powdered skimmed milk | |

*I use Fisher Count Down Cheese Spread (Fisher Cheese Co., Wapakoneta, Ohio 45895) which contains only 1% fat. I buy this in a local diet food store.

1. Mix the water and dry milk in a saucepan and bring to a boil. Let cool to lukewarm.
2. Mix the yogurt with about ½ cup of milk. Then mix thoroughly with the remaining milk. Pour into an ovenproof container (I use a 1-quart wide-mouthed jar).
3. Place in a 275° oven for 10 minutes. Turn the oven off but leave container in the oven. Let stand at least 6 hours or overnight. Refrigerate. Save ¼ cup yogurt as starter for a new batch.

SPAGHETTI SAUCE

2 tablespoons oil
1½ cups chopped onion
2 cloves garlic chopped
¼ cup thinly sliced carrot
¼ cup chopped celery
1 2-pound, 3-ounce can Italian tomatoes

¼ cup chopped parsley
1½ teaspoons salt
dash pepper
¾ teaspoon orégano
¾ teaspoon basil

1. Heat the oil in a large pot. Sauté the onion, garlic, carrot, and celery for about 10 minutes.
2. Drain the can of tomatoes. Add the tomatoes only to the vegetables. Add the parsley and seasonings. Stir and bring to a boil. Lower the heat and simmer covered about 45 minutes.
3. Purée in a blender. Return to the pot and re-heat.

About 3 cups of sauce

FISH

Fish is an ideal food for inclusion in a low-cholesterol diet because it is high in protein and polyunsaturated fats and low in total fat and calories. It would therefore be wise to substitute fish for some of the meat you eat.

To make this dietary change a pleasurable one, only two things have to be remembered:

1) Make sure that the fish you buy is fresh, and

2) Don't dry out and toughen the fish by overcooking.

Besides its dietary benefits, fish has the added advantage of not requiring the time-consuming trimming away of fat which is necessary for meat and poultry. Fish also has a short cooking time which makes it a good choice for a quick supper.

My own inclusion of considerably more recipes for fish than for meat reflects my own eating habits. I generally serve fish for supper 3-4 times per week, poultry once or twice, a meatless main dish once or twice, and meat once.

Buying Fish

Fish odor is the simplest and most reliable test for freshness of fish. Newly caught fish has practically no odor. The fish odor strengthens with the passage of time. When buying fish, always check that it has a mild smell and no strong "fishy" odor. Never buy fish without first smelling it, no matter how much the person behind the fish counter may growl.

Other indications for freshness of a whole fish are bright and bulging eyes, reddish gills, shiny scales adhering tightly to the skin, and firm flesh which springs back when pressed.

Fish fillets should have a firm texture and no drying out around the edges. I've found that in supermarkets the fish on special or the fish present in largest quantity is usually the freshest. When only a few pieces of a particular variety are present, the odds are that they are the remaining pieces of a large lot. Probably the safest way to insure getting high-quality fresh fish is to find a reputable fish store with a high turnover.

For maximum flavor, fresh fish should be eaten as soon as possible after purchase, preferably on the same day. It should be stored well-wrapped in the coldest part of the refrigerator until used.

Frozen fish is usually cheaper than fresh fish but you may find as I do that the texture and flavor of fresh fish are worth the price differential. If you use frozen fish, it should be defrosted in the refrigerator or in cold water to prevent draining away of fish juices. For the same reason, it is sometimes advised to cook frozen fillets when they're only partially defrosted.

Some knowledge of fish nomenclature may facilitate shopping. Whole fish are fish just as they come from the water. Drawn fish are whole fish minus their insides or entrails. Dressed fish have both entrails and scales removed. Usually the head, tail and fins are removed as well. Small dressed fish are called pan-dressed. Splitting a dressed fish means cutting it in half horizontally. The split fish may also have its backbone removed. I usually remove the backbone after cooking when it can be easily lifted out with minimal loss of fish flesh.

Fish fillets are the sides of fish cut lengthwise away from the backbone and may or may not be skinless. Fish steaks are cross-section cuts (usually ½-1 inch thick) of large dressed fish. A piece of backbone in the center of the steak is the only bone present.

When deciding how much fish to buy, it is usually advised to plan for each person 1 pound of whole fish, ½ pound of dressed fish and ⅓ pound of fillets or steaks.

Kosher fish have both scales and fins. There is a great variety of kosher fish from which to choose. Some common non-kosher fish are shellfish, catfish, eels and shark.

For those interested in reducing caloric intake as well as intake of saturated fats, the following fish are usually considered the "fat" or high calorie fish: butterfish, herring, mackerel, salmon, shad, smelt, tuna, trout, whitefish.

Cooking Fish

Fish has very little connective tissue and requires considerably less cooking time than poultry or meat. Fish flesh is naturally tender and does not need long cooking to tenderize it.

Fish is done or cooked when it loses its translucent look and becomes opaque. White-fleshed fish becomes milky white. At this point the flesh flakes easily with a fork. Check for doneness during cooking and remember that once it's overdone, there's little you can do to improve it.

Baking is the most frequent fish preparation method I use, probably because of its simplicity. At least once a week, I bake fish fillets on a greased baking pan in a 350° oven just until the fish flakes with a fork. The cooking time is generally very short, about 10 minutes, depending on the thickness of the fillet. I usually serve the fish with a sauce of lemon juice and margarine flavored with dill or parsley. Chopped walnuts or almonds browned in margarine are other easy toppings for baked fish. Fresh fish properly cooked is naturally flavorful and requires very little in the way of fancy cookery to make it enjoyable.

Most of the baked fish dishes included in this chapter are very good served cold the following day. Since my husband doesn't like sandwiches, I usually bake enough fish to have leftovers for lunch for him.

Poaching, or cooking in a simmering liquid, is another simple and quick method to prepare fish. The poaching liquid may be salted water or a mixture of wine and water. Onions, carrots, celery, bay leaf, parsley, peppercorns, etc. may be added to flavor the cooking liquid. The fish is added to the simmering liquid and cooked covered just until the fish flakes. As with baking, the cooking time is very short, usually about 5-10 minutes. Poached fish is excellent served hot with a "cream" sauce or cold in salads.

Fish may also be broiled, fried, or steamed. Always keep

in mind the basic principle that fish should be cooked only until it becomes opaque and can be flaked with a fork.

Although fish is pareve, it may not be cooked together with meat. Fish may, however, be cooked in or with milk.

See the appetizer and salad chapters for additional fish recipes.

❧⧉☙

Cold Fish

HERRING-CRANBERRY SURPRISE

This unusual combination is actually quite delicious with neither flavor predominating. It's a very elegant first course or brunch dish.

1 8- or 12-ounce jar herring fillets in wine sauce
1 1-pound can whole berry cranberry sauce
1 small or medium red onion, sliced very thin
1 cup low-fat yogurt

1. Remove the herring fillets from the jar and drain on a paper towel. Discard the onions which were packed with the herring. Cut the herring into bite-size pieces.

2. Mash the cranberry sauce in a medium-sized bowl. Blend in the remaining ingredients. Serve chilled.

6-8 servings as a first course

SWEET AND SOUR SALMON or HALIBUT

An excellent main dish or first course. To serve as a first course, remove the center bone after cooking and cut the steaks in half. A festive Jewish holiday dish when you don't feel like making gefilte fish.

4 salmon or halibut steaks	½ cup brown sugar
1 medium onion, sliced	⅓ cup raisins
1 large lemon, sliced	½ teaspoon salt
2 cups water	

1. Place the onion and lemon slices, water, brown sugar, raisins, and salt in a large shallow pan. Bring to a boil, reduce heat, and simmer covered 10 minutes.
2. Add the fish steaks and simmer covered about 15-20 minutes or until the fish can be flaked with a fork.
3. Allow to cool and then refrigerate. The poaching liquid jells and is delicious.

4 main-dish servings
8 first-course servings

SEVICHE (MARINATED FISH)

Seviche appears in both Spanish and French cuisines and is a very refreshing appetizer. Serve it with either toothpicks or small plates and forks.

1 pound flounder or sole
fillets
¾ cup lime juice
¼-½ cup chopped green
peppers
¼-½ cup chopped celery

¼-½ cup chopped scallions
¼-½ cup chopped parsley
3 medium tomatoes, cubed
2 tablespoons wine vinegar
2 tablespoons oil
1 teaspoon salt

1. Cut the fish into 1½-inch pieces.
2. Marinate the fish overnight in the lime juice and drain well.
3. Mix the fish with the peppers, celery, scallions, parsley and tomatoes.
4. Beat the oil, vinegar and salt together and pour over the other ingredients. Stir gently.

8 first-course servings

GEFILTE FISH

Gefilte fish has the reputation of being difficult to make, but if the fish store grinds the fish, its preparation is almost as easy as meatballs. Home-made gefilte fish is however considerably more expensive than already prepared fish and I usually save it for a special holiday treat.

Any combination of fresh-water fish can be used, but whitefish, pike and carp are the most common. Whitefish is usually about twice as expensive as carp, with pike somewhere in the middle.

1½ pounds whitefish
1½ pounds pike

3 pounds carp or buffle carp

Fish Broth

Fish bones and heads
3 medium onions, sliced
water to cover

2 teaspoons salt
2 teaspoons sugar
¼ teaspoon white pepper

Fish Balls

ground fish
1 medium onion, grated*
4 egg whites
1½ teaspoons salt
1 tablespoon sugar

¼ teaspoon white pepper
½ cup ice water
3 tablespoons matzo meal
2 sliced carrots

1. Fillet and grind the fish. Save the bones and heads. To prepare the cooked broth, put the fish bones and heads in a large pot (at least 5- or 6-quart). Put the sliced onions on top and add water to cover everything, about 5-6 cups. Add the salt, sugar and pepper. Bring to a boil and simmer, covered, while preparing the ground fish balls.
2. Put the ground fish in a wooden chopping bowl and add the remaining ingredients except the carrots. Chop until the fish is fine and very well blended. Refrigerate for about 10 minutes and shape into 3-inch balls.
3. Place the fish balls in the broth and add the sliced carrots. Bring to a boil, reduce heat and simmer covered for 1½ hours. Stir once or twice so the balls get uniformly cooked.
4. Let the fish balls cool in the broth for about ½ hour and then remove the fish balls and carrots.
5. Adjust the seasoning in the broth and strain. Save both the broth and bones. Chill the broth until it's jellied and serve with the gefilte fish. The fish still on the bones is delicious so let the bone pickers in your family enjoy themselves.

12-14 balls

*My friend, Nechama, who makes the best gefilte fish I've tasted, suggests this alternative to grating the onion by hand: Chop the onion and purée it in an electric blender with the egg whites. Rinse out the blender with the ½ cup ice water and add the water to the ground fish.

SALMON OR FISH MOUSSE

An excellent summer dish to make in the cool morning or the day before.

2 envelopes unflavored gelatin
½ cup water
¼ cup fresh lemon juice
1 small onion, chopped
1 1-pound can salmon, drained or 1 pound fish fillets, poached and drained

¼ cup mayonnaise
1 teaspoon dried dill
1 teaspoon salt (only if using fish fillets)
½ cup evaporated skimmed milk or ⅓ cup skimmed milk powder plus water to give ½ cup milk, chilled

1. If the skimmed milk is not ice cold, pour it into a medium bowl and place it in the freezer to chill. For faster whipping, chill until crystals just begin to form around the edges.
2. Sprinkle the unflavored gelatin over the water in a small saucepan and let stand for 5 minutes. Slowly bring to a boil, stirring to dissolve the gelatin.
3. Put the lemon juice and onion into the blender. Pour in the hot gelatin mixture. Blend to grate the onion. Add the mayonnaise, salmon or fish, dill, and salt (if using). Blend just until the salmon or fish is puréed. Pour into a large bowl and refrigerate.
4. Beat the skimmed milk until it stands in peaks. Fold ⅓ of the whipped milk into the salmon or fish mixture. Then fold in the remaining whipped milk.
5. Pour into a lightly oiled 1-quart mold. Chill until firm, and unmold. Decorate with lettuce, parsley, unpeeled cucumber slices, etc.

6 servings

TUNA MOUSSE

2 envelopes unflavored gelatin
½ cup water
2 7-ounce cans tuna, undrained

1 cup low-fat yogurt
¼ cup mayonnaise
¼ cup fresh lemon juice
1 teaspoon dried dill

1. Sprinkle the unflavored gelatin over the water in a small saucepan and let stand for 5 minutes. Slowly bring to a boil, stirring to dissolve the gelatin.
2. Place all the ingredients including the dissolved gelatin into a blender container. Blend until the mixture is smooth.
3. Pour into a 1-quart mold. Chill until firm. Decorate with lettuce, parsley, unpeeled cucumber slices, tomato slices, etc.

6 servings

MOCK LOBSTER SALAD

1 pound fish fillets (any white fish)
½ cup finely chopped celery (optional)

¼ cup mayonnaise
3 tablespoons chili sauce
1 tablespoon horseradish

1. Add the fillets to boiling salted water, reduce heat, and simmer covered for about 5 minutes or until they can be flaked with a fork. Drain, flake, and chill. Add the celery, if desired.

2. Mix together the mayonnaise, chili sauce, and horseradish. Gently mix into the fish and celery.
3. Arrange the fish on individual beds of lettuce leaves.

3 main-dish servings
6-8 appetizer servings

MOCK SHRIMP SALAD

1 pound fish fillets (any white fish)
½ cup chili sauce

2-4 tablespoons horseradish
lettuce

1. Add the fillets to boiling salted water, reduce heat, and simmer covered for about 5 minutes or until they can be flaked with a fork. Drain, flake and chill.
2. Mix the chili sauce and horseradish together.
3. Arrange the fish on individual beds of lettuce leaves. Spoon a few tablespoonfuls of sauce over the fish and pass the rest around.

3 main-dish servings
6-8 appetizer servings

SAUCES FOR COLD POACHED FISH

Green Mayonnaise

½ cup mayonnaise
¼ cup chopped fresh parsley
3 tablespoons finely chopped scallions

½-¾ teaspoon dried dill
⅛ teaspoon salt
1 tablespoon lemon juice

Mix all the ingredients together and serve from a small bowl.

Caper-Anchovy Mayonnaise

½ cup mayonnaise
1 tablespoon capers

1-2 teaspoons anchovy paste
1 tablespoon lemon juice

Blend all ingredients well and serve from a small bowl.

Hot Fish

SCROD WITH WALNUT SAUCE

This is an excellent choice for a company or family dinner. It's exceedingly simple yet still festive. The thick scrod is hard to overcook and can be put in the oven while guests are having cocktails.

3 pounds boneless scrod,
 ¾-1 inch thick
salt
pepper

garlic powder
½ cup margarine
¾ cup chopped walnuts

1. Place the scrod in a greased baking dish. Season with salt, pepper and garlic powder and bake in a 400° oven for

about 15-20 minutes or until the fish flakes when pricked with a fork. Start checking for doneness at 15 minutes.

2. While the fish is cooking, heat the margarine and stir in the walnuts. Continue cooking until the margarine has browned slightly, about 5 minutes.

3. When the fish is done, drain off any liquid which may have formed in the bottom of the baking dish. Pour the sauce over the fish and serve.

8 servings

OVEN-FRIED FISH FILLETS

These fish fillets have a nice crisp crust without all the bother of frying. The wine adds a delicate and pleasant flavor but the dish can also be made without first marinating the fillets in wine.

1 pound thin fish fillets—flounder or perch are very good

½ cup dry white wine or vermouth

1½ teaspoons salt

½ cup bread crumbs, flavored or unflavored, or ½ cup cornflake crumbs

2-3 tablespoons melted margarine

1. Arrange the fish in a single layer in a shallow baking dish. Mix the wine and the salt and pour over the fish. Let stand about ½ hour.

2. Remove the fish and coat with bread crumbs. Place on a well-greased baking pan. Spoon the melted margarine over the fish fillets. Bake at 500° for 7-10 minutes or until the fish flakes easily.

4 servings

BROILED CODFISH STEAKS

Don't ignore this recipe because it's so simple. It's quite delicious. Remember that if you start off with really fresh fish, there's very little you have to do to it.

4 small codfish steaks,
  ½-¾ inch thick
salt
3 tablespoons oil

½ cup breadcrumbs, seasoned or unseasoned
chopped parsley for garnish

1. Sprinkle the codfish steaks lightly with salt and brush on both sides with oil. Coat the steaks with breadcrumbs.
2. Preheat an oiled broiler pan for 5-10 minutes. Place the steaks on the pan. Broil without turning until the topping is crisp and golden brown. Bake at 400° to 450° for 5 minutes or until the fish flakes when pricked with a fork.
3. Garnish with parsley and serve with lemon margarine sauce, if desired.

Lemon Margarine Sauce

3 tablespoons margarine,
  melted

3 tablespoons fresh lemon
  juice

BAKED FISH WITH BARBECUE SAUCE

Any leftovers of this dish are excellent served cold the following day.

1 tablespoon corn oil
3-4 tablespoons chopped onion
3-4 tablespoons chopped green pepper
1 8-ounce can tomato sauce
2 tablespoons brown sugar

2 tablespoons fresh lemon juice
¼ teaspoon Worcestershire sauce
1 pound fish fillets
salt and pepper

1. Heat the oil in a small saucepan and sauté the onion and green pepper over low heat for 10 minutes.
2. Add the tomato sauce, brown sugar, lemon juice and Worcestershire sauce. Bring to a boil and simmer covered 15 minutes.
3. Season the fish fillets with salt and pepper and place them in a shallow baking dish.
4. Spoon the sauce over the fish and bake uncovered at 350° or 400° just until the fish can be flaked with a fork (about 10 minutes for fish fillets less than ½ inch thick).

3-4 servings

HUNGARIAN FISH BAKE

An easy and delicious "different" kind of fish dish.

1 pound fish fillets
salt, pepper
1 cup low-fat yogurt

¾ teaspoon paprika
1 teaspoon caraway seeds
1 tablespoon grated onion

1. Season the fish fillets and place them in a shallow baking dish.
2. Stir together the yogurt, paprika, caraway seeds, and onion. Spoon the mixture over the fish fillets.
3. Bake uncovered at 350° or 400° just until the fish can be flaked with a fork (about 10 minutes for fish fillets less than ½ inch thick).

3-4 servings

FISH WITH TOMATO SOUP AND YOGURT

Try this simple variation of baked fish when you're looking for something different requiring little effort.

1 pound fish fillets—cod, scrod, haddock, flounder, or any white fish
salt
garlic powder

¾ cup undiluted canned tomato soup
¾ cup low-fat yogurt
1½ tablespoons fresh lemon juice

1. Season the fillets with salt and garlic powder and place in a single layer in a greased baking dish.
2. Stir the tomato soup, yogurt, and lemon juice together and spoon over the fish.

3. Bake uncovered at 350° until the fish flakes when touched with a fork, about 10 minutes, depending on the thickness of the fillets.

3-4 servings

TOMATO-FISH CASSEROLE

As soon as I tasted this dish at a friend's house, I knew I was going to ask for the recipe. I was pleased to find that it's so easy to prepare.

1 pound fish fillets (flounder, scrod or any white fish), cut into 2-inch pieces
20 crackers broken into coarse pieces (Manischewitz Tam Tam or Rokeach Snackers or saltines or a combination of crackers)
⅛ teaspoon garlic powder
½ teaspoon salt
3 tablespoons melted margarine
1 8-ounce can tomato sauce

1. Mix together the fish, broken crackers, garlic powder, salt and margarine and put into a 1½-quart greased casserole.
2. Bake covered at 350 degrees for 20 minutes.
3. Pour the tomato sauce over the fish. Reduce the heat to 300° and bake covered for 20 minutes.

4 servings

"CREAM" SAUCE FOR POACHED FISH

This amount of sauce is enough for one pound of poached fish. For added richness, use evaporated skimmed milk. For added flavor substitute ¼ cup white wine or sherry for ¼ cup of milk. The variations are endless so use your imagination and devise some of your own.

3 tablespoons oil or margarine	1½ cups skimmed milk
3 tablespoons flour	¾ teaspoon salt
	dash white pepper

1. Heat the oil or margarine in a medium saucepan. Stir in the flour. Gradually stir in the milk, beating with a wisk until the sauce is thickened and comes to a boil.
2. Stir in the salt and any additional ingredients (see below). Stir in flaked poached fish and heat through for 3-4 minutes.

3 servings

Possible Additions

½ pound sautéed mushrooms	cooked sliced carrots
few tablespoons capers	1-2 teaspoons Dijon mustard
minced anchovies	dill or other herbs
	artichoke hearts

FISH IN "EGG" LEMON SAUCE

This version of Greek egg lemon sauce is, of course, without the eggs. I generally use the sauce for poached fish but it's also excellent over any plain baked or broiled fish.

3 tablespoons oil or margarine	¼ cup lemon juice
3 tablespoons flour	¾ teaspoon salt
1¼ cups milk	2-3 cups cooked fish

1. Heat the oil or margarine in a medium saucepan. Stir in the flour. Gradually stir in the milk, beating with a wisk until the sauce is thickened and comes to a boil.
2. Stir in the lemon juice, salt and fish. Heat through about 3-4 minutes. Serve over rice.

3 servings

SMOKED COD IN CREAM SAUCE

Served with baked or mashed potatoes, this is an easy "different" fish supper.

1 pound boneless smoked
  cod
1 cup skimmed milk
2 tablespoons margarine or
  oil

2 tablespoons flour
1/8 teaspoon white pepper
salt to taste

1. Soak the cod in cold water for about one hour to remove excess salt. Drain well and cut into several pieces.
2. Bring the milk to a simmer and add the fish. Cover and simmer until the fish flakes, about 5-10 minutes. Remove the fish from the milk with a slotted spoon and set aside. Save the milk for the sauce.
3. In another pot heat the margarine or oil and stir in the flour. Add the reserved milk slowly, stirring constantly with a wisk until the sauce comes to a boil and thickens. Add the fish and pepper and heat a few minutes. Season to taste with salt.

3-4 servings

TUNA CREOLE

2 tablespoons oil
2 medium or 1 large onion
1 green pepper, chopped
2 celery stalks, chopped
1 1-pound can tomatoes
1 bay leaf
2-3 sprigs parsley, chopped

1½ teaspoons sugar
¾ teaspoon salt
¼ teaspoon Worcestershire sauce
1 7-ounce can water-packed tuna, drained

1. Heat the oil in a medium saucepan. Sauté the onion, green pepper, and celery for 10-15 minutes.
2. Add the tomatoes, bay leaf, parsley, sugar, salt, and Worcestershire sauce. Bring to a boil, reduce the heat, and simmer covered for 20-30 minutes.
3. Break the tuna fish into chunks and stir into the tomato mixture. Heat through for a few minutes. Remove the bay leaf and serve over rice.

3-4 servings

CURRIED TUNA

The raisins and chutney add a sweet flavor.

5 tablespoons oil or margarine
¼ pound sliced or coarsely chopped mushrooms
½ cup chopped onion
4 tablespoons flour
1½ cups skimmed milk
½ teaspoon salt

¾ teaspoon curry powder
⅓ cup raisins
1 7-ounce can water-packed solid white tuna, drained and flaked
2 tablespoons chutney (optional)

1. Sauté the mushrooms and onion in 2 tablespoons oil or margarine for 10 minutes. Set aside.
2. In a separate pan heat the remaining 3 tablespoons oil or margarine. Stir in the flour. Gradually stir in the milk, beating with a wisk until the sauce comes to a boil and thickens. Add the sautéed mushrooms and onion.
3. Stir in the salt, curry powder, raisins, tuna, and chutney, if desired. Heat through. Serve with rice.

3 servings

FISH CAKES

These fish cakes are vastly superior to the commercially prepared ones and are well worth the time and effort involved in making them. They can be frozen and are likely to appeal to children. The recipe is modeled after one suggested by my Aunt Lillie, whose delicious fish cakes convinced me to try to make some myself.

1 small carrot
1 small onion
2 teaspoons salt
6 cups water
2 pounds fish fillets (scrod, cod, haddock or any white fish or boneless chowder fish)

3 medium potatoes, cooked and mashed—about 2 cups
¼ teaspoon white pepper
2 egg whites
bread crumbs or corn flake crumbs
corn oil for frying

1. Bring the carrot, onion, 1 teaspoon salt and water to a boil and simmer covered for 15 minutes.
2. Add the fish and simmer another 5-10 minutes or until the fish is just cooked.
3. Drain the fish and vegetables and chop them together in a wooden chopping bowl.
4. Mix in the mashed potatoes, 1 teaspoon salt, and white pepper. Form into 3- to 4-inch patties.

5. Dip the patties into the egg whites and then in the bread crumbs or corn flake crumbs.
6. Heat 2 tablespoons corn oil in a frying pan over medium heat and fry the patties until they're crisp on both sides. Add additional oil as needed. Or even fry the patties on a very well greased pan at 400° for 20 minutes. Turn once.

14 fish cakes, 7 servings

FISH FILLETS VÉRONIQUE

A delicately flavored dish in which the fish is not overpowered by the sauce.

1½ pounds thin fillets (sole, flounder, or any white-fleshed fish)
½ cup dry white wine
4 tablespoons margarine or 3 tablespoons oil

4 tablespoons flour
1 cup skimmed milk
½ teaspoon salt
1½ cups halved seedless green grapes

1. Sprinkle the fillets lightly with salt and arrange them in a large shallow flameproof pan. Fold very thin fillets in half to make attractive serving portions. Pour the wine over the fish. Bring to a simmer and cook covered just until the fish can be flaked with a fork, about 10 minutes.
2. When the fish is done, pour off and save all of the poaching liquid. Hold the fillets back with your hand. I generally need help with this step. If you have a large baster it would probably be useful in removing the liquid. Cover the fish and set aside.
3. While the fish is cooking, begin to prepare a thick cream sauce. Melt the margarine in a saucepan. Stir in the flour. Gradually stir in the milk while beating with a wisk. Stir in the salt. Cook until the sauce reaches a simmer and is smooth and thickened.
4. Gradually stir no more than one cup of the reserved poaching liquid into the cream sauce. Usually there is

about ¾ cup of poaching liquid, but with frozen or thick fillets there may be considerably more. Stir in the halved grapes. Bring to a boil, stirring. Taste and adjust the seasoning.

5. Remove any additional liquid which may have accumulated in the pan containing the fish. Pour the sauce over the fish. Cover and heat through for about 5 minutes.

4 servings

FISH FILLETS BONNE FEMME

Substitute ½-¾ pound sautéed fresh mushrooms for the green grapes in the recipe for Fish Fillets Véronique.

FLOUNDER–ASPARAGUS ROLL-UPS

This elegant dish is a good choice for a spring dinner. The asparagus-cooking liquid gives the sauce a mild, pleasing flavor.

1 pound fresh asparagus
3 cups water
1 teaspoon salt
1 pound flounder fillets
salt and pepper
3 tablespoons oil or margarine
3 tablespoons flour

½ cup evaporated skimmed milk or ⅓ cup skimmed milk powder plus enough water to give ½ cup milk
¾ teaspoon curry powder (optional) or
¼ pound sautéed fresh mushrooms or 1 4-ounce can mushrooms, drained (optional)

1. Snap off and discard the lower, tough portions of the stalks. Cut the asparagus into about 3-inch lengths.
2. Bring the water and salt to a boil. Add the asparagus and cook for 5 minutes. Drain immediately and save 1 cup of the cooking liquid for the "cream" sauce.
3. Season the fillets with salt and pepper. Place a few pieces of asparagus at the broad end of each fillet and roll up the fillets around the asparagus. Place seam-side-down in a greased 8- or 9-inch square baking dish.
4. Heat the oil or margarine in a saucepan over medium heat. Stir in the flour. Gradually add 1 cup of the asparagus-cooking liquid while stirring constantly with a wisk. Gradually stir in the milk. Continue heating and stirring until the sauce comes to a boil and thickens. Add the mushrooms or curry powder, if desired.
5. Pour the sauce over the fish and bake covered for 15 minutes at 350 degrees or until the fish flakes with a fork.

4 servings

FILLET OF SOLE WITH SALMON STUFFING

Another elegant dish which looks and tastes as if it came from a fine French restaurant. Serve with rice so that none of the delicious sauce will be lost.

Stuffing

1 3½-ounce can salmon
1 egg white
1 tablespoon bread crumbs
1 tablespoon chopped fresh parsley

½ cup white vermouth or dry white wine
3 tablespoons margarine
4 tablespoons flour
1 cup skimmed milk
¾ teaspoon salt

1 pound (4) fillets of sole
salt and pepper

1. Empty the salmon can with its liquid into a bowl. Remove the skin and bones. Add the egg white and mash until very smooth. Stir in the bread crumbs and parsley.
2. Sprinkle the fillets lightly on both sides with salt and pepper. Place a few tablespoonfuls of the salmon mixture at the broad end of each fillet and roll up. Place seam-side-down in a 10-inch frying pan.
3. Pour the white wine or white vermouth over the fish and bring to the simmering point. Simmer covered over low heat until the fish is opaque and flakes when pricked with a fork—about 5-10 minutes.
4. While the fish is cooking, begin to prepare the sauce. Melt the margarine in a small saucepan. Stir in the flour and cook for a minute or two. Gradually add the milk, stirring constantly with a wisk and bring to the simmering point.
5. When the fish is cooked, pour its cooking liquid into the sauce, holding the rolled fillets back with your hand or a spatula. Heat the sauce, stirring, until it is smooth and thick. Add the salt and adjust the seasonings to taste. If the fish is to be prepared in advance, stop here. Shortly before serving, reheat the sauce and go to the next step.
6. Drain off any more liquid which may have accumulated in the pan holding the fish. Spoon the sauce over the fish and reheat over a low flame for about 5 minutes.

4 servings

FISH FILLETS WITH CAPERS AND LEMON

Fried fish with a difference.

1 pound thin fish fillets (sole, flounder, perch, mackerel)
salt and pepper
⅓-½ cup bread crumbs

oil for frying
4 tablespoons margarine
½ medium lemon, peeled and cut into ¼-inch cubes
2 tablespoons capers, drained

1. Sprinkle the fish fillets lightly with salt and pepper. Coat with bread crumbs.
2. Heat 2 tablespoonfuls oil in a frying pan. Add the fish fillets and fry for a few minutes on each side until the crumbs are golden brown. Add more oil to the pan as needed. Remove the fillets to a serving plate as they're done.
3. Add the margarine, diced lemon, and capers. Stir until the margarine melts and spoon the sauce over the fillets.

3 servings

FISH MOUSSE

This unusual dish is far easier to make than one might guess when tasting it. I use ground chowder fish as the main ingredient but any white fish could be used.

1 pound ground fish
¾ teaspoon salt
⅛ teaspoon white pepper
4 egg whites (keep one separate)

1 cup evaporated skimmed milk or ¾ cup powdered skimmed milk plus enough water to make 1 cup milk

Sauce

2 tablespoons margarine
2 tablespoons flour
¾ cup skimmed milk
¼ cup white vermouth or white wine

½ teaspoon salt
white pepper
¼ teaspoon dry mustard (optional)

1. Mix the fish with the salt, pepper and one of the egg whites. Beat in the evaporated skimmed milk with a wooden spoon until the mixture is smooth.
2. Beat the remaining 3 egg whites until stiff and fold them into the fish mixture.
3. Pour the mixture into a well-greased 8-inch square baking

dish and bake uncovered at 325° for 25 minutes or until the top is firm and golden brown and a knife inserted into the mousse comes out clean.

4. While the mousse is baking, prepare the sauce. Melt the margarine in a small saucepan and stir in the flour. Cook for a minute or two. Gradually add the milk, constantly stirring with a wisk, and bring the sauce to a boil. Stir in the vermouth. Stir in the seasonings and adjust to taste.

4 servings

FISH STEW

A hearty one-dish meal for a cold winter day. My husband sometimes takes it in a wide-mouth thermos for lunch.

2 tablespoons oil	1½-2 teaspoons salt
2 cups chopped onion	dash pepper
½ cup chopped celery	1 teaspoon orégano or basil
½ cup chopped carrot	¼ teaspoon crumbled saffron
½ cup chopped green pepper	(optional)
2 cloves garlic, minced	2 pounds fish (scrod, cod,
3 cups diced potatoes	haddock, pollock) cut into
2 cups water or fish stock	1½- to 2-inch chunks
1 28-ounce can tomatoes	

1. In a large pot (at least 3-quart), sauté the onions, celery, carrots, green pepper and garlic in the oil over medium heat for 10 minutes.
2. Add the potatoes, water, tomatoes, salt, and seasonings. Bring to a boil, reduce heat, and simmer covered until the potatoes are cooked—15-30 minutes.
3. Add the fish. Bring to a boil again and simmer until the fish flakes, about 5-10 minutes.

6-8 servings

CORN-FISH CHOWDER

2 tablespoons oil or margarine
1 cup chopped onion
1 clove garlic, chopped
1 1-pound can tomatoes or stewed tomatoes
2 bay leaves

1 12-ounce can corn, undrained
2½-3 cups skimmed milk
¾ teaspoon salt
dash white pepper
1 pound fish fillets, cut into 2- or 3-inch pieces

1. Heat the oil in a 2- to 3-quart pot and sauté the onion and garlic until the onion is wilted, about 10 minutes.
2. Add the tomatoes and bay leaves. Bring to a boil, reduce heat, and simmer covered 10-15 minutes.
3. Add the undrained corn, milk, salt and pepper. Bring to a boil.
4. Add the fish pieces and continue cooking just until the fish flakes with a fork, about 5 minutes.

4 servings

FISH FONDUE

1½ pounds firm thick fish fil-   duck sauce
     lets cut into ¾-inch pieces   chutney

Fondue Batter

½ cup flour   or:
½ cup cornstarch   egg whites
½ teaspoon salt   corn flake crumbs
1 tablespoon baking powder   bread crumbs
2 egg whites
½ cup water

Follow the same procedure as for Chicken Fondue (see page 205).

4-6 servings

POULTRY

You will probably find chicken appearing on your shopping list more frequently when you change to a low-cholesterol diet. Fortunately, there is such a huge variety of healthy ways to prepare chicken that you need never become bored with it.

Turkey is another form of poultry which may be eaten often. Turkey parts can frequently be purchased separately, so you need not wait for company to have turkey. Since larger fowl seem to me to have proportionately more fat, I use small chickens (under 3 pounds) and turkeys (under 10-12 pounds). Duck and goose contain large amounts of fat and should be avoided.

Much of the poultry fat is concentrated in or just beneath the skin so avoiding the skin is a good idea. The white flesh is leaner than the dark but the dark is still lean compared to meat.

Boneless chicken breasts with the fat and skin removed make the healthiest, most elegant chicken dishes. Boning chicken breasts is a skill which can be acquired easily, so don't be afraid to try it. Just remember to cut toward the bone while pulling the flesh away from the bone. Your butcher is undoubtedly the best person to approach for a demonstration of the boning technique and he may be willing to do it for you altogether (for a price, of course). The leftover bones should be saved for soup.

All poultry and turkey should be very well trimmed of fat before using. This does take a good amount of time and I quickly acquired the knack of trimming while talking on the telephone.

I bake or broil chicken on a rack which fits into a Teflon pan so that fat drippings go into the pan. Putting about ½ inch of water into the pan before cooking makes cleaning much easier. The chicken is done when the juices which run out when a fork is inserted are clear and colorless instead of pinkish.

Many chicken recipes call for browning chicken pieces in oil. I generally prefer to brown the chicken pieces under the broiler instead. This method is easier and part of the chicken fat is left in the broiler pan.

Chicken dishes which call for cooking chicken in liquid are healthiest prepared a day ahead of when they will be served so that the fat can be removed from the cooking liquid. After cooking, remove the chicken from the cooking liquid and refrigerate each separately overnight. The next day, skim off the congealed fat from the surface of the liquid. Return the chicken to the liquid and re-heat.

Some commercial barbecue sauces (i.e. Open Pit) are acceptable for low-cholesterol cooking. As always, check the ingredients on the label carefully. Chinese duck sauce makes a very easy and pleasant chicken barbecue sauce. For a tangy tomato barbecue sauce, see the recipe for Baked Fish with Barbecue Sauce.

I find cooked chicken left over from preparing chicken soup very useful. I freeze it in a ½-pound package to have ready for quick meals.

See the Appetizer and Salad chapters for additional chicken recipes.

CHICKEN WITH CURRANT-JELLY SAUCE

Whenever my friends ask me for a good chicken recipe, this is the one I offer first. It could hardly be easier, yet it has an elegant touch.

1 3-pound chicken, cut into serving pieces or 2 Cornish hens cut in half	pepper
	garlic powder
	¾ cup currant jelly
salt	2 tablespoons sherry

1. Season the chicken with salt, pepper and garlic powder and bake on a rack at 350° for 45-55 minutes.
2. Just before serving, melt the current jelly in a small saucepan over low heat. Stir in the sherry; bring to a boil and spoon over the chicken.

4-6 servings

CRISPY BAKED CHICKEN

This is another recipe of the quick and easy variety.

1 2½- to 3-pound chicken, cut into serving pieces
salt

pepper
garlic powder
¾ cup corn flake crumbs

1. Season the chicken with salt, pepper, and garlic powder.
2. Coat with crumbs and bake on a rack at 350° for 45-55 minutes.

4-6 servings

ORANGE-HONEY CHICKEN

This is a quick and easy Shabbat dish. Grease the measuring cup lightly with oil before using to help get all of the honey out of the cup.

½ cup honey
2 tablespoons orange juice
1 tablespoon grated orange rind

1 2½- to 3-pound chicken cut into serving pieces
salt

1. Mix together the honey, orange juice, and orange rind.

2. Place the chicken pieces on a rack. Sprinkle lightly with salt. Spoon about ⅓ of the honey mixture over the chicken pieces. Bake at 350° for 45-55 minutes. Baste twice with the remaining honey mixture.

4-6 servings

TERIYAKI CHICKEN

A friend once gave me the following tip for the economical use of soy-sauce marinades. Save the marinade after it has been used for one batch of chicken and freeze it until you want to use it again. This saves both time and ingredients.

1 2½- to 3-pound chicken, cut into serving pieces
½ cup soy sauce
1 tablespoon sherry

1 large clove garlic, crushed
1½ tablespoons brown sugar
½ teaspoon ginger
⅛ teaspoon cinnamon

1. Mix together the ingredients for the marinade.
2. Pour the marinade over the chicken and refrigerate at least 3 or 4 hours or preferably overnight. Move the chicken pieces around several times so that they all have equal contact with the marinade.
3. Place the chicken pieces on a rack. Bake at 350° for 45-55 minutes or broil about 20 minutes on each side.

4-6 servings

CHICKEN WITH ORANGE STUFFING

This dish has a marvelous aroma as well as taste.

¾ cup orange juice
2 tablespoons lemon juice
3 tablespoons sherry
2 teaspoons grated orange rind
1 teaspoon grated lemon rind
⅔ cup brown sugar, firmly packed

2 quarts 1- to 1½-inch bread cubes
1 cup celery or parsley, chopped
1 2½- to 3-pound chicken, cut into serving pieces
salt

1. Combine the orange juice, lemon juice, sherry, orange rind, and lemon rind in a small pot; bring to a boil and simmer a few minutes.
2. Put the bread cubes and parsley or celery in a greased baking pan large enough for the chicken parts to be placed in it in one layer. Sprinkle the chicken parts with salt and place them on top of the bread cubes.
3. Pour half of the sauce over the chicken and bake uncovered for 1 hour at 350°. Baste the chicken with the remaining half of the sauce several times during the baking.

4-6 servings

CHICKEN JUBILEE

This is an excellent company dish that's easy enough to make often just for the family.

3-pound chicken cut into serving pieces
salt
1 1-pound, 13-ounce can dark, sweet pitted cherries in syrup
½ cup sherry
orange juice
¾ teaspoon grated lemon rind
3 tablespoons cornstarch
3 tablespoons orange juice

1. Sprinkle the chicken pieces lightly with salt and spread them in a single layer in a broiling pan. Broil until the skin is light gold, about 10 minutes on each side. This is an effortless, low-calorie way to brown chicken.
2. Place the chicken pieces in a large casserole.
3. Drain the cherries and save the syrup. Add ½ cup sherry to the syrup and add enough orange juice to make 2¼ cups of liquid. Stir the lemon rind into the liquid and pour over the chicken. Bring to a boil and simmer covered over low heat until tender, about 30 minutes.
4. Stop at this point if the dish is being prepared a day ahead. Remove the chicken and refrigerate the chicken and cooking liquid separately overnight. Skim off the congealed fat from the surface of the liquid. Return the chicken to the liquid and reheat.
5. Stir in the cherries.
6. Mix the cornstarch and 3 tablespoons orange juice together and stir slowly into the cooking liquid. Continue cooking a few minutes until the sauce thickens. Serve with rice.

4-6 servings

COQ AU VIN (CHICKEN IN WINE)

2½- to 3-pound chicken cut into serving pieces

3 tablespoons oil

2-3 carrots cut into ½-inch slices (optional)

1 medium onion, chopped

1 clove garlic, crushed or finely minced

½ pound mushrooms, sliced

1 cup chicken broth

1¼ cups red wine

½ teaspoon salt

⅛ teaspoon pepper

3 tablespoons cornstarch

3 tablespoons water

1. Brown the chicken pieces either by broiling about 10 minutes on each side or by frying in oil. Dry the chicken pieces well with paper towels before frying. Set the browned chicken pieces aside.
2. In a large pot or casserole sauté the carrots in oil over medium heat for a few minutes. Add the onion and garlic and sauté until the onion is wilted. Add the mushrooms and sauté 5 minutes longer.
3. Add the chicken pieces, chicken broth, wine, salt, and pepper to the casserole. Bring to a boil and simmer covered until the chicken is tender, about 30 minutes. Stop at this point if the chicken is being prepared a day ahead. Follow Step 4 in Chicken Jubilee (page 196).
4. Mix the cornstarch and water together and stir slowly into the hot liquid. Continue cooking a few minutes until the sauce thickens.

4-6 servings

CHICKEN WITH MIDDLE-EASTERN SPICES

2½- to 3-pound chicken cut into serving pieces
salt and pepper
2 tablespoons oil
1 large onion, chopped
1 large or 2 medium cloves garlic, minced or crushed
2 cups water or chicken broth

1½ teaspoons cumin
¾ teaspoon coriander
½ teaspoon turmeric
½ teaspoon allspice
6 tablespoons fresh lemon juice
½-¾ teaspoon salt
3 tablespoons cornstarch
3 tablespoons water

1. Sprinkle the chicken pieces lightly with salt and pepper. Brown by broiling about 10 minutes on each side.
2. Sauté the onion and garlic in a large casserole until the onion is golden brown. Add the chicken, water or chicken broth, spices, salt and lemon juice. Bring to a boil, lower the heat, and simmer covered for about 30 minutes or until the chicken is tender. Stop at this point if the chicken is being prepared a day ahead. Follow Step 4 in Chicken Jubilee (page 196).
3. Mix the cornstarch and water and stir into the hot liquid. Cook another minute or two until the sauce is thickened. Serve with rice.

4-6 servings

CHICKEN WITH TARRAGON AND WINE

A simple but elegant addition to your chicken repetoire.

2½- to 3-pound chicken cut into serving pieces
salt
pepper
garlic powder
1½ cups dry white wine

1½ teaspoons tarragon
½ pound sliced fresh mushrooms, sautéed in oil, or
2 4-ounce cans mushrooms, drained (optional)

1. Season the chicken pieces with salt, pepper and garlic powder. Brown by broiling about 10 minutes on each side.
2. Transfer the browned chicken to a large flameproof casserole. Sprinkle on the tarragon and wine. Bring to a boil and simmer covered over low heat for 30 minutes or until the chicken is tender. Spoon the sauce over the chicken several times during the cooking period. If desired, add the mushrooms during the last 10 minutes of cooking. Serve with rice.

4-6 servings

SAUTÉED CHICKEN BREASTS

For a quick, elegant dinner, I can't think of anything better than sautéed boned chicken breasts.

4 boned and skinned chicken
breasts from 2½- to 3-
pound chickens
salt
pepper
1-2 egg whites
bread crumbs

3 tablespoons oil
2 tablespoons fresh lemon
juice
2 tablespoons chopped fresh
parsley

1. Season the chicken breasts with salt and pepper. Dip them in the egg whites and then in bread crumbs.
2. Heat the oil in a large frying pan and sauté the breasts over medium heat for 3 minutes on each side.
3. Sprinkle with parsley and lemon juice and serve immediately.

4 servings

CHICKEN BREASTS WITH TARRAGON

4 boned and skinned chicken
breasts from 2½- to 3-
pound chickens
salt
pepper
1 clove garlic, crushed
3 tablespoons oil

½ teaspoon tarragon
2 tablespoons fresh lemon
juice
2 tablespoons brandy
3 tablespoons white wine
chopped fresh parsley

1. Season the breasts with salt and pepper.
2. Heat the oil in a large frying pan and add the breasts and the crushed garlic. Sauté the breasts for 2 minutes on each side over medium heat.
3. Mix the tarragon, brandy, lemon juice, and white wine and pour over the chicken. Sauté 2-3 minutes longer.
4. Sprinkle with chopped parsley and serve.

4 servings

CHICKEN BREASTS WITH GRAPES

4 boned and skinned chicken breasts from 2½- to 3-pound chickens
salt
pepper
flour

3 tablespoons oil
¾ cup seedless green grapes
¾ cup white wine
1½ teaspoons cornstarch
1½ teaspoon water

1. Season the chicken breasts with salt and pepper. Coat them with flour.
2. Heat the oil in a large frying pan and sauté the breasts over medium heat for 3 minutes on each side. Remove the breasts from the pan and pour off any excess oil. Keep the breasts warm in a very low oven.
3. Add the grapes and wine to the pan. Bring rapidly to a boil and scrape the bottom of the pan.
4. Stir the cornstarch and water into a smooth paste and stir into the wine. Heat briefly until the sauce is thickened and pour over the breasts.

4 servings

HERBED BAKED CHICKEN BREASTS

A very good company dish.

6 boned and skinned chicken breasts from 2½- to 3-pound chickens
salt
pepper
2 egg whites
bread crumbs

⅓ cup oil
¼ teaspoon rosemary
¼ teaspoon sage
2 teaspoons chopped fresh parsley
½ cup dry white wine

Filling

2 tablespoons oil
¼ pound fresh mushrooms, chopped

¼ teaspoon salt
few tablespoons bread crumbs

1. Sauté the chopped mushrooms in 2 tablespoons oil until the mushrooms are soft, about 7-10 minutes. Stir in ¼ teaspoon salt. Add a few tablespoons of bread crumbs to absorb any liquid and to bind the mushroom mixture.
2. Season the chicken breasts on both sides with salt and pepper.
3. Place 1-2 tablespoons of filling on each breast and roll up. Secure with a toothpick if desired.
4. Dip each breast in egg white and then in bread crumbs. Place in a greased shallow baking pan.
5. Mix the oil, rosemary, sage and parsley together. Pour over the chicken breasts. Bake uncovered for about 25 minutes, at 350°.
6. Pour the wine over the breasts and bake another 15 minutes. Spoon the sauce over the chicken a few times while baking.

6 servings

ORIENTAL CHICKEN WITH MUSHROOMS AND PEPPERS

I thank Susan Dreyfuss for the recipe for this delicious delicately flavored dish.

2 skinned and boned chicken breasts from 3-pound chickens, cut into ¾-inch pieces (about ½ pound chicken meat)
1 teaspoon sherry
½ teaspoon soy sauce
2 teaspoons cornstarch
¾ teaspoon salt
1 4-ounce can mushrooms or ¼ pound sliced fresh mushrooms, lightly sautéed in oil
1 large or 2 small green peppers, cut into ¾-inch cubes
3 tablespoons oil

1. Mix the chicken pieces, sherry, soy sauce, 1 teaspoon cornstarch, and ¼ teaspoon salt. Marinate for 15-20 minutes.
2. If using canned mushrooms, drain them and save the liquid. Mix 1 teaspoon cornstarch with 2 tablespoons of the mushroom-packing liquid (or 2 tablespoons of water if using fresh mushrooms).
3. Warm 2 tablespoons of the oil over medium to high heat in a pan or wok. Add the chicken to the hot oil and stir constantly for a few minutes until the chicken almost completely loses its pink color and turns white. Remove the chicken, leaving as much oil as possible in the pan or wok.
4. Add the remaining 1 tablespoon of oil to the pan or wok. Add the pepper. Sprinkle with the remaining ½ teaspoon of salt. Stir for about a minute. Quickly stir in the mushrooms. Add the cooked chicken and stir for another 30-60 seconds. Add the cornstarch mixture and stir briefly until the liquid thickens. Serve at once with hot rice.

2-3 servings

CHICKEN AND SNOW PEAS

Once the chicken breasts are boned, this dish takes practically no time to prepare. Fresh snow peas are expensive but have a marvelous flavor and texture. Be sure not to overcook them.

2 skinned and boned chicken breasts from 2½- to 3-pound chickens (½ pound breast meat)
1½ tablespoons soy sauce
1½ tablespoons sherry
½ teaspoon cornstarch
dash salt

dash sugar
3 tablespoons oil
6 ounces fresh snow peas or 1 6-ounce package frozen pea pods, defrosted and drained

1. Cut the chicken breasts into bite-sized pieces and marinate them in a mixture of the soy sauce, sherry, cornstarch, salt, and sugar for 15-20 minutes.
2. If using fresh snow peas, remove the strings attached to the stem end of the peas. Warm 1 tablespoon of oil in a pan or wok over medium heat. Add the fresh or defrosted snow peas. Sprinkle lightly with salt and stir constantly for 15-30 seconds. Remove from the pan and set aside.
3. Warm 2-3 tablespoons of oil in a pan or wok over medium heat. Lift the chicken pieces out of the marinade and add them to the hot oil. Save the marinade. Fry the chicken pieces and stir constantly for a few minutes or until the chicken is almost cooked. Add the pea pods and reserved marinade and stir fry another minute or two to heat through. Serve at once.

2 servings

Variation

Substitute ½ pound of sautéed mushrooms for the pea pods.

CHICKEN FONDUE

We have our friends, the Bergmans, to thank for introducing us to fondue as an enjoyable, relaxing way of entertaining.

4-6 chicken breasts, skinned, boned, and cut into ¾-inch pieces

oil for frying
Chinese duck sauce
chutney

Fondue Batter

½ cup flour
½ cup cornstarch
½ teaspoon salt
1 tablespoon baking powder
2 egg whites
½ cup water

or:
egg whites
corn flake crumbs
breadcrumbs

1. Prepare the batter. Stir the dry ingredients together. Beat in the egg whites and water to form a smooth batter.
2. Place enough oil in a fondue pot to reach a depth of at least 2 inches. Heat the oil until it sizzles when a bread cube is dropped in it.
3. Secure a piece of raw chicken on a fondue fork. Dip the chicken into the batter and let any excess batter drip off. Place in the hot oil and cook for about 5 minutes or until the batter is golden brown. Remove from the oil and serve with Chinese duck sauce or chutney. The chicken pieces can, instead, be dipped in egg white and then in corn flake crumbs or bread crumbs. Fry until the crust is golden brown and serve with duck sauce or chutney.

4-6 servings

CHICKEN À LA KING

This is one of my mainstays for a fast, easy supper.

3 tablespoons oil
3 tablespoons flour
1 4-ounce can mushrooms or ¼ pound fresh mushrooms sautéed in oil
1¼ cups water or mushroom-packing liquid plus water to make 1¼ cup liquid

1 teaspoon powdered instant chicken soup or 1 chicken bouillon cube
¾ teaspoon salt
1-2 tablespoons sherry
½ pound chicken, shredded or diced
cooked drained peas (optional)

1. Drain the mushrooms and save the liquid. Add enough water to measure 1¼ cups.
2. Warm the oil over medium heat and stir in the flour. Gradually add the water while stirring constantly with a wisk. Bring to a boil and stir in the salt and powdered chicken soup or bouillon cube. Simmer a few minutes longer.
3. Stir in the sherry, mushrooms, chicken and peas (if desired). Cook a few minutes until heated through. Serve with rice.

3-4 servings

CHICKEN OR TURKEY TETRAZZINI

This is a superb buffet dish and an excellent choice for feeding a large group. It can be prepared through Step 3 and refrigerated for several days.

6 tablespoons oil
1 medium onion, chopped
1 large clove garlic, mashed
¾ pound mushrooms, sliced
6 tablespoons flour
2 cups chicken stock or 2 cups water plus 2 teaspoons powdered chicken soup
¼ cup sherry
½ cup dry white wine or white vermouth

2 tablespoons chopped fresh parsley (optional)
½ cup whole or slivered almonds
2-3 cups cooked chicken or cooked turkey, cut into small pieces
1 teaspoon salt
dash pepper
8 ounces tetrazzini or very thin spaghetti

1. Warm 2 tablespoons of oil in a 9-inch frying pan and sauté the onion over medium heat until wilted. Add the mashed garlic and sauté another minute or two. Add the sliced mushrooms and sauté until they're soft. Set aside.
2. Heat the remaining 4 tablespoons of oil in a medium saucepan. Stir in the flour. Gradually add the chicken stock, sherry and white wine while stirring constantly with a wisk. Cook, stirring until the sauce comes to a boil and thickens. Stir in the mushroom mixture, parsley, almonds, chicken, salt and pepper. Taste and adjust the seasonings.
3. Cook the tetrazzini until done but still firm, about 6 minutes. Drain. Spread the cooked pasta in a large shallow greased casserole—about 9 by 13 inches. Spoon the sauce over the pasta.
4. Cover and bake at 350° for 30 minutes.

5-6 servings

MEATS

Because of their high saturated-fat content, meats should be eaten much less frequently and in smaller portions in a low-cholesterol diet than in the usual American diet. I serve meat to my family no more than once a week.

Only the leanest cuts of meat should be used. Avoid cuts which are heavily marbled with fat. Ask the butcher to trim away all visible fat. At home, trim off any remaining fat before using. Freeze small bits or chunks of meat left over from trimming for use in oriental-style dishes.

Do not buy already ground meat. Instead, have it ground to order from lean, well-trimmed cuts.

Use a rack underneath meat when broiling or roasting so that the fat can drip off.

Veal, which is very young beef, is leaner than beef or lamb and should be eaten more frequently than the other meats. I use veal in most of my meat meals.

For veal roast I use a thick, boneless shoulder cut which is very lean and has no waste. You may have to ask your butcher to cut the roast especially for you. I prefer this cut to the somewhat less expensive rolled roast which requires considerably more time-consuming trimming away of fat. Veal scallops and veal chops are also usually lean cuts. For veal stew or ground veal, I choose the less expensive leg cuts. Breast of veal contains more fat and I generally do not prepare it.

For roast beef, I choose lean 2-3 pound eye roasts which usually require little trimming. I use shoulder steak or London broil, cut from shoulder steak, for broiling. I occasionally prepare Oriental-style beef-and-vegetable dishes with beef sliced from shoulder steak or eye roast.

I use lamb only for shishkebab and then choose lean shoulder pieces. I do not use liver or organ meat because of their high cholesterol content.

Stews are healthiest when prepared a day ahead of serving so that the fat can be removed from the cooking liquid. After cooking the meat, but before thickening the sauce, remove the meat from the cooking liquid and refrigerate each separately overnight. The next day skim off the congealed fat from the surface of the liquid. Return the meat to the liquid and re-heat.

'Lower Fat' frankfurters, salami, and baloney (Best's Kosher Sausage Co., Chicago, Ill. 60608) have recently appeared on the market. The frankfurters contain "at least 33% less fat than the 30% fat allowed by the USDA standard for franks." This still probably leaves about 20% fat so it would be wise to use these products infrequently.

Using lower grades of meat can help cut meat-fat intake since the amount of fat-marbling decreases with decreasing meat grade. 'Standard' is leaner than 'good' which is leaner than 'choice' which is leaner than 'prime'. I've found very lean steaks from a lower beef grade than my butcher usually carries quite satisfactory. A lower-grade meat can be made more tender by putting it through a tenderizer machine.

CRANBERRY-VEAL ROAST

A superb dish that's wonderfully easy to make.

2- or 3-pound shoulder veal roast, well-trimmed
salt, pepper, garlic powder

1 8-ounce can whole berry cranberry sauce
¼ cup sherry

1. Sprinkle the veal roast with salt, pepper, and garlic powder. Place in an 8- or 9-inch square baking pan.
2. Mash the cranberry sauce in a small saucepan. Add the sherry and warm to melt the gel.
3. Pour the sauce over the veal. Bake uncovered at 350° 20-

25 minutes for each pound. For a juicier roast, use the shorter baking time. Baste a few times with the sauce.

5-7 servings

HERBED VEAL ROAST

The cooking liquid has a marvelous aroma and flavor.

2- or 3-pound shoulder veal roast, well trimmed
salt, pepper, garlic powder
⅔ cup orange juice

⅓ cup white vermouth or dry white wine
¼ teaspoon marjoram
¼ teaspoon rosemary

1. Season the roast with salt, pepper, and garlic powder. Place in an 8- or 9-inch baking pan.
2. Combine the orange juice, wine, and spices and pour over the meat. Bake uncovered at 350° for 20-25 minutes for each pound. For a juicier roast, use the shorter baking time. Baste a few times with the sauce.

5-7 servings

COLD VEAL ROAST

Perfect for a summer buffet.

3-pound shoulder veal roast, well-trimmed

salt, pepper, garlic powder
lettuce leaves

Sauce

1 7-ounce can tuna fish, drained
6-8 anchovies

6 tablespoons fresh lemon juice
½ cup corn oil
chopped parsley

1. Season the roast with salt, pepper, and garlic powder. Place it on a rack and roast at 350° for 20 minutes to the pound. Let cool.
2. Place all the ingredients for the sauce in a blender container and whirl until the contents are very smooth. Transfer to an attractive bowl and garnish with chopped parsley.
3. Slice the veal roast and arrange on a serving dish. Surround with lettuce leaves. Serve with the tuna sauce.

8 servings

VEAL SCALLOPS WITH LEMON

1 pound veal scallops, pounded thin
salt and pepper
2 tablespoons oil

¼ cup white wine
2½ tablespoons fresh lemon juice
chopped parsley

1. Season the veal scallops with salt and pepper. Heat the oil in a frying pan and quickly brown the scallops on both sides. Remove to a plate as they're done.
2. Add the wine and lemon juice to the pan. Stir and bring to a boil.
3. Return the veal to the pan and spoon the sauce over the scallops. Cover and simmer for 1-2 minutes. Serve garnished with chopped parsley.

3-4 servings

VEAL SCALLOPS WITH SHERRY

1 pound veal scallops, pounded thin
salt, pepper, garlic powder

2 tablespoons oil
½ cup sherry
chopped parsley (optional)

1. Season the veal scallops with salt, pepper, and garlic powder. Heat the oil in a frying pan and quickly brown the scallops on both sides. Remove to a plate as they're done.
2. Add the sherry to the pan. Stir and bring to a boil.
3. Return the veal to the pan and spoon the sherry over the scallops. Cover and simmer for 1-2 minutes. Serve garnished with chopped parsley if desired.

3-4 servings

Variation:

Add ¼ -½ pound of sautéed fresh mushrooms to the pan in Step 3 along with the veal.

SWEET-AND-SOUR VEAL AND CABBAGE, CHINESE STYLE

1 pound lean veal, cut into very thin strips about 1 inch by 2 inches.
3 tablespoons oil

1 pound Chinese cabbage cut on the diagonal into ¼-inch shreds

Veal Marinade

4 teaspoons sherry
4 teaspoons soy sauce

½ teaspoon salt
¼ teaspoon sugar

Sweet And Sour Sauce

¼ cup vinegar
¼ cup water
1 tablespoon soy sauce

¼ cup sugar
4 teaspoons cornstarch
1 teaspoon salt

1. Combine the veal strips with the veal marinade and let stand 20-30 minutes.
2. Mix together the ingredients for the sweet and sour sauce and set aside.
3. Warm 2 tablespoons of oil over medium-high heat in a very large pan or a wok. Add the veal strips. Fry and stir constantly until the veal almost loses its pink color. Remove the veal to a bowl, leaving as much oil in the pan as possible.
4. Add the remaining 1 tablespoon of oil to the pan or wok. Add the shredded cabbage. Fry and stir for about 3-5 minutes or until the cabbage is cooked but still crisp. Add the veal and sweet and sour sauce. Continue cooking another few minutes until the veal is done and the sauce is thickened.

4 servings

SPINACH-VEAL MEAT LOAF

This delicious meat loaf is a fine company or buffet dish.

1 10-ounce package frozen chopped spinach
1½ pounds lean ground veal
1 small onion, grated
1 clove garlic, crushed

2 egg whites
1½ teaspoons salt
½ teaspoon dried rosemary
dash pepper

1. Cook the spinach according to package directions. Drain in a strainer or colander and press out as much moisture as possible.
2. Combine the spinach with all of the other ingredients and blend well.
3. Shape into a loaf and bake at 375° for 45 minutes or until cooked but still juicy.

6 servings

VEAL LOAF

A quick and easy family-style meat loaf. A 1.65-ounce package of textured soy protein meat extender, hydrated according to package directions, can be substituted for ½ pound of the meat. If this is done, a slightly shorter cooking time may be required.

1½ pounds ground veal
1 small onion, grated
2 egg whites
1¼ teaspoon salt

¾ teaspoon orégano
¼ teaspoon garlic powder
3 tablespoons bread crumbs

1. Mix all the ingredients together in a large bowl.
2. Shape into a round loaf on a baking pan.
3. Bake at 350° about 45 minutes or until cooked but still juicy.

4-6 servings

SWEET AND SOUR MEATBALLS

1 pound lean ground veal
1 small onion, grated
1 teaspoon salt
1 egg white
1 16-ounce can whole-cran-berry sauce

½ jar of chili sauce (⅝ cup)
2 tablespoons lemon juice
2 tablespoons brown sugar

1. Mix together the veal, grated onion, salt, and egg white.
2. Bring the cranberry sauce, chili sauce, lemon juice and brown sugar to a boil in a medium saucepan.
3. Shape the meat mixture into 1-inch balls and drop into the hot sauce.
4. Cover and simmer about ½ hour or until the meatballs are cooked.

3-4 servings

VEAL MEATBALLS

1 pound ground lean veal
1½ teaspoons Dijon mustard
1 teaspoon fresh lemon juice
½ teaspoon salt

dash pepper
1 clove garlic crushed
2-3 tablespoons oil

1. Thoroughly blend the veal, mustard, lemon juice, salt, pepper, and garlic together. Shape into 1-inch balls.
2. Heat the oil in a frying pan and brown the meatballs over moderately high heat. Remove and serve as a main dish or with toothpicks as a hot hors d'oeuvre.

3-4 servings

VEAL TZIMMES

An excellent Shabbat or Jewish holiday dish.

2 tablespoons oil	1 teaspoon salt
2 pounds veal cut into 1½-inch cubes	1 11-ounce package mixed dried fruit
4 carrots cut into 1-inch slices	2 tablespoons cornstarch mixed with 2 tablespoons water
2 cups water	

1. Brown the veal cubes in hot oil. Add the carrots, water, and salt. Bring to a boil, lower the heat, and simmer covered for about one hour.
2. Add the package of mixed fruit. Cover and simmer another 30 minutes or until the meat and fruit are tender.
3. If a thickened sauce is desired, stir in the cornstarch mixture and cook for a few mintues longer.

6 servings

MIDDLE EASTERN-STYLE VEAL STEW

2 tablespoons oil
1 large or 2 medium onions, chopped
1 large or 2 small cloves garlic, minced or crushed
2 pounds veal cut into 1- to 1½-inch cubes
1½ cups water

2 tablespoons fresh lemon juice
½ teaspoon cumin
½ teaspoon coriander
½ teaspoon turmeric
½ teaspoon allspice
½ teaspoon salt
2 tablespoons cornstarch
2 tablespoons water

1. Sauté the onion and garlic in the oil until the onion is golden brown.
2. Add the veal and sauté until light brown.
3. Add the water, lemon juice, and seasonings. Bring to a boil, reduce heat, and simmer covered 1-1½ hours or until the meat is tender.
4. If a thickened sauce is desired, mix the cornstarch and water and stir into the cooking liquid. Cook another few minutes. Serve with rice.

6 servings

VEAL STEW WITH MUSHROOMS AND SHERRY

A delicately flavored veal dish.

3 tablespoons oil
1 medium onion, chopped
1 large clove garlic, minced or crushed
¾ pound fresh mushrooms, sliced
2 pounds veal cut into 1- to 1½-inch cubes

¾ cup chicken broth or ¾ cup water plus ¾ teaspoon powdered instant chicken soup
¾ cup sherry
¾ teaspoon salt
2 tablespoons cornstarch dissolved in 2 tablespoons water

1. Sauté the onion and garlic in the oil in a 2½-quart casserole for about 5 minutes. Add the mushrooms and sauté about 5 minutes longer. Add the veal and sauté until light brown.
2. Add the broth, sherry, and salt. Bring to a boil, lower the heat, and simmer covered 1-1½ hours or until the veal is tender.
3. If a thickened sauce is desired, stir in the cornstarch mixture and cook for a few minutes longer.

6 servings

VEAL STEW SUPREME

The stew is equally good with or without the mint jelly, which adds a sweet, intriguing flavor. If you want to find out how you like the mint flavor before adding the jelly to the stew, stir a bit of jelly into a few tablespoons of stewing liquid and taste. The potatoes make this a one-dish meal. Otherwise serve with rice or noodles.

3 tablespoons oil
¾ cup chopped onion
2 cloves garlic, minced or crushed
2 pounds veal cut into 1½-2-inch cubes
¼ cup flour
2 cups water

1½ teaspoons salt
1 teaspoon rosemary
¼ teaspoon ginger
6 carrots cut in 1- to 1½-inch chunks
6 small new potatoes, peeled (optional)
½ cup mint jelly (optional)

1. Sauté the onion and garlic in the oil until golden.
2. Add the veal and brown on all sides.
3. Sprinkle on the flour and stir over low heat for a few minutes.
4. Add the water, salt, and spices. Bring to a boil and simmer covered over low heat for 30 minutes.
5. Add the carrots and potatoes, bring to a boil again, and simmer covered for about one hour or until the veal and vegetables are tender. Stir in the mint jelly during the last 15 minutes of cooking, if desired.

6 servings

ITALIAN-STYLE VEAL STEW

2 tablespoons oil
2-3 cups chopped onions
2 cloves garlic, minced or chopped
2 pounds lean veal, cut into 1½-inch cubes

1½ cups tomato sauce
½ cup red or white wine
orégano, basil, salt and pepper to taste

1. Sauté the onions and garlic in the oil in a 2½- or 3-quart pan until the onions are soft. Add the veal cubes and sauté until they are light brown on all sides.

2. Add the tomato sauce, wine and seasonings to taste, depending on the tomato sauce used. Bring to a boil, lower the heat, and simmer covered for about 1-1½ hours or until the veal is tender.

MARINADE FOR LONDON BROIL OR BEEF SHISHKEBAB

This amount of marinade is enough for about 2 pounds of beef.

½ teaspoon powdered ginger
¼ teaspoon dry mustard
⅛ teaspoon pepper
3 tablespoons sherry

½ cup soy sauce
1 tablespoon oil
1 medium onion, chopped
2 cloves garlic, crushed

1. Beat the ginger, mustard, and pepper into the sherry. Mix in the soy sauce, oil, onion and garlic.
2. Pour over the meat and marinate 3-4 hours or overnight. Thread beef cubes on skewers with onions, cherry tomatoes, green pepper cubes, etc. and grill.

6 servings

MARINADE FOR LAMB SHISHKEBAB

1 pound lean lamb, cut into 1- or 1½-inch cubes
4 tablespoons fresh lemon juice
2 tablespoons oil

1 large clove garlic, mashed
½ teaspoon orégano
¼ teaspoon basil
½ teaspoon salt
dash pepper

Beat together all the ingredients for the marinade. Pour over the lamb and marinate for 3-4 hours or overnight. Thread on skewers with onions, cherry tomatoes, green peppers, etc. and grill.

3 servings

CHINESE PEPPER STEAK

1 pound lean beef, i.e., shoulder steak or eye roast
2 tablespoons soy sauce
1 tablespoon sherry
¾ teaspoon salt
¼ teaspoon sugar
1 teaspoon cornstarch

3 tablespoons oil
1 pound green peppers (2 large or 3 medium) cut into 1-inch cubes
1 clove garlic, crushed or minced

1. Trim off any fat from the meat. Slice into thin strips. Slicing is somewhat easier if the meat is partially frozen.
2. Combine the meat with the soy sauce, sherry, ¼ teaspoon salt, sugar, and cornstarch. Let stand for 30 minutes, turning occasionally.
3. Warm 2 tablespoons of oil in a wok or large pan over medium-high heat. Add the green peppers. Sprinkle with the remaining ½ teaspoon of salt. Fry and stir constantly for 2 minutes. Remove the green peppers, leaving as much oil in the wok or pan as possible.
4. Add the remaining 1 tablespoon of oil and the garlic to the pan or wok. Add the beef slices. Fry and stir constantly until the beef slices lose almost all of their redness.
5. Add the green peppers and heat through for about a minute or two. Serve at once with hot rice.

4 servings

BREAKFAST FOODS

We are all aware of the importance of a well-balanced breakfast in meeting our nutritional needs and preparing us for the day's activities. Nutritionists advise having at least one-fourth of the day's food at breakfast and including a good source of protein. I hope that this section will help you to plan enjoyable and healthy breakfasts.

People accustomed to having two eggs every morning will have to change their breakfast eating habits when they switch to a low-cholesterol diet. The American Heart Association recommends that egg yolks be limited to three per week, including those used in cooking. The number of egg whites which can be eaten is, however, not limited.

Fortunately, scrambled eggs prepared with a combination of one whole egg and 2 egg whites differ only slightly from those made entirely from whole eggs. Scrambled eggs can even be made without any egg yolk at all by beating egg whites with a small amount of milk and a few drops of yellow food coloring.

Commercial egg substitutes can also be used to make scrambled eggs. I personally prefer the taste of whole eggs plus egg whites or egg whites alone. I do use the egg substitutes for omelets with well-flavored fillings such as mushrooms or green peppers.

My family very much enjoys pancakes for breakfast. Over the weekend I frequently prepare more pancakes than we need and then reheat the leftovers in a low oven on weekdays. If you're really rushed, cooked pancakes can even be reheated by briefly popping them in the toaster. Another time-saver for breakfast pancakes is to prepare the batter without the baking powder the evening before and store in the refrigerator. Stir in the baking powder thoroughly in the morning.

Most pancake recipes call for only 1 or 2 eggs and can easily be adapted to a low-cholesterol diet by using skimmed milk and substituting 2 egg whites for 1 whole egg and 3 egg whites for 2 whole eggs. See the section on meatless main dishes for pancake recipes in addition to those in this chapter.

Lingonberries are among our favorite pancake accompaniments. This tart, deep red topping is expensive but only a small amount is needed for a strong flavor. It can be found in the foreign foods section of most supermarkets. Blueberry Sauce (see page 318) is also excellent with pancakes.

All cereals, except for those granola-type cereals with coconut, can be included on a low-cholesterol diet. One friend's healthy breakfast is a mixture of granola, whole-bran cereal, and low-fat yogurt.

Muffins are a quick and easy breakfast food which pleases everyone. See the breads section (page 230) for recipes. If time is precious in the morning, mix the dry ingredients together the evening before.

The Morningtar Farms breakfast patties, links, etc. are soy products with acceptable ratios of polyunsaturates/saturates. You might want to try them to add interest to your breakfast menus.

Fresh fruits at breakfast time make for an extremely easy, healthy meal—one to look forward to.

FRENCH TOAST

My children's favorite breakfast. The cooked slices can be frozen and reheated in the oven or toaster.

3 egg whites	10 slices bread (4 inches square)
1 cup skimmed milk	
¼ teaspoon cinnamon	oil for frying

1. Beat the egg whites, milk, and cinnamon together.
2. Dip the bread slices into the milk mixture.

3. Fry in hot oil until golden brown on both sides. Serve with syrup, preserves, or sugar.

10 slices

GRANOLA

Add raisins, chopped dates, or chopped apricots, if you want, to the baked granola.

4 cups rolled oats
2 cups wheat germ
¼ cup sunflower seeds (optional)
¼-½ cup sesame seeds (optional)
¾ cup walnuts
¾ cup oil
2 tablespoons water
4 teaspoons vanilla or almond extract
⅔ cup brown sugar or honey

1. In a large bowl combine the oats, wheat germ, sunflower seeds, sesame seeds, and walnuts.
2. In another bowl mix together the oil, water, and vanilla or almond extract. Add the mixture to the dry ingredients and mix well.
3. Stir in the honey or brown sugar. Spread the mixture out into 2 large (10-inch by 15-inch) greased baking pans. Bake at 275° for one hour. Stir a few times during baking so that the granola will brown evenly.

PUFFY ORANGE OMELET

The orange juice and orange rind give a yellow color plus a very pleasing flavor to this dish made with egg whites.

3 egg whites
2 tablespoons orange juice
2-3 teaspoons grated orange rind
dash salt
1 tablespoon margarine

1. Beat the egg whites, orange juice, orange rind, and salt together with a wisk or electric beater until light and fluffy—about 3-4 minutes at medium speed with an electric beater.
2. Melt the margarine in a small frying pan which has a cover. Tilt to cover the bottom of the pan with margarine. Pour the egg mixture over the melted margarine. Cover and cook over low heat about 5-8 minutes or until firm on the top and browned on the underside.

2 servings

PANCAKES

For an extra-special breakfast, add ¾ cup of blueberries or drained crushed pineapple to the batter.

1½ cups flour or 1¼ cups flour plus ¼ cup wheat germ	2 tablespoons sugar
	3 egg whites
	3 tablespoons oil
¾ teaspoon salt	1¼ cups skimmed milk
2½ teaspoons baking powder	corn oil for frying

1. Stir the dry ingredients together.
2. Beat the egg whites, oil, and milk with a fork or a wisk until well mixed. Stir the dry ingredients into the milk mixture until thoroughly blended.
3. Drop the batter onto a hot, oiled pan or griddle. When bubbles appear on the top surface and the underside is golden, turn and brown the other side. Remember that the second side takes much less time to cook than the first. Add more oil sparingly as needed.

24 3½-inch pancakes

Variation:

Cornmeal Pancakes—Substitute ½ cup corn meal for ½ cup of the flour.

BUTTERMILK PANCAKES

The buttermilk flavor really comes through and makes these pancakes quite different.

2½ cups flour
4 teaspoons baking powder
1 teaspoon salt

3 egg whites
2¼ cups buttermilk
2 tablespoons oil

1. Stir the flour, baking powder and salt together.
2. Beat the egg whites, buttermilk and oil with a fork or wisk.
3. Pour the buttermilk mixture into the dry ingredients and mix well until thoroughly blended.
4. Spoon the batter onto a hot, oiled frying pan or griddle. When the underside is brown, turn and brown the other side. Serve with syrup.

24 3½-inch pancakes

ORANGE JUICE PANCAKES

1½ cups flour
3 teaspoons baking powder
¾ teaspoon salt
2 tablespoons sugar
1¼ cups skimmed milk

6 tablespoons (½ of a 6-ounce can) frozen orange juice concentrate, thawed
2 egg whites
3 tablespoons oil

1. Stir together the flour, baking powder, salt, and sugar.
2. Beat the egg whites, milk, orange juice concentrate, and oil with a fork or wisk. Pour into the flour mixture and mix until thoroughly blended.

3. Spoon the batter onto a hot oiled frying pan or griddle. When bubbles appear on the top and the underside is light brown, then turn and brown the other side. Watch these pancakes closely as they cook, since they tend to brown rapidly.

24 3½-inch pancakes

BANANA PANCAKES

These delicious pancakes are golden brown outside and slightly moist in the center. Contrast their sweetness with a topping of tart lingonberries for a special breakfast treat.

1 cup flour	3 small or 2 medium very
1½ teaspoons baking powder	ripe bananas
¼ teaspoon salt	⅓ cup skimmed milk
½ teaspoon cinnamon	2 egg whites
2 tablespoons sugar	

1. Stir the dry ingredients together and set aside.
2. Mash the bananas. Beat in the milk and egg whites with a fork or wisk.
3. Pour the banana mixture into the dry ingredients and mix well until thoroughly blended.
4. Spoon the batter onto a hot, oiled frying pan or griddle. When bubbles appear on the top of the pancakes and the underside is brown, turn and brown the other side.

16 3-to-3½-inch pancakes

flour mixture. Stir until completely blended. Stir in the
corn.
3. Heat 2 tablespoons of oil in a frying pan. Drop spoon
the batter into the oil and fry until golden on both
sides.

APPLESAUCE PANCAKES

A very flavorful and healthy way to start the day.

1½ cups flour	3 egg whites
3 tablespoons sugar	2 tablespoons oil
1 tablespoon baking powder	¾ cup skimmed milk
½ teaspoon salt	1 cup applesauce
1 teaspoon cinnamon	

1. Stir the dry ingredients together.
2. Beat the egg whites, oil, milk, and applesauce together
   with a wisk until thoroughly blended.
3. Pour the milk mixture into the dry ingredients and stir until completely blended.
4. Fry on a lightly oiled griddle or frying pan until both sides
   are golden brown.

24 3-to-3½-inch pancakes

CORN FRITTERS

1 cup flour	3 egg whites
1¼ teaspoons baking powder	1 cup drained corn
½ teaspoon salt	oil for frying
½ cup plus 1 tablespoon skimmed milk	

1. Stir the flour, baking powder, and salt together.
2. Lightly beat the egg whites and milk and pour into the

flour mixture. Stir until completely blended. Stir in the corn.
3. Heat 2 tablespoonfuls of oil in a 9-inch frying pan. Spoon the batter into the hot oil and fry until golden on both sides. Serve with maple syrup.

14 3- or 3½-inch fritters

APPLE SYRUP

This syrup is a pleasant bonus you can easily make from apple peels and cores which otherwise might be thrown away. It can be served on sherbet and fruits as well as on pancakes or French toast.

apple peels and cores
water
piece of cinnamon stick (optional)

sugar or artificial sweetener

1. Place the apple cores and peels and cinnamon stick, if desired, in a saucepan. Add water to cover them. Bring to a boil and simmer covered 30-40 minutes.
2. Remove the solid material in a strainer or with a slotted spoon.
3. Boil the syrup down to about ½ its original volume or until it's slightly thickened. Sweeten to taste with sugar or artificial sweetener. Cool and refrigerate.

about ¾ cup syrup from 3 pounds apples

BREADS

Breads differ from cookies, pies and cakes in that a good number of commercially baked bread products can be eaten on a low-cholesterol diet. Some French and Middle-Eastern style breads contain no shortening or eggs at all. Plain white, whole wheat, rye, and pumpernickel breads and rolls and English muffins are all acceptable.

Commercial biscuits, muffins, butter rolls, sweet rolls and sweet breads should, however, be avoided. I generally concentrate my bread baking on those bread types where the commercially available products are not acceptable.

My family especially enjoys the various "quick breads" whose recipes are included in this chapter. "Quick breads" depend on baking powder and baking soda instead of yeast for rising and can be prepared and baked in a relatively short time. Muffins require even less preparation and baking time and make marvelous breakfast treats.

See General Baking Hints in the section on cakes and pies. (page 246).

When making yeast breads, do not use yeast packages after the suggested date on the package. A good spot for yeast dough to rise is an unlit oven in which a large pan of hot water has been placed on the bottom or lowest shelf. Test to see if a yeast dough has risen to double in bulk by making a ½-inch indentation with 2 fingers. If the indentation remains and the dough does not spring up again, it has risen enough.

Breads and rolls should be reheated in a very low oven to prevent their drying out.

APPLE BREAD

An easy way to add interest to an everyday meal.

2 cups flour
1½ teaspoons baking powder
1 teaspoon baking soda
½ teaspoon salt
1½ teaspoons cinnamon
¼ cup oil

3 egg whites
2 tablespoons skimmed milk
⅔ cup sugar
2 cups finely chopped peeled apples
½ cup walnuts (optional)

1. Stir the flour, baking powder, baking soda, salt and cinnamon together.
2. Beat the oil, egg whites, milk, and sugar with a fork or wisk. Stir the dry ingredients into the oil mixture until well blended. Stir in the apples and walnuts.
3. Bake in a greased 9- by 5-inch loaf pan at 375° for 40 minutes.

APRICOT-NUT BREAD

An excellent bread that's very easy to make.

1 cup dried apricots
1½ cups warm water
2 cups flour
2 teaspoons baking powder
¾ teaspoon baking soda
½ teaspoon salt

¾ cup sugar
2 tablespoons oil
2 egg whites
¾ cup orange juice
½ cup chopped walnuts

1. Soak the apricots in the warm water for 30 minutes. Drain and cut the apricots into small pieces.
2. Stir the flour, baking powder, baking soda and salt together.
3. Beat the sugar, oil, and egg whites with a wisk or fork. Stir in the flour mixture alternately with the orange juice and blend well after each addition.
4. Pour the batter into a greased 9- by 5-inch loaf pan and bake at 350° for 55 minutes.

BANANA BREAD

My husband loves banana bread and this is his favorite recipe. Remember that the riper the banana the more flavorful the bread.

2 cups flour
1 teaspoon baking powder
1 teaspoon baking soda
½ teaspoon salt
½ cup margarine
½ cup sugar
1 cup mashed ripe bananas (2 medium or 3 small bananas)

3 tablespoons skimmed milk or low-fat yogurt
1 teaspoon vanilla
½ cup chopped walnuts
raisins, chopped dates (optional)

1. Stir the flour, baking powder, baking soda, and salt together and set aside.
2. Cream the sugar and margarine. Add the bananas, milk or yogurt, and vanilla. Mix well. Blend in the dry ingredients. Stir in the nuts and raisins or dates if desired.
3. Bake in a greased 9- by 5-inch baking pan at 350° for about 45 minutes or until the top is firm and golden brown and a toothpick inserted in the center comes out dry.

CHALLAH

Since children are great kneaders, challah-making is an excellent bad-weather activity with a delicious end product. I'm quite happy with the challah obtained by using all egg whites and I would suggest your trying it this way first. If you prefer a stronger egg flavor or color, you could try 1 whole egg plus 3 egg whites, or 2 whole eggs plus 2 egg whites, or 3 whole eggs.

1½ cups warm water
1 package yeast
½ teaspoon sugar
6-6½ cups flour (approximately)
2½ teaspoons salt
6 tablespoons sugar
5 egg whites or ¾ cup egg substitute
¼ cup oil

Glaze

1 egg yolk + 1 tablespoon water

1. Pour the warm water into a small bowl. Sprinkle in the yeast and ½ teaspoon sugar. Stir to dissolve.
2. In a large bowl, stir together 5 cups of flour, salt, and the remaining sugar. Make a well in the center of the flour mixture. Pour in the yeast mixture, egg whites, and oil. Mix together until smooth.
3. Slowly add flour to form a soft dough. Add as much flour as can be stirred in with a spoon and then turn the dough out onto a floured surface.
4. Knead the dough for at least 10 minutes until it is smooth and elastic. The dough is quite sticky at first. Frequently sprinkle the kneading surface and your hands with flour as long as necessary to prevent the dough from sticking. Scrape sticky dough from your fingers with the back of a knife.

5. Place the dough in a large, lightly oiled bowl. Turn the dough over so that the top and bottom are lightly oiled. Cover and place in a warm place to rise. I generally put the bowl in an unlit oven with a large pan of warm water on the bottom shelf.
6. When the dough has doubled in size, punch it down and knead a few times. Cut in half and then cut each half into 3 pieces. Roll each piece into a strip about 12 to 15 inches long. Braid the strips into 2 challahs.
7. Place the challahs on a greased cookie sheet. Let rise until doubled in bulk. Brush with the egg yolk-and-water mixture for a shiny glaze.
8. Bake at 350° for 30-35 minutes.

2 large challahs

CORN BREAD

1¼ cups corn meal	2 egg whites
¾ cup flour	1 cup skimmed milk
¼ cup sugar	¼ cup oil or melted marga-
¾ teaspoon salt	rine
4 teaspoons baking powder	

1. Stir the corn meal, flour, sugar, salt, and baking powder together.
2. Add the egg whites, milk, and oil or margarine. Beat until smooth.
3. Bake in a greased 8- or 9-inch square pan at 425° for 20 minutes.

CRANBERRY BREAD

The cranberries, fresh or frozen, can be chopped in a blender.

2 cups flour
2 teaspoons baking powder
½ teaspoon baking soda
½ teaspoon salt
2 egg whites
2 tablespoons oil
¾ cup orange juice

⅔ cup sugar
1 tablespoon grated orange rind
1½ cups cranberries, chopped
½ cup chopped walnuts

1. Stir the flour, baking powder, baking soda, and salt together in a large bowl.
2. Beat the egg whites, oil, orange juice, sugar, and orange rind together. Pour into the dry ingredients and stir just until completely blended. Stir in the chopped cranberries and nuts.
3. Bake in a greased 9- by 5-inch loaf pan at 350° for about 45-50 minutes or until a toothpick inserted in the center comes out clean.

DATE AND NUT BREAD

1 cup chopped dates
1½ teaspoons baking soda
¾ cup boiling water
1½ cups flour
½ teaspoon salt
3 tablespoons oil

2 egg whites
½ cup white or firmly packed brown sugar
1 teaspoon vanilla
½ cup chopped walnuts

1. Pour the boiling water over the dates and baking soda. Let cool.
2. Stir the flour and salt together.
3. Beat the oil, egg whites, sugar, and vanilla together. Stir in the flour mixture alternately with the date mixture and blend well after each addition. Stir in the nuts.
4. Bake in a greased 9- by 5-inch loaf pan at 350° for 40-45 minutes.

ORANGE–NUT BREAD

2¼ cups flour
2 teaspoons baking powder
½ teaspoon baking soda
½ teaspoon salt
2 egg whites
3 tablespoons oil
¾ cup sugar

1 cup orange juice
½ teaspoon vanilla
2 tablespoons grated orange rind
¾-1 cup chopped walnuts
¼-½ cup raisins (optional)

1. Stir the flour, baking powder, baking soda, and salt together in a large bowl.
2. Beat the egg whites, oil, sugar, orange juice, vanilla, and orange rind together. Pour into the dry ingredients and stir just until completely blended. Stir in the chopped nuts and raisins (if desired).
3. Bake in a greased 9- by 5-inch loaf pan at 375° for 45 minutes.

PUMPKIN BREAD

A firm, moist, flavorful loaf.

2 cups flour
1 teaspoon baking soda
½ teaspoon baking powder
1 teaspoon salt
1 teaspoon cinnamon
½ teaspoon nutmeg
1 cup canned pumpkin

½ cup oil
3 egg whites
1 cup brown sugar, firmly packed
¼ cup water
½ cup raisins
½ cup chopped walnuts

1. Stir the flour, baking soda, baking powder, salt, cinnamon, and nutmeg together.
2. Beat the pumpkin, oil, egg whites, sugar, and water together. Stir in the dry ingredients until well blended. Stir in the raisins and nuts.
3. Spoon into a greased 9- by 5-inch loaf pan. Bake at 350° in the lower half of the oven for 60-70 minutes or until a toothpick inserted in the center comes out clean. If the top begins to brown before the bread is done, cover loosely with aluminum foil for the remainder of the baking time.

BAKING POWDER BISCUITS

2 cups flour
1 tablespoon baking powder
1 teaspoon salt

¼ cup margarine
⅔ cup skimmed milk

1. Stir the flour, baking powder and salt together.
2. Blend in the margarine with a fork or pastry blender until

the mixture resembles coarse crumbs. Add the milk and mix into a soft dough.
3. Knead about ½ dozen times on a lightly floured surface. Pat the dough out to ½-inch thickness.
5. Cut into 2-inch rounds. Dip the cutter into flour frequently to prevent dough from sticking to it. Place the rounds on an ungreased cookie sheet and bake at 450° for 12 minutes or until golden brown.

18 biscuits

SCONES

These British-style biscuits are delicious with preserves.

2 cups flour	¼ cup margarine
4 teaspoons baking powder	2 egg whites
½ teaspoon salt	⅓ cup milk
2 tablespoons sugar	

1. Stir together the flour, baking powder, salt and sugar. Mix in the margarine with a pastry blender or fork until the mixture resembles coarse crumbs.
2. Lightly beat the egg whites and milk and add all at once to the flour mixture. Stir to make a soft dough.
3. Turn the dough out onto a lightly floured surface and pat or roll into a circle about ½ inch thick. Cut into 10 or 12 wedges.
4. Bake on a greased cookie sheet at 425° for 10-12 minutes or until golden brown.

10-12 scones

NO-KNEAD CINNAMON BUNS
OR CRESCENTS

The recipe for these delicious, light-as-a-feather rolls is my adaptation of a family recipe given to me by my friend, Ann Parmenter. Ann remembers her mother awakening early to prepare the rolls in time for breakfast. This is an especially handy dough because after the first rising it can be stored in the refrigerator for several days. If you don't need so many rolls, cut the recipe in half, but still use a full package of dry yeast.

1½ cups skimmed milk
1 cup margarine
½ cup sugar
1 teaspoon salt
1 package dry yeast
¼ cup warm water
4 egg whites
5½ cups flour

Filling

4 tablespoons melted margarine
½ cup sugar mixed with
2 teaspoons cinnamon
chopped nuts, raisins

1. Scald the milk, Add the margarine, sugar, and salt and let cool to lukewarm.
2. Stir the dry yeast into the warm water and let stand 5-10 minutes or until dissolved.
3. Beat the egg whites into the milk mixture one at a time with a fork or wisk. Beat in the yeast mixture. Stir in the flour vigorously with a wooden spoon until thoroughly mixed. Cover with a dish towel and let rise until double in bulk. Punch down and refrigerate overnight or as long as 3-4 days.
4. To make crescents, divide the dough into quarters. On a lightly floured surface, roll each quarter into a 10- or 12-inch circle. Brush with melted margarine and sprinkle with 2 tablespoons of the sugar-cinnamon mixture. Cut into 8 wedges. Roll up each wedge starting from the wide end.

Shape into a crescent and place point down on a greased baking sheet. Sprinkle with a little sugar and cinnamon if desired. Allow at least 1½ inches of space between the crescents for rising. Let rise for 2 hours or until the dough does not spring back when lightly touched with a fingertip. Bake at 375° for 12-15 minutes or until the tops and bottoms of the crescents are lightly browned.

5. To make spiral buns, divide the refrigerated dough in half. On a lightly floured surface, roll each half into a 12- by 18-inch rectangle. Brush with melted margarine and sprinkle with half of the sugar-cinnamon mixture. Starting with one of the long sides, roll up the rectangle. Cut into 18 1-inch slices. Place 9 slices cut-side-down into a greased 8-inch square pan or a 9-inch round pan. Do the same thing with the other 9 slices. Let rise for 2 hours or until the dough does not spring back when lightly pressed with a fingertip. Bake at 375° for 12-15 minutes or until the tops and bottoms of the buns are lightly browned.

36 spiral buns or
32 crescents

BASIC MUFFIN RECIPE

These are extremely easy and good. Try making up your own variations.

2 cups flour
¾ teaspoon salt
4-6 tablespoons sugar
3½ teaspoons baking powder

2 egg whites
1 cup skimmed milk
3 tablespoons oil

1. Stir the dry ingredients together.
2. Beat the egg whites, milk and oil together lightly and pour over the dry ingredients. Stir only until the dry ingredients are moistened thoroughly. The batter will be lumpy. Spoon into greased muffin tins or aluminum foil cupcake tin liners until they are about ⅔ full. Sprinkle a few teaspoons

of sugar over the tops of the muffins, if desired. Bake at 400° for 20 minutes or until golden brown.

12 muffins

Variations

Blueberry—For delicious cake-like blueberry muffins, increase the amount of sugar to ½-⅔ cup, beat in ½ teaspoon vanilla with the liquids, and stir 1 cup of blueberries into the final batter.

Pineapple—Stir one cup of thoroughly drained crushed pineapple into the final batter.

Apple—Use 6 tablespoons sugar and stir 1½ teaspoons cinnamon in with the dry ingredients. Stir 1 cup finely chopped apples into the final batter.

Surprise Muffins—Prepare Basic Muffin batter and fill greased muffin tins ⅓ full. Put a teaspoon of jam, raisins, or chopped dates in the center and top with the remaining batter.

Nut or Dried Fruit Muffins—Stir ½-¾ cup chopped nuts or chopped apricots or dates into the final batter.

BRAN MUFFINS

These muffins have a strong bran flavor. If you prefer a less prominent bran taste, substitute ¼-½ cup flour for ¼-½ cup bran.

¾ cup flour	1½ cups whole bran cereal
1 tablespoon baking powder	1 cup skimmed milk
½ teaspoon salt	2 egg whites
¼ cup white or firmly packed brown sugar	3 tablespoons oil

1. Stir the flour, baking powder, salt and sugar together.
2. Pour the milk over the bran and let stand for 5 minutes.

Mix in the egg whites and oil. Add the dry ingredients and mix just until completely blended.

3. Fill greased muffin cups or foil cupcake holders ⅔ full. Bake at 400° for 20 minutes.

12 muffins

Variations

Applesauce-Bran Muffins—Mix ½ teaspoon cinnamon in with the dry ingredients. Substitute ¾ cup applesauce and ⅓ cup milk for the 1 cup milk. Follow mixing and baking directions for Bran Muffins.

Banana-Bran Muffins—Stir ½ teaspoon cinnamon in with the dry ingredients. Substitute 1 cup mashed ripe banana and ¼ cup milk for the 1 cup milk. Follow mixing and baking directions for Bran Muffins.

PUMPKIN MUFFINS

Try this unusual muffin around Thanksgiving time.

3 cups flour
2 tablespoons baking powder
1 teaspoon salt
1½ teaspoons cinnamon
¼ teaspoon nutmeg
3 egg whites
6 tablespoons oil

½ cup skimmed milk or water
1 cup firmly packed dark brown sugar
1 14-ounce can pumpkin (Be sure to get plain cooked pumpkin and not pumpkin-pie mix.)

1. Stir the flour, baking powder, salt, and cinnamon together in a large bowl.
2. Beat the egg whites, oil, milk, sugar, and pumpkin with a wisk until thoroughly blended.
3. Pour the milk mixture into the dry ingredients and stir just until all of the dry ingredients are moistened. Spoon into greased muffin tins. Bake at 400° for 20-25 minutes.

2 dozen muffins

OATMEAL MUFFINS-I

1 cup flour or ⅞ cup flour plus 2 tablespoons wheat germ	¾ teaspoon cinnamon
	2 egg whites
	3 tablespoons oil
1 cup uncooked oats	¼ cup brown sugar
1 tablespoon baking powder	¾ cup skimmed milk
¾ teaspoon salt	

1. Stir together the flour, oats, baking powder, salt, and cinnamon.
2. Beat the egg whites, sugar, oil, and milk together with a wisk until thoroughly blended.
3. Pour the milk mixture into the flour mixture and stir just until the dry ingredients are moistened.
4. Spoon into greased muffin cups and bake at 425° for 18-20 minutes.

12 muffins

OATMEAL MUFFINS-II

These are sweet and crisp, actually more like a cookie than a muffin.

2¼ cups uncooked oats	¼ cup wheat germ or chopped nuts or bran (optional)
½ cup margarine	
¾ cup brown sugar, firmly packed	

1. Cream the margarine and sugar together. Stir in the oats and optional ingredient, if desired.

2. Spoon into 12 ungreased cupcake tins. Bake at 375° for 15 minutes. Allow to cool about 15 minutes. To remove muffins from the tins, insert a knife at one point along the edge and the entire muffin will become loosened.

12 muffins

2. ... 12 ... cupcake ...
... Allow ... about ...
... from the ... a knife
... the entire ... will ...

CAKES AND PIES

Commercial cakes and pies, except for angel food cake, are not suitable for a low-cholesterol diet because they contain whole eggs and butter or hydrogenated vegetable shortening. So, unless you're willing to forego cakes and pies almost completely, it's likely that you'll want to do more home baking.

Many of your present recipes can be easily adapted to meet low-cholesterol requirements. Polyunsaturated margarine can usually be used when butter or shortening is called for. In some recipes, corn oil can even be substituted for shortening. Use slightly less oil than the amount of shortening listed in the recipe, i.e., ⅓ cup oil for ½ cup shortening.

Egg whites or commercial egg substitute (Egg Beaters, Second Nature, Scramblers, etc.) can be used in place of whole eggs. When making substitutions, be sure to remember that each commercial egg substitute has a different volume of product corresponding to one egg. I find egg whites more convenient to stock and use than egg substitutes, except perhaps in recipes calling for a large number of eggs. Since the volume of egg whites is greater than that of egg yolks, I substitute 2 whites for one whole egg and 3 whites for 2 eggs.

If it bothers you to throw egg yolks away, you can buy powdered egg white from Henningsen Foods, Inc., 2 Corporate Park Drive, White Plains, New York, 10604. I find reconstituting the powdered egg white with water a bit difficult and use this product infrequently and only when large numbers of egg whites are called for.

Since I don't like to spend much time hovering over an oven or mixing bowl, most of the recipes in this chapter are simple and quick. They can be rapidly mixed together and put into the oven before you start your other supper preparations. Then you can crown your meal with a home-made cake.

I've included a good number of recipes for cakes which contain no eggs and many recipes for oil-based rather than margarine-based cakes. The oil cakes have the dual virtues of being pareve and high in polyunsaturates. I've also included a few speedy and easy frosting recipes.

Yeast cakes are an excellent idea for persons on a low-sodium diet since they lack the sodium contained in baking powder and baking soda. I usually bake non-yeast cakes myself because they're faster to prepare. Fleishmann's (Standard Brands) puts out excellent recipe booklets for yeast baking which can usually be obtained for a nominal charge with a few yeast wrappers.

To boost the nutritive value of your cakes, substitute 2 tablespoons of wheat germ for 2 tablespoons of flour in each cup of flour called for.

Low-fat yogurt can often be successfully substituted for sour cream in baking, and 3 tablespoons of cocoa plus one tablespoon of margarine can be substituted for one square of unsweetened chocolate. You can be certain that your family and friends will be happy to sample the products of your experimentation and most likely everyone will be very pleased with the results.

General Baking Hints

1. Prepare your own cake mixes by mixing up an extra batch of dry ingredients each time you bake a cake.
2. Separate egg whites from yolks when the eggs are cold, but beat egg whites when they've come to room temperature. They whip up to a greater volume at room temperature than they do when cold.
3. When separating egg whites from yolks, crack and separate each egg over a cup. Then add each egg white to the others in a bowl. This way an incompletely separated egg will not spoil the previously separated ones. Egg whites will not whip properly when contaminated by egg yolk.
4. Grease pans by pouring in a few teaspoons of oil and spreading the oil around with a napkin or tissue.

5. Use a 25° lower baking temperature with a glass baking dish than with a baking pan.
6. Measure margarine by starting with a fresh container and marking off quarters or thirds of a cup.
7. Bake cakes and pies near the center of the oven and away from the sides.
8. Cool cakes completely before frosting.
9. Cool baked pie shells completely before filling.
10. Put thin strips of aluminum foil around the edges of pie crusts during baking to prevent burning.
11. Roll pie crusts between 2 sheets of waxed paper which have been placed on a damp surface to which the bottom surface of waxed paper can adhere.
12. Prick a one-crust pie shell all over with a fork before baking.
13. Prick the top crust of a 2-crust pie with a fork in many spots to allow steam to escape.
14. A cake is done when a toothpick inserted in the center comes out dry and clean or when the top feels firm and the edges are just starting to pull away from the sides of the pan.
15. Store opened brown sugar in a tightly covered container to avoid hardening. Buy only as much as you can anticipate using soon and press the box to make sure it's soft. Hardened brown sugar can be softened for measuring by heating on a baking pan in a warm oven for a few minutes. It rehardens after cooling, though.
16. Rolled-out pie crusts can be frozen flat between layers of foil. This is one way to get ready for apple-picking time.
17. Grease a measuring cup lightly with oil before using it to measure honey or peanut butter.
18. When baking a cake to be frozen, press a large sheet of aluminum foil into the bottom and sides of the baking pan. Fold excess foil over the edges of the pan. Grease the foil and bake as usual. After baking and cooling, remove the cake from the pan by lifting up the edges of the foil. The cake can now be frozen in the foil and you have one less pan to wash.

Cakes

BASIC APPLE CAKE

Second helpings of this simple, flavorful cake are very hard to resist.

2 cups flour
½ teaspoon salt
2 teaspoons baking soda
1 teaspoon cinnamon
¼ teaspoon nutmeg
¾ cup oil
1 cup white or firmly packed brown sugar

3 egg whites
4 cups peeled and diced apples (4-5 large apples)
chopped nuts, raisins, chopped dates (optional)

1. Stir the flour, salt, baking soda and spices together.
2. Beat the oil, sugar and egg whites together. Mix in the dry ingredients until thoroughly blended. Stir in the chopped apples. Stir in the nuts, raisins, or dates if desired.
3. Bake in a greased 9 × 13-inch baking dish at 325° for 30 minutes.

12-16 servings

1-2-3 BANANA CAKE

Just about all you need to make this easy cake are 3 ripe bananas and a few minutes' preparation time, so don't wait for a special occasion to try it.

1½ cups flour
1 teaspoon baking soda
1 teaspoon salt
½ teaspoon cinnamon
1 cup mashed very ripe bananas (3 medium)
¼ cup margarine or 3 tablespoons corn oil

⅔ cup sugar
2 egg whites
½ teaspoon vanilla
½ cup chopped walnuts (optional)

1. Stir the flour, baking soda, salt and cinnamon together.
2. Beat the oil, sugar, egg whites, and vanilla into the mashed bananas. Mix in the flour mixture. Stir in the nuts, if desired.
3. Bake in a greased 8-inch square baking dish at 325° for 35-40 minutes.

6 servings

QUICK BLUEBERRY COFFEE CAKE

This cake can be made with fresh, frozen, or drained canned blueberries. My family enjoys it so much that I make 3 at a time and freeze 2. See General Baking Hints #18 on baking cakes for the freezer (page 247).

1½ cups flour
2 teaspoons baking powder
¼ teaspoon cinnamon
½ teaspoon salt
½ cup sugar
¼ cup corn oil
2 egg whites
½ cup water or milk
¾ teaspoon vanilla
1 cup blueberries

Optional Topping

½ cup flour
6 tablespoons white or
  brown sugar
¾ teaspoon cinnamon
2 tablespoons oil

1. Stir together the flour, baking powder, cinnamon, and salt.
2. Beat the sugar, oil, water or milk, egg whites, and vanilla together with a whisk. Stir the flour mixture into the oil mixture until well blended. Stir in the blueberries.
3. Pour into a greased 8-inch square baking dish. Sprinkle with topping, if desired, and bake at 350° for 35 minutes.

6-8 servings

BROWN SUGAR CAKE

You get a large, light cake here for a little time input.

1½ cups dark brown sugar
1 cup corn oil
3 egg whites
3 cups flour
1 teaspoon baking powder
1 teaspoon baking soda
¾ teaspoon salt
½ teaspoon cinnamon
¼ teaspoon nutmeg
¼ teaspoon cloves
1 cup strong coffee
½ cup raisins
½ cup chopped walnuts

1. Mix the oil, sugar, and egg whites together with a wisk.
2. Stir the dry ingredients together and add alternately with the coffee to the oil mixture. Stir vigorously until well blended. Stir in the raisins and nuts.
3. Bake in a greased 9 × 13-inch baking dish for 30 minutes at 350°.

12-16 servings

BAKED CHEESECAKE

An excellent dessert for a Shavuot meal or for any dairy meal. If you're in a hurry, serve the cake without a topping or with a topping of canned pie filling. Corn flake crumbs can be used in place of oats in the crust, but I find oats more flavorful.

Crust

1½ cups uncooked oats
¾ teaspoon cinnamon
6 tablespoons sugar

6 tablespoons melted margarine

Filling

1 pound dry or low-fat cottage cheese or pot cheese
½ cup plus 2 tablespoons sugar
2 tablespoons flour
⅛ teaspoon salt
3 egg whites

¾ cup evaporated skimmed milk or
½ cup powder milk plus enough water to yield ¾ cup milk
½ teaspoon grated lemon rind or
½ teaspoon vanilla

1. Stir the oats, cinnamon, and sugar together. Stir in the melted margarine and blend well. Press the mixture into a 9½-inch pie plate.
2. Put all the filling ingredients into a blender and whirl until completely smooth and no trace of graininess remains.
3. Pour the filling into the prepared crust and bake at 350° for 35 minutes or until the filling is set and firm. Allow to cool.
4. If desired, cover the cake with either Strawberry or Pineapple Topping (recipes follow).

8 servings

STRAWBERRY TOPPING FOR CHEESECAKE

8-12 sliced fresh strawberries
6 tablespoons apricot preserves

2 teaspoons water
2 teaspoons sugar
2 teaspoons rum or cognac

Arrange the sliced berries over the cooled cheesecake. Heat the apricot preserves, sugar, and water in a small saucepan until the preserves are melted. Stir in the rum or cognac. Spoon the sauce over the top of the cheesecake. Refrigerate until ready to serve.

PINEAPPLE TOPPING FOR CHEESECAKE

1 cup undrained crushed
  pineapple
2 tablespoons orange juice

1 teaspoon cornstarch
1 teaspoon kirsch

1. Heat the crushed pineapple, orange juice, and cornstarch in a small saucepan, stirring continuously just until the mixture comes to a boil and thickens. Remove from the heat and stir in the kirsch. Cool and spread over the cake.

NO-BAKE CHEESECAKE

Serve the cheesecake alone or with the toppings suggested for baked cheesecake. The pineapple-lemon flavoring goes very well with cottage cheese.

2 egg whites
2 tablespoons unflavored gelatin
1 cup pineapple juice or water
12 ounces pot cheese or dry cottage cheese

2 teaspoons lemon juice
1 teaspoon grated lemon rind
6 tablespoons sugar
9-in pre-baked cornflake crumb or oatmeal pie shell

1. Separate the egg whites and set aside.
2. In a small saucepan, sprinkle the gelatin on ½ cup of the juice or water and let stand 5 minutes.
3. Slowly bring the liquid to a boil and stir to dissolve the gelatin.
4. Put the gelatin mixture, remaining ½ cup of juice, cottage cheese, lemon juice, lemon rind, and 4 tablespoons of sugar into a blender. Whirl until very smooth and no trace of graininess remains. Pour into a large bowl. Refrigerate while performing the next step.
5. Beat the egg whites until frothy. Add the remaining 3 tablespoons of sugar gradually and continue beating until the egg whites are thick and glossy. Fold ⅓ of the beaten egg whites into the cottage cheese mixture. Then fold in the remaining egg whites. Pour into the pie shell. Chill until firm, about 2-3 hours.

8 servings

OLD-FASHIONED CHEESECAKE

This is a European-style cheesecake which has a heavier filling than the American variety. Either kind is very good, too good in fact to remain around the house for long.

1½ cups flour
2 teaspoons baking powder
dash salt
2 tablespoons margarine

½ cup sugar
2 egg whites
2 tablespoons milk
1 teaspoon vanilla

Filling

1 pound dry or low-fat cottage cheese or pot cheese
½ cup sugar
2 egg whites
¼ teaspoon cinnamon

2 tablespoons melted margarine
¼ cup milk
raisins (optional)

1. Stir the flour, baking powder, and salt together and set aside.
2. Cream the margarine and sugar. Beat in the egg whites, milk, and vanilla. Stir in the flour mixture and blend until smooth.
3. Press about ⅔ of the dough onto the bottom and sides of a greased 8-inch square baking pan.
4. Blend the filling ingredients until completely smooth in an electric blender. Spread the filling over the dough.
5. Roll the remaining dough with floured hands into strips about as wide as a pencil. Arrange the strips in a crisscross pattern over the filling.
6. Bake 45 minutes at 350°.

6-8 servings

CHERRY OR BLUEBERRY
PIE-FILLING CAKE

This recipe makes a lovely large cake which seems to be a universal favorite.

3 cups flour
1 tablespoon baking powder
½ teaspoon salt
¾ cup oil
¾ cup sugar

1 teaspoon vanilla
½ cup orange juice
5 egg whites or ¾ cup Egg Beaters
1 can pie filling

Topping

2 tablespoons sugar
2 tablespoons chopped walnuts

½ teaspoon cinnamon

1. Stir the flour, baking powder, and salt together.
2. Blend the oil and sugar with a wisk. Beat in the vanilla and orange juice. Beat in the egg whites. Stir in the flour mixture until well blended.
3. Spread half of the batter in a greased 9 × 13-inch baking dish. Spoon the pie filling over the batter, spreading it to ½ inch from the edge of the batter. Spoon the remaining batter over the pie filling. Some of the pie filling will probably show through. Sprinkle with topping.
4. Bake at 325° for 45 minutes.

12-16 servings

EGGLESS SPICE CAKE

This is so easy that it takes less time to make than some packaged mixes.

1½ cups flour	¼ teaspoon cloves
⅔ cup sugar	1 cup water
1 teaspoon baking soda	6 tablespoons oil
¼ teaspoon salt	1 tablespoon vinegar
1 teaspoon cinnamon	1 teaspoon vanilla
½ teaspoon nutmeg	

1. Mix the dry ingredients together in a bowl.
2. Add the water, oil, vinegar, and vanilla and stir vigorously until well-blended.
3. Bake at 350° in a greased 8- or 9-inch square baking pan for 35 minutes or until a toothpick inserted in the center comes out dry.

6-8 servings

EGGLESS COCOA CAKE

Variations of this cake have been appearing in cookbooks and magazines as long as I can remember. Sometimes it's called Wacky Cake or Cockeyed Cake or even Mother's Day Cake. No matter what the name, it's easy, good and the healthiest chocolate cake I've come across. The recipe usually calls for mixing right in the pan, but I find mixing in a bowl easier.

1½ cups flour
3 tablespoons cocoa
⅔ cup sugar
1 teaspoon baking soda

5 tablespoons oil
1 teaspoon vanilla
1 tablespoon vinegar
1 cup water

1. Stir the dry ingredients together. Mix in the remaining ingredients until well blended.
2. Bake in a greased 8- or 9-inch square pan at 350° for about 30 minutes.

6-8 servings

EGGLESS APPLESAUCE CAKE

This is a rich, moist, flavorful cake.

1¾ cups flour
1¼ teaspoons baking soda
¼ teaspoon salt
1 teaspoon cinnamon
½ teaspoon nutmeg
¼ teaspoon cloves
½ cup oil

⅔ cup dark brown sugar, firmly packed
1 cup applesauce
½ cup raisins (optional)
½ cup chopped walnuts (optional)

1. Stir the flour, baking soda, salt, and spices together.
2. Mix the oil, brown sugar, and applesauce. Stir in the dry ingredients, then stir in the walnuts and raisins if desired. Bake in a greased 8- or 9-inch square pan at 350° for 35-40 minutes.

6-8 servings

HONEY CAKE

This honey cake is light in texture and marvelous in taste.

3 cups flour
2¼ teaspoons baking powder
1 teaspoon baking soda
½ teaspoon cloves
½ teaspoon cinnamon
¾ teaspoon allspice
¾ teaspoon ginger
1 cup strong coffee or 2 teaspoons instant coffee dissolved in 1 cup water

¾ cup sugar
5 egg whites or ¾ cup Egg Beaters
¼ cup corn oil
1 cup honey
½ cup raisins
½ cup chopped walnuts

1. Stir together the flour, baking powder, baking soda, and spices.
2. Beat the egg whites or egg substitute until frothy, with an electric beater. Continue beating and gradually add the sugar. Beat in the honey and oil.
3. Add the dry ingredients and the coffee alternately to the honey mixture. Beat until smooth after each addition.
4. Stir in the nuts and raisins.
5. Bake at 325° in a well-greased 9- by 13-inch baking dish for 45-50 minutes.

12-16 servings

MANDARIN ORANGE CAKE

This easily prepared, flavorful cake has the additional virtues of containing no shortening and keeping very well for several days. The recipe can be doubled and baked in a 9- by 13-inch pan.

1 cup flour
⅔ cup sugar
1 teaspoon baking soda
¼ teaspoon salt

2 egg whites
1 11-ounce can mandarin oranges, drained

Syrup

½ cup orange juice
¼ cup sugar

1 teaspoon grated orange rind

1. Stir together the flour, ⅔ cup sugar, baking soda, and salt. Add the egg whites and drained mandarin oranges and stir vigorously until everything is well blended. Don't worry that there won't be enough liquid for a batter; the mandarin oranges break into pieces and give off juice.
2. Pour into a greased 8-inch square pan and bake at 350° for 30 minutes. Prick holes all over the warm cake with a fork.
3. Stir the orange juice, ¼ cup sugar, and orange rind together in a small saucepan and bring to a boil. Spoon over the cake. Best served warm.

6-8 servings

PINEAPPLE-BANANA CAKE

An excellent choice for a large party since it can easily be cut into many slices. My husband likes to add a third fruit flavor by topping this with applesauce.

3 cups flour
1¼ teaspoon baking soda
¾ teaspoon salt
1½ teaspoons cinnamon
3 egg whites
1¼ cups oil
1½ teaspoons vanilla

1¼ cups sugar
3 small or 2 medium very ripe bananas, mashed
1 cup unsweetened crushed pineapple, undrained
½ cup chopped walnuts (optional)

1. Stir the flour, baking soda, salt, and cinnamon together.
2. Beat the egg whites, oil, vanilla, and sugar together with a wisk until thoroughly blended. Beat in the mashed bananas and crushed pineapple. Stir in the dry ingredients until thoroughly mixed. Stir in the walnuts, if desired.
3. Bake in a greased 10-inch tube pan at 350° for 1 hour.

12-16 servings

PLUM CAKE

A delicious cake to prepare when plums are in season. The recipe can be doubled and baked in a 9- by 13-inch pan.

1½ cups flour
1 teaspoon baking powder
¼ teaspoon salt
½ cup corn oil
6 tablespoons sugar

2 egg whites
10-12 prune plums, pitted and quartered
2 tablespoons sugar
½ teaspoon cinnamon

1. Stir the flour, baking powder, and salt together.
2. Beat the oil, sugar, and egg whites together with a wisk until well blended. Stir the flour mixture into the oil mixture until thoroughly mixed.
3. Pat the dough into a greased 8- or 9-inch square baking pan, pressing dough about ½ inch up the sides of the pan. Arrange the plum quarters in rows on top of the dough.
4. Stir the sugar and cinnamon together and sprinkle over the plums. Bake at 350° for 35-40 minutes.

6-8 servings

PUMPKIN SPICE CAKE

A perfect end to Thanksgiving or any dinner.

3 cups flour or 2 cups flour plus 1 cup whole-bran cereal
2 teaspoons baking powder
2 teaspoons baking soda
½ teaspoon salt
1½ teaspoons cinnamon
½ teaspoon nutmeg
¼ teaspoon ginger
¼ teaspoon cloves

1 cup oil
1 14½-ounce can pumpkin (1¾ cups)
1½ cups brown sugar, firmly packed
6 egg whites or 1 cup Egg Beaters
raisins, chopped walnuts (optional)

1. Stir together the flour, baking powder, baking soda, salt and spices.
2. In a large bowl beat the oil, pumpkin, and sugar together with an electric mixer. Beat in the egg whites gradually. Stir in the flour mixture and beat until smooth. Stir in the raisins and nuts if desired.
3. Bake at 350° in a greased 9- by 13-inch baking pan for about 45 minutes or in a greased 10-inch tube pan for about 55 minutes.

12-16 servings

RHUBARB CAKE

A good cake to make in the spring when fresh rhubarb is still plentiful.

2½ cups flour
1 teaspoon baking soda
¼ teaspoon salt
1¼ teaspoons cinnamon
½ cup margarine
1¼ cups brown sugar
3 egg whites

1¼ teaspoons vanilla
1 cup skimmed milk
1 tablespoon white vinegar
or lemon juice
2½ cups thinly sliced fresh
rhubarb

1. Stir the flour, baking soda, salt, and cinnamon together.
2. Cream the margarine and sugar. Beat in the egg whites and vanilla.
3. Add the vinegar or lemon juice to the milk and let the mixture stand for 5 minutes to sour.
4. Stir the dry ingredients alternately with the sour milk into the creamed margarine mixture. Stir in the sliced rhubarb.
5. Bake in a greased 9- by 13-inch baking dish at 350° for 35 minutes.

12-16 servings

BASIC WHITE CAKE

I often call this "birthday party cake" since it's what I make for my children's parties. They have a grand time frosting, decorating, and eating it. The same recipe can be used to make 20 cupcakes.

2¼ cups flour
¾ teaspoon salt
4 teaspoons baking powder
½ cup oil
1 cup sugar

2 teaspoons vanilla
1 cup skimmed milk or
water
4 egg whites at room temperature

1. Stir the flour, salt, and baking powder together.
2. In a large bowl, beat the oil, ¾ cup of sugar, and vanilla together with a wisk. Add the dry ingredients alternately with the water or milk, stirring vigorously until well blended.

3. Beat the egg whites until frothy. Gradually add the remaining ¼ cup of sugar and continue beating until the egg whites are thick and glossy. Fold about ¼ of the beaten egg whites into the batter to lighten the batter. Then fold in the remaining egg whites.
4. Pour into 2 greased 9-inch round pans and bake at 350° for 25-30 minutes. Or spoon into 20 greased cupcake tins and bake for the same time at 350°.
5. Cool completely before frosting or spreading with filling.

2 9-inch layers or
20 cupcakes

VARIATIONS ON BASIC WHITE CAKE

Poppy Seed Cake
1. Mix ⅓ cup poppy seed with the dry ingredients and proceed as for basic white cake.
2. Split the cooled cake layers horizontally and spread with Orange Filling (below) or with Pineapple Topping for Cheesecake.

Orange Filling for One 9-Inch Layer

1 cup orange juice
3 tablespoons cornstarch
⅔ cup sugar

2 teaspoons grated orange rind
2 teaspoons fresh lemon juice

Stir all the ingredients together in a small saucepan. Slowly bring to a boil while stirring constantly. Simmer a minute or two until thickened.

Maraschino Cherry Cake
1. Substitute ⅓ cup maraschino cherry juice for ⅓ cup water or milk.
2. Stir ½ cup finely chopped maraschino cherries into the batter just before baking.

3. Prepare cherry frosting by substituting maraschino cherry juice for milk in Basic Frosting and stirring in a few tablespoons of finely chopped cherries.

BASIC FROSTING

For orange frosting, substitute orange juice for milk and 1-2 teaspoons grated orange rind for the vanilla. For sherry frosting (which I highly recommend), substitute sherry for the milk.

3 tablespoons margarine   5-6 teaspoons skimmed milk
1½ cups confectioner's sugar   ½ teaspoon vanilla

1. Soften the margarine with the back of a spoon. Mix in the confectioner's sugar and milk alternately. Stir in the vanilla.

*Frosting for 1 8-inch square or
9-inch round layer*

STRAWBERRY FROSTING

3 tablespoons margarine   2 tablespoons strawberry
1½ cups confectioner's sugar   preserves
1 tablespoon skimmed milk

1. Stir the sugar, preserves, and milk into the margarine and mix until very well blended.

*Frosting for one 8-inch square
or 9-inch round layer*

YOGURT BABKA

Excellent for a brunch or when having people in for coffee and cake.

1 package yeast	6 tablespoons sugar
¼ cup lukewarm water	¼ cup melted margarine
3 cups flour (approximately)	½ cup low-fat yogurt
½ teaspoon salt	3 egg whites

Filling

2 tablespoons melted margarine	¼ cup sugar mixed with 1 teaspoon cinnamon

1. Sprinkle the yeast over the lukewarm water in a small bowl. Stir to dissolve.
2. In a large bowl, stir the salt, sugar, and 2¼ cups of the flour together.
3. Make a well in the center of the flour mixture. Pour in the dissolved yeast, melted margarine, yogurt, and egg whites. Mix well. Gradually stir in about ¾ cup additional flour to make a soft but not sticky dough. Cover and refrigerate overnight.
4. Punch the dough down. Roll out on a lightly floured surface to a rectangle about 11 by 14 inches. Brush with 2 tablespoons melted margarine. Sprinkle with the sugar-cinnamon mixture.
5. Starting from the 14-inch side, roll up as for a jelly roll. Cut into 10 slices.
6. Place the slices cut side down in a greased 10-inch tube pan. Let rise until double in bulk.
7. If desired, brush the top with additional melted margarine and sprinkle with more sugar-cinnamon mixture.
8. Bake at 350° for about 40 minutes or until golden brown.

YOGURT CAKE

This is a moist and substantial cake with excellent keeping properties. To make it more festive, use 1¼ cups orange juice in the syrup and then stir in ¼ cup rum.

2½ cups flour
1½ teaspoons baking soda
½ teaspoon salt
½ cup margarine
1¼ cups sugar

3 egg whites
1 tablespoon grated orange rind
1 teaspoon vanilla
1 cup low-fat yogurt

Syrup

1½ cups orange juice

¾ cup sugar

1. Stir the flour, baking soda, and salt together.
2. Cream the sugar and margarine. Beat in the egg whites, orange rind, and vanilla.
3. Stir the flour mixture into the sugar mixture alternately with the yogurt until completely mixed.
4. Bake at 375° in a greased 9-inch tube pan for 40 minutes.
5. While the cake is baking, prepare the syrup. Bring the orange juice and sugar to a boil in a small saucepan and simmer uncovered for 3-5 minutes over low heat.
6. Let the cake cool for about 5 minutes and remove from pan. Prick the cake in many spots with a fork and slowly spoon the hot syrup all over it.

10 servings

Pies

BAKLAVA

An absolutely marvelous dessert, well worth the effort involved in making it. This is a low-cholestrol adaptation of a recipe given to me by my friend, Denise Telio. Orange Blossom has a pleasing exotic taste and can be purchased in Middle-Eastern or Armenian groceries. Take care to use only a few drops since the flavor is quite strong. See Filo-Pastry Hors d'Oeuvres (page 45) in the chapter on appetizers for information on using fiilo dough.

Sugar Syrup

1 cup water
2 cups sugar

1 teaspoon lemon juice
few drops of Orange Blossom

Pastry

1 pound filo dough

1-1¼ cups melted margarine

Filling

2½ cups walnuts
3 tablespoons melted margarine

3 tablespoons sugar
¼ teaspoon cinnamon

1. Bring the water and sugar to a boil. Add the lemon juice and boil uncovered for 15 minutes or until a candy thermometer reaches 230°. Let cool and refrigerate. The

syrup can be prepared days ahead and stored in the refrigerator.

2. Stir all the ingredients for the filling together and set aside.
3. With a pastry brush, spread melted margarine on the bottom and sides of a 9- by 13-inch Pyrex dish. Line the dish with a sheet of filo dough, pressing some of the dough up on the sides of the dish. Brush with melted margarine. Continue layering the filo sheets and brushing them with margarine until half of the dough has been used. To save time, some of the sheets may be folded in half and layered that way.
4. Spread the filling over the dough. Continue layering filo sheets and brushing with margarine until the remainder of the dough is used. Brush the top sheet with margarine.
5. Refrigerate at least one hour covered. Cut into 2-inch diamond-shaped pieces. Bake at 350° in the middle of the oven for 35-45 minutes or until golden brown.
6. Stir a few drops of Orange Blossom into the cold sugar syrup and pour over the hot pastry. Serve at room temperature and enjoy.

TWO-CRUST PIES

Here are two recipes for oil pie crusts which I've found equally successful. The first contains less oil and might be favored by calorie watchers. Both are very good.

Pie Crust I
2 cups flour   ½ cup corn oil
1 teaspoon salt   6 tablespoons ice water

Pie Crust II
2 cups flour   ⅔ cup corn oil
1 teaspoon salt   4 tablespoons ice water

1. Stir in the flour and salt together. Beat the oil and water together with a fork and pour over the flour. Mix very

well and then shape into a large ball. Divide the ball in half.

2. Cut two 12-inch pieces of waxed paper. Place one sheet on a slightly dampened surface such as a kitchen counter top on which you're going to roll the pastry. Dampening the surface helps to hold the waxed paper in place. Place one of the pastry balls on the paper and flatten with the palm of your hand. Cover with the other sheet of waxed paper. Roll out the dough into a circle reaching to the edges of the paper. Peel off the top sheet of paper. Pick up the bottom sheet of paper with the crust and invert over a 9-inch pie pan. Press into the pan and very gently peel off the paper.

3. Place the desired filling in the pie crust.

4. Roll the second ball of dough as described in Step 2. Peel off the top sheet of paper. Lift up the bottom sheet with the crust and invert over the filled pie. Gently peel off the waxed paper. Trim off any excess dough. Pinch the edges of the top and bottom crusts together forming a crease about every inch or so. Prick the top crust with a fork in 8 or 10 places to allow steam to escape. I like to cover the rim of the pie crust with a 2 or 3 inch sheet of aluminum foil at this point to prevent excess browning of the edge.

5. Bake in a 425° oven for 45 minutes or until the crust is golden brown.

APPLE PIE FILLING

5-6 cups sliced, peeled cooking apples—Cortland, Rome, Baldwin (about 2 pounds)

½ cup firmly packed brown sugar
1 tablespoon cornstarch
½-1 teaspoon cinnamon

1. Stir the sugar, cornstarch and cinnamon together. Pour over the apples just before filling and mix together.

ONE-CRUST PIES

1. Use half the amount of ingredients listed for 2-crust pies. Prepare, roll out, and press the dough into the pan as directed for 2-crust pies. Remove the waxed paper and trim off any excess dough.
2. Pinch the edges of the dough into waves on the rim of the pan. Prick the dough with a fork all over the pie shell.
3. Bake at 425° for 10-12 minutes or until golden brown. Cool before filling.

Besides the fillings suggested in this chapter, try Lemon-Pineapple Chiffon from the dessert section (page 310).

CORN FLAKE-CRUMB OR OATMEAL PIE CRUST

1¼ cups corn flake crumbs
    or uncooked oats
¾ teaspoon cinnamon

3-4 tablespoons sugar
6 tablespoons melted margarine

1. Stir the dry ingredients together. Mix in the melted margarine.
2. Firmly press the crumb mixture onto the bottom and sides of a 9-inch pie plate. If an 8-inch pie plate is available, place it on top of the crumbs and press down firmly.
3. Bake at 350° for 10-12 minutes. Cool completely before filling.

FLUFFY STRAWBERRY-RHUBARB PIE

A luscious way to announce that spring is here.

1 pound fresh rhubarb
⅔ cup water
⅓ cup sugar
2 envelopes unflavored gelatin
1 16-ounce package frozen sliced strawberries, partially defrosted

½ cup skimmed evaporated milk or ⅓ cup powdered milk plus enough water to make ½ cup milk chilled
9-inch pre-baked pie shell

1. If the skimmed milk is not ice cold, pour it into a bowl and place it in the freezer. For faster whipping, chill until crystals begin to form around edges.

2. Cut the rhubarb into ¾-inch slices and place in a saucepan with ⅓ cup of water and ⅓ cup sugar. Bring to a boil and simmer covered over low heat until tender, about 10-15 minutes.
3. While the rhubarb is cooking, sprinkle the gelatin over the remaining ⅓ cup water and let soften for at least 5 minutes. Stir the gelatin into the hot cooked rhubarb until thoroughly mixed. Add the berries and stir until they're completely thawed. Refrigerate until the mixture begins to set.
4. Beat the chilled milk until it is very thick and stands in peaks.
5. Fold ⅓ of the whipped milk into the rhubarb mixture. Then fold in the remaining ⅔. Pour into a pre-baked pie shell. Refrigerate until the filling is firm.

6-8 servings

FRESH STRAWBERRY PIE

This is the simplest pie that I know of and also one of the best. Be sure to try it.

1 quart fresh strawberries, washed, hulled and drained
2-4 tablespoons sugar (optional)
¾ cup currant jelly
1 9-inch pre-baked pie shell

1. Place the berries in the pie shell and sprinkle with sugar, if desired.
2. Warm the currant jelly in a pan over low heat until it is completely melted.
3. Spoon the melted jelly over all of the berries to form a glaze. Refrigerate until ready to serve.

6-8 servings

LUSCIOUS CHOCOLATE PIE

Serve only thin slices of this rich and delicious dessert.

1¼ cups margarine
1¼ cups sugar
⅔ cup cocoa

1½ teaspoons vanilla
3 egg whites
pre-baked 9-inch pie shell

1. Cream the margarine, sugar, cocoa, and vanilla together.
2. Add the egg whites one at a time and beat very well with an electric mixer after each addition.
3. Spoon into the pie shell and chill.

12 servings

GELATIN FLUFF PIE

A breeze of a pie to make and eat.

1 3-ounce package flavored gelatin
1½ cups water

⅓ cup powdered milk
⅓ cup ice water

1. Bring 1 cup water to a boil and dissolve the gelatin in it. Add ½ cup cold water. Cool and refrigerate until just beginning to jell.
2. For fast whipping, chill the ice water and powdered milk in a bowl in the freezer until crystals begin to form at edges. Whip on high speed until thick and stiff. Fold thoroughly into the gelatin. Pour into a pre-baked pie shell and refrigerate until firm.

6-8 servings

COOKIES

Since most commercial cookies are made with whole eggs and butter or hydrogenated vegetable shortening, cookie lovers will probably find themselves baking their own.

See General Baking Hints in the chapter on cakes and pies for suggestions on how to adapt recipes to meet low-cholesterol criteria.

See Shopping Guide in the Introduction for two permissible commercial cookies I've come across.

A helpful trick for making roll cookies is to dip the cookie cutters frequently into flour to prevent dough from sticking inside them.

Extra-large eggs have been used in the following recipes and the cookies have been baked in the top half of the oven.

ALMOND KISSES

These easy and attractive meringue cookies are especially good served with fruit compotes or fruit macédoines.

3 egg whites at room temperature
⅔ cup sugar

½ teaspoon vanilla
1 cup chopped almonds

1. Beat the egg whites until frothy with an electric mixer on high speed. Gradually add the sugar and continue beating until the mixture stands in peaks—about 10 minutes with

a hand beater. Beat in the vanilla. Stir in the chopped nuts.
2. Drop by heaping teaspoonfuls onto baking sheets lined with brown paper. Bake at 300° for 35-40 minutes or until the kisses are light brown and crisp throughout. Remove carefully with a thin, wide spatula.

48 cookies

ALMOND MACAROONS

Commercial macaroons usually contain highly saturated coconut and don't taste nearly as good as these.

8 ounces almond paste   ½ cup sugar
2 egg whites

1. Cut the almond paste into small pieces and soften with a spoon.
2. Mix in the egg whites and beat at medium speed with an electric mixer until the mixture is smooth. Since this is a thick mixture, it will be necessary to scrape the beaters several times so that no lumps remain. Beat the sugar in gradually.
3. Drop by tablespoonfuls on a greased cookie sheet. Bake at 325° for 25-30 minutes or until lightly browned.

18 macaroons

BANANA COOKIES

My favorite kind of cookie recipe—quick, easy, high-yield, and very good. Try substituting a few tablespoons of wheat germ for an equivalent amount of flour if you want to boost its nutritional value.

¾ cup margarine
⅔ cup sugar
3 egg whites
1 teaspoon vanilla
1 cup mashed ripe bananas (2 medium or 3 small)

2¼ cups flour
2½ teaspoons baking powder
½ teaspoon salt
½ teaspoon cinnamon
¾ cup chopped walnuts

1. Cream the margarine and the sugar in a large bowl. Beat in the egg whites, mashed bananas and vanilla.
2. Stir together the flour, baking powder, salt and cinnamon. Stir the flour mixture into the banana mixture until well blended. Stir in the chopped walnuts.
3. Drop by teaspoonfuls about 1 to 1½ inches apart on greased cookie sheets. Bake at 350° in the upper half of the oven for 15 minutes or until golden brown.

6-7 dozen cookies

COTTAGE CHEESE RUGELACH

Just as good as cream cheese rugelach but much healthier.

Dough

1 cup (8 ounces) dry cottage cheese
1 cup margarine

6 tablespoons sugar
1 teaspoon vanilla
2¾ cups flour

Filling

¾ cup firmly packed brown sugar

1 teaspoon cinnamon
½ cup chopped walnuts
½ cup raisins

1. Cream the cottage cheese, margarine, sugar, and vanilla until well blended. Blend the flour into the cheese mixture. Chill several hours.

2. Divide the dough into 4 parts. Roll each part into a thin circle (8- or 9-inch diameter) on a lightly floured surface. Chill the remaining dough until it is to be used.
3. Stir the cinnamon and brown sugar together. Sprinkle the circle of dough with ¼ of the brown sugar, 2 tablespoons chopped walnuts and 2 tablespoons raisins. Cut the circle into 8 wedges. Roll up each wedge starting with the wide end. Curve into a crescent and place on a greased cookie sheet with the tip underneath. Repeat with the remaining portions of dough. Bake at 350° for 25 minutes or until light brown.

32 rugelach

GINGERBREAD PEOPLE

My 8-year-old daughter prepares these cookies from start to finish with aplomb.

½ cup margarine	½ teaspoon salt
¾ cup sugar	¾ teaspoon cinnamon
2 egg whites	½ teaspoon cloves
2½ cups flour	¼ teaspoon ginger
¾ teaspoon baking soda	

1. Cream the sugar and margarine. Beat in the egg whites until thoroughly blended.
2. Stir the flour, salt, baking soda and spices together. Stir the flour mixture into the margarine mixture. Knead for a minute or so into a smooth dough. Refrigerate for ½ hour.
3. Roll out portions of the dough on a lightly floured surface to about a 3/16-inch thickness. Keep the remaining dough refrigerated. Cut out shapes and remove to lightly greased cookie sheets. Decorate with sprinkles, raisins, etc.
4. Bake at 375° for 10 minutes.

About 12 6-inch gingerbread people

HAMANTASCHEN

Since these freeze well, I usually start baking several weeks before Purim and have many yummy hamantaschen to celebrate with.

4¼ cups flour
1 tablespoon baking powder
½ teaspoon salt
6 egg whites or 1 cup Egg Beaters
¾ cup oil

¾ cup sugar
1 teaspoon vanilla
1 egg yolk (if glaze is desired)
2 tablespoons water

1. Mix the flour, baking powder and salt together.
2. Beat the egg whites, oil, sugar and vanilla together.
3. Stir the flour mixture into the egg mixture. Mix well and knead a few times into a smooth dough.
4. Roll out portions of the dough on a lightly floured surface and cut into 3½-inch circles with an empty tuna fish can.
5. Place a teaspoon of filling in the center of each circle of dough. Bring up the edges of dough to cover the filling and pinch them together to form a triangle.
6. If a glaze is desired, beat the egg yolk with 2 tablespoons water and brush the mixture on the tops of the hamantaschen.
7. Bake on greased cookie sheets at 350° for 18-20 minutes in the center of the oven.

A 12-ounce (1¼ cups) can or jar of commercial lekva is just enough for this recipe. Any extra dough can be rolled out to make Jewish star cookies. Sprinkle with sugar and bake about 10 minutes at 350°.

40 hamantaschen

HAMANTASCHEN FILLINGS

These flavorful fillings are far superior to the commercial varieties. Be sure to try them if you have the time.

Apricot

11 ounces dried apricots
2 cups water

3 tablespoons sugar or to taste

1. Bring the apricots and water to a boil and simmer covered for 20-25 minutes or until soft.
2. Drain the cooked apricots, being sure to save the liquid. If you can resist drinking the liquid immediately, it can be used in gelatin desserts.
3. Purée the cooked apricots in a blender or just mash well with a fork. Mix in the sugar.

2 cups filling

Prune

12 ounces pitted prunes
2 cups water

1-2 teaspoons grated lemon rind (optional)

1. Bring the prunes and water to boil and simmer covered for 20 minutes.
2. Drain, saving the juice for other uses.
3. Purée the cooked prunes in a blender or mash well with a fork. Mix in the lemon rind.

2 cups filling

HOLIDAY SUGAR COOKIES

My mother-in-law gave this recipe to me when I was newly married and I've been using it ever since.

2 cups flour
1½ teaspoons baking powder
½ teaspoon salt
⅓ cup oil
⅔ cup sugar

1 teaspoon vanilla
2 egg whites plus enough water to make ⅓ cup liquid

1. Stir the flour, baking powder, and salt together.
2. Beat the remaining ingredients together.
3. Stir the flour mixture into the egg mixture and mix well. Knead a few times into a dough.
4. Roll out on a lightly floured surface. Dust the rolling pin with flour if the dough sticks to it. Cut into desired shapes with holiday-cookie cutters.
5. Lift up with a pancake turner and transfer to greased cookie sheets. Bake at 400° for 9-10 minutes or until lightly browned.

36 2-inch Star of David cookies

MANDEL BROT

This is one of my favorite recipes. It's easy and yields a lot of very good cookies. I usually prepare several batches for any large party. Mandel brot can be stored in a covered container for almost any length of time.

3 cups flour
2 teaspoons baking powder
¼ teaspoon salt
1 cup oil
1 cup sugar

½ teaspoon vanilla
½ teaspoon almond extract
6 egg whites or 1 cup Egg Beaters
1 cup chopped almonds

Topping (Optional)
2 tablespoons sugar mixed with ½ teaspoon cinnamon

1. Stir the flour, baking powder, and salt together.
2. Beat the oil, sugar, vanilla, and almond extract together. Gradually beat in the egg whites or egg substitute.
3. Stir the flour mixture into the egg mixture until thoroughly blended. Stir in the almonds.
4. Form 4 long rolls by dropping the batter from a large spoon onto 2 greased cookie sheets. If desired, sprinkle with topping. Place the rolls far apart since they spread to about double their original size in baking.
5. Bake at 350° for 20 minutes in the upper half of the oven. Cut into ¾-inch slices and turn onto the cut side. Return to the oven and bake 10-15 minutes more depending on how dry you like your mandel brot.

60 ¾-inch slices

MOHN COOKIES

These disappear very rapidly in our house on Purim. An excellent addition to Shalach Manot trays.

¼ cup poppy seeds
3¼ cups flour
2½ teaspoons baking powder
½ teaspoon salt
3 egg whites

¾ cup sugar
½ cup plus 2 tablespoons oil
3 tablespoons orange or pineapple juice
1 teaspoon vanilla

1. Stir the poppy seeds, flour, baking powder and salt together.
2. Beat the egg whites, sugar, oil, juice, and vanilla together.
3. Stir the flour mixture into the egg white mixture. Knead a few times into a smooth dough. Chill ½ hour.
4. Roll out small batches on a floured surface until very thin. Cut into 1-inch diamonds or into holiday shapes.
5. Lift up with a pancake turner or thin spatula and place on greased cookie sheets. Bake at 375° for 7-8 minutes.

About 120 1½-inch cookies.

MOLASSES-GINGER COOKIES

A not-too-sweet cookie.

2 cups flour	½ cup margarine
1½ teaspoons baking soda	6 tablespoons sugar
1 teaspoon cinnamon	2 tablespoons molasses
½ teaspoon ginger	2 egg whites

1. Mix together the flour, baking soda, cinnamon and ginger.
2. Cream the margarine and sugar. Mix in the molasses and egg whites.
3. Stir the flour mixture into the margarine mixture.
4. Shape the dough into 1-inch balls. Place them on greased cookie sheets and flatten with the bottom of a glass dipped in sugar after each pressing.
5. Bake at 350° for 10 minutes.

3½ to 4 dozen 2-inch cookies

OATMEAL COOKIES I

This is a pareve adaption of the recipe on the oats box.

1 cup flour
1 teaspoon salt
½ teaspoon baking soda
⅔ cup oil
1 cup firmly packed brown sugar

2 egg whites
2 tablespoons water
1 teaspoon vanilla
3 cups uncooked oats

1. Stir the flour, salt and baking soda together in a medium bowl.
2. Beat the oil, sugar, egg whites, water and vanilla together with a wisk in a large bowl.
3. Add the flour mixture to the egg mixture. Stir until all the flour is mixed in. Add the oats and stir well.
4. Drop by teaspoonfuls onto greased cookie sheets and bake at 350° for 10-12 minutes.

60 cookies

OATMEAL COOKIES II

Making these cookies is a marvelous activity for children who have nothing to do or for adults who happen to like thin, crisp oatmeal cookies.

1 cup margarine
1 cup brown sugar
2 teaspoons vanilla
1¼ cups flour

1 teaspoon baking soda
2 cups oats

1. In a large bowl cream the margarine, brown sugar, and vanilla together.
2. Stir the flour and baking soda together and then stir into the margarine mixture. Stir in the oats until well blended. For children, the final blending can be done by squishing together by hand.
3. Form 1-inch balls and place at least 2 inches apart on ungreased cookie sheets (these cookies spread widely in baking). Flatten the balls with the bottom of a drinking glass dipped in sugar after each pressing.
4. Bake at 400° for 10 minutes.

48 cookies

OATMEAL-WHEAT GERM COOKIES

The person who gave me this recipe says that it's the one cookie she doesn't feel guilty about letting her children eat. The recipe can be doubled without problems.

¾ cup whole wheat flour
½ teaspoon salt
½ teaspoon baking soda
1 teaspoon cinnamon
1 cup oats

½ cup wheat germ
½ cup oil
⅔ cup brown sugar
2 egg whites
1 teaspoon vanilla

1. Stir together all the dry ingredients except the sugar.
2. Beat the oil, sugar, egg whites and vanilla together with a wisk.
3. Stir the dry ingredients into the egg mixture.
4. Drop by teaspoonfuls onto a greased cookie sheet and bake at 375° for 7-8 minutes. Remove immediately from the cookie sheet with a spatula.

24 cookies

ORANGE OR LEMON COOKIES

Easy pareve drop cookies. Very good anytime but I like them especially with fruit ices for a simple summer dessert.

2 cups flour
2 teaspoons baking powder
½ teaspoon salt
3 egg whites
⅔ cup oil

1 teaspoon vanilla
2 teaspoons grated orange or lemon rind
⅔ cup sugar

1. Stir the flour, baking powder and salt together.
2. Beat the remaining ingredients together with a wisk until blended. Stir in the dry ingredients.
3. Drop by teaspoonfuls about 2 inches apart onto ungreased cookie sheets. Flatten with the bottom of a glass dipped into sugar after each pressing.
4. Bake at 400° for 10 minutes or until the cookies are crisp around the edges.

60 1½-inch cookies

NO-BAKE PEANUT BUTTER COOKIES I

Healthy, easy, fun for children to make. Lightly oil the measuring cup before adding peanut butter and honey to aid in their removal from the cup.

½ cup peanut butter (preferably unhydrogenated)
½ cup honey

¾ cup powdered milk
¾ cup uncooked oats

1. Mix the peanut butter and honey together.
2. Stir in the powdered milk.
3. Stir in the oats. Batter will be very stiff. Mix well.
4. Shape into small (about 1-inch) balls.

30 cookies

NO-BAKE PEANUT BUTTER COOKIES II

A good summer cookie. Can be made in just a few minutes without heating up the kitchen. Also a good activity for restless children.

¼ cup margarine
¼ cup peanut butter (preferably unhydrogenated)
1 tablespoon skimmed milk

½ cup sugar
¾ teaspoon vanilla
1½ cups uncooked oats

1. Bring the first 4 ingredients to a boil in a small saucepan, stirring.
2. Remove from the heat. Stir in vanilla and oats.
3. Drop by teaspoonfuls onto waxed paper. Cool.

3 dozen 1-inch cookies

PUMPKIN COOKIES

Our eighty-year-old neighbors introduced us to these pleasing, elusively flavored cookies.

2 cups flour
4 teaspoons baking powder
¼ teaspoon nutmeg
¾ teaspoon cinnamon
¼ teaspoon ginger
½ teaspoon salt
½ cup margarine

¾ cup brown sugar, firmly packed
3 egg whites
1 cup cooked pumpkin
½ cup raisins
1 cup chopped nuts

1. Stir the flour, baking powder, nutmeg, cinnamon, ginger and salt together.
2. Cream the margarine and sugar. Add the egg whites and pumpkin and beat until thoroughly mixed.
3. Stir in the raisins and nuts. Drop by teaspoonfuls onto greased cookie sheets. Bake 10 minutes at 350°.

7 or 8 dozen 1½-inch cookies

REFRIGERATOR SPICE COOKIES

1½ cups flour
1 teaspoon baking soda
¼ teaspoon salt
1½ teaspoons cinnamon
¼ teaspoon ginger
¼ teaspoon nutmeg
¼ teaspoon cloves

½ cup margarine
½ cup brown sugar, firmly packed
1 egg white
1 teaspoon orange juice
1-2 tablespoons grated orange rind

1. Mix the flour, baking soda, salt, and spices together.
2. Cream the margarine and brown sugar. Thoroughly mix in the egg white, orange juice and orange rind.
3. Stir the flour mixture into the margarine mixture.
4. Shape the dough into 2 rolls of 1-inch diameter. Wrap in waxed paper and chill several hours or overnight.
5. Cut into ¼-inch slices and bake at 350° on greased cookie sheets for 10-12 minutes.

About 4 dozen cookies

TAGLACH I

Taglach are small bits of cooked or baked dough coated with a sticky, ginger-flavored honey mixture, altogether delicious and very habit-forming. A delightful way to start off the new year. In this recipe, the pieces of dough are cooked in the honey. The honey will be easier to remove from the measuring cup if the cup is lightly oiled first. The saucepan will be easier to wash if it's lightly oiled before using.

Syrup

1 cup honey
½ cup brown sugar

½ teaspoon ginger
½ cup strong tea

Dough

6 egg whites or 1 cup Egg Beaters
1 tablespoon oil

2¾ cups flour
¼ teaspoon ginger
¼ teaspoon salt
1¼ teaspoons baking powder

1. Combine the honey, sugar, and ginger in a large saucepan. Bring to a boil and simmer covered over very low heat for 7-10 minutes.
2. Mix the flour, ginger, salt and baking powder. Lightly beat the egg whites and oil and stir into the flour mixture. Knead into a soft dough. If the dough is too sticky to handle, add a little flour. If the dough is dry or flaky, knead in a little oil. Roll the dough between your palms into strips ½ inch in diameter. Cut the strips into ½-inch pieces.
3. Drop the little pieces of dough into the boiling honey. Bring to the boiling point again if necessary. Cover and simmer over low heat without uncovering for 30 minutes. Uncover and with a wooden spoon bring the pieces of

dough on the bottom of the pan to the surface. Break up any clumps. Cover and cook another 10 minutes.

4. Take the pan off the heat and stir in the tea. Cool and spoon into aluminum-foil muffin cups or small tart pans for individual servings.

TAGLACH II

In this method, the pieces of dough are first baked in the oven and then coated with the honey. Since no liquid is added to the honey mixture, this method yields a stickier product. See introduction to Taglach I.

Dough

2 cups flour
¾ teaspoon baking powder
¼ teaspoon salt
⅛ teaspoon ginger

2 tablespoons oil
4 egg whites or ⅔ cup Egg Beaters

Syrup

1 cup honey
½ cup brown sugar

½ teaspoon ginger

1. Stir the flour, baking powder, salt and ginger together. Beat the oil and egg whites together and stir into the flour mixture. Knead gently to form a dough. Add a little more flour if necessary to give a soft, not sticky dough. Roll the dough between your palms into strips ½ inch in diameter. Cut the strips into ½-inch lengths.
2. Place the bits of dough on a greased baking pan and bake at 350° for 20 minutes or until the pieces of dough are light brown. Turn the pieces of dough over during the baking or shake the pan a few times.
3. Meanwhile, combine the honey, sugar and ginger in a large saucepan. Bring to a boil and simmer covered over very low heat 7-10 minutes.

4. Drop the pieces of baked dough into the honey mixture. Cook about 5 minutes longer. Stir to coat all the pieces with honey.
5. Spoon into aluminum-foil muffin cups or pour into a lightly oiled pie plate, let cool until comfortable to handle, and shape into balls with moistened hands.

TWO-WAY COOKIE DOUGH

This dough produces the sweet, melt-in-your-mouth kind of cookies.

2 cups flour
1 teaspoon baking powder
½ teaspoon salt
¾ cup margarine

¾ cup sugar
2 egg whites
1 teaspoon vanilla

1. Stir the flour, baking powder, and salt together.
2. Cream the margarine and sugar. Beat in the egg whites and vanilla. Stir in the flour mixture to form a dough. Use this dough for either of the cookies below.

Drop Cookies

If desired, stir in chopped nuts, raisins, chopped dates, grated orange or lemon rind. Drop by teaspoonfuls onto lightly greased baking sheets. Bake at 375° for about 10 minutes or until the cookies are light brown.

About 5 dozen cookies

Thumbprint Cookies

Shape dough into small round balls. If the dough is sticky, stir in a little flour until it is just firm enough to work with. Place the balls on lightly greased baking sheets. Press a finger into the center of each ball. Bake at 375° for about 10 minutes or until light brown. When cookies are cool, fill the centers with jam, jelly, or apple butter.

About 4 dozen cookies

WALNUT-BRANDY COOKIES

The only trouble with these cookies is that they're so hard to resist.

½ cup margarine
⅓ cup sugar
¼ teaspoon salt
¾ teaspoon vanilla

1 tablespoon brandy
1 cup flour
½ cup chopped walnuts

1. Cream the margarine, sugar, and salt. Blend in the vanilla and brandy.
2. Mix in the flour. Stir in the nuts. Roll into 1-inch balls.
3. Bake on ungreased cookie sheets at 350° for 15-20 minutes or until light brown.

24 cookies

WALNUT OR PECAN MACAROONS

These unusual-tasting macaroons are very nice to have when guests drop in during Passover.

1 cup ground walnuts or
  pecans
¾ cup sugar

¼ teaspoon cinnamon
1 egg white

1. Stir the ground nuts, sugar and cinnamon together. Mix in the unbeaten egg white.
2. Shape the mixture into ¾-inch balls. If the mixture is crumbly rather than sticky and you have difficulty shaping the balls, stir in 1 or 2 teaspoons additional egg white.

Place the balls 1 to 1½ inches apart on a greased baking sheet.

3. Bake at 300° for 20 minutes. The top of the cookie should be firm but the remainder somewhat soft. Remove very carefully with a thin, wide spatula or pancake turner and place on a flat plate to cool.

24 macaroons

APRICOT SQUARES

A delicious cookie likely to please any palate.

Filling
1 cup dried apricots
1 cup water

3 tablespoons sugar
1 teaspoon lemon juice

Pastry
1 cup flour
½ teaspoon baking soda
pinch salt
⅔ cup brown sugar

1 cup uncooked oats
½ cup margarine, melted
½ teaspoon vanilla

1. Bring the apricots and water to a boil. Simmer covered 20-30 minutes or until the apricots are soft. Add more water if necessary. Remove the cover; continue cooking until the water evaporates and the apricots form a paste. Remove from heat and stir in the sugar and lemon juice.
2. Stir the flour, baking soda, salt, brown sugar and oats together. Mix in the margarine and vanilla until crumbly.
3. Press ⅔ of the mixture into a greased 8-inch square baking pan. Spread with the apricot paste. Sprinkle with remaining ⅓ of the crumbly mixture and press lightly.
4. Bake at 375° for 25 minutes.

16 2-inch squares

BANANA BROWNIES

These are a good choice for a bake sale or large party since they're a bit unusual and the recipe can be successfully doubled.

1¾ cups flour
2 teaspoons baking powder
½ teaspoon salt
½ cup margarine
⅔ cup sugar

3 egg whites
1 teaspoon vanilla
3 small or 2 medium ripe
    bananas, mashed
¾ cup chopped walnuts

Topping
2 tablespoons sugar

½ teaspoon cinnamon

1. Stir together the flour, baking powder and salt.
2. Cream the margarine and sugar. Beat in the egg whites, vanilla and mashed bananas.
3. Stir the flour mixture into the banana mixture until well blended. Stir in the chopped walnuts.
4. Spread into a greased 9- by 13-inch baking dish. Sprinkle with the sugar-cinnamon topping. Bake at 350° for 30-35 minutes.

24-28 bars

BRAN-APPLE BARS

If you're in a rush or don't like apples, omit them and bake a few minutes less. Excellent either way.

1 cup flour
1 teaspoon baking powder
½ teaspoon baking soda
1 teaspoon cinnamon
½ teaspoon nutmeg
¼ teaspoon salt
½ cup margarine

¾ cup sugar
3 egg whites
1 teaspoon vanilla
1 cup whole-bran cereal
1½ cups finely chopped apples (2 medium apples)

1. Stir the flour, baking powder, baking soda, cinnamon, nutmeg, and salt together.
2. Cream the margarine and sugar. Beat in the egg whites and vanilla. Stir in the flour mixture.
3. Stir in the bran and apples. Bake in a greased 9- by 13-inch pan at 350° for 25 minutes. Cut into bars.

24-28 bars

COCOA BROWNIES

A rich, chewy brownie which tastes just like those made with solid chocolate.

1 cup flour
¾ teaspoon baking powder
6 tablespoons cocoa
½ teaspoon salt
½ cup margarine

¾ cup sugar
2 egg whites
1 teaspoon vanilla
¾ cup chopped walnuts (optional)

1. Stir the flour, baking powder, cocoa and salt together.
2. Cream the margarine and sugar. Beat in the egg whites and vanilla.
3. Stir the flour mixture into the margarine mixture. Stir in the nuts, if desired.
4. Spread into a greased 8-inch square pan and bake for 18 minutes at 350°. Cut into squares when cool.

16 2-inch brownies

DATE SQUARES

1 cup flour
1¼ teaspoons baking powder
½ teaspoon salt
3 egg whites
¾ cup brown sugar

¾ cup oil
2 cups (8 ounces) chopped dates
¾ cup chopped walnuts

1. Stir the flour, baking powder, and salt together.
2. Beat the egg whites, sugar and oil together. Stir in the flour mixture and mix well.
3. Stir in the dates and walnuts.
4. Bake in a greased 9- by 13-inch Pyrex dish for 30 minutes at 325°. When cool, cut in squares.

24-28 squares

FRUIT DESSERTS, GELATINS, ICES, AND CRÊPES

This chapter includes fruit desserts, gelatin desserts, puddings, ices, and sherbets, all of which are light and simple and provide a refreshing end to any meal. They can be accompanied by plates of cookies for those who aren't watching their waistlines. Don't be at all hesitant about serving these light desserts to company. Most guests will welcome the change from the calorie-rich desserts so often served.

For those times when you want a really smashing dessert, I've included recipes for crêpes and meringues.

Almost any combination of diced fresh fruit flavored with a small amount of liqueur or brandy makes an excellent, easy dessert. In case you don't know (I didn't until I started to write this chapter), a macédoine is a mixture of diced fresh fruits while a compote is a mixture of fresh or dried fruit which has been poached in hot syrup.

Evaporated skimmed milk can be substituted for cream in many gelatin recipes calling for whipped cream. Chilled evaporated skimmed milk whips up very easily to a consistency resembling whipped cream. To prepare the equivalent of evaporated skimmed milk from dry powdered skimmed milk, use twice the amount of skimmed milk powder as directed on the box.

To unmold gelatin desserts, run a sharp knife around the top of the mold to loosen the gel. Dip the mold up to its rim in warm (not hot) water for 10 seconds. Place a moistened serving plate on top of the mold. Invert the mold and plate together and shake gently to release the gelatin. Center the gelatin if necessary. Lightly oiling the mold before pouring in the gelatin makes unmolding easier. Plastic Tupperware molds do not require dipping in warm water and are very convenient to use.

If a gelatin recipe calls for "chilling until slightly thickened" and the gelatin becomes firm, place the container in a large bowl of warm water until the gelatin reaches the right consistency.

Some commercial frozen products are acceptable for use on a low-cholestrol diet. Baskin Robbins's flavored ices and Dorothy Muriel sherbets contain no milk. Usually sherbets do contain milk, however, so be sure to check the labels. Some diet frozen desserts (i.e., Thin's Inn) are made with skimmed milk and would be acceptable. If your children want ice cream, convince them to have ice milk instead. Homemade ices or sherbets are harder than the commercial kind and should be taken out of the freezer to soften 5 to 10 minutes before serving.

Hints for Buying Fruit

Berries: Check for mold and leaky berries which stain the container. These are extremely perishable. Refrigerate and use as soon as possible.

Citrus fruits: Look for firm, thin-skinned fruits which are heavy for their size. Refrigerate at once.

Canteloupe and honeydew melons: Press the end of the melon opposite the stem end. Softening is an indication of ripeness. Be especially wary of very hard honeydew melons. I've had too many which never ripened.

Peaches: Look for firm but not hard peaches. Very hard peaches with a greenish color may never ripen. Ripen at room temperature out of the sunlight.

Pears are picked before they reach maturity. Choose firm pears and let them ripen at room temperature out of the sunlight.

Pineapple: Look for one heavy for its size. It's ripe when it has a brownish color and when a top leaf can be pulled out easily. It should be refrigerated at this point and used within a few days. If it feels soft it's probably overripe.

Plums: Choose firm plums which yield slightly to pressure. Keep at room temperature until soft enough for eating and then refrigerate.

BAKED APPLES

I think that the aroma of baking apples is almost reason enough to make them. They're also an extremely easy way to add a special touch to the end of any meal. Don't use McIntosh apples since they become mushy very quickly when baked.

large baking apples (Cortland or Rome Beauty)
1 tablespoon brown sugar per apple

¼ teaspoon cinnamon per apple
raisins (optional)
chopped walnuts (optional)

1. Core the apples with an apple corer, being careful not to cut all the way through to the bottom of the apple. Prick the skins with a fork in several places.
2. Mix the brown sugar and cinnamon together. Stir in the raisins and walnuts if desired. Stuff the hollow cores with the mixture.
3. Place the apples in a baking dish and pour water in to a level of ½ inch.
4. Bake at 375° for 40-60 minutes or until tender. Check the apples frequently after 40 minutes.

APPLE CRISP WITH OATMEAL TOPPING

This is my family's favorite winter Shabbat dessert. The only time-consuming part about it is peeling the apples, and even that goes quickly if you can convince someone to help you. If I expect to be really pressed for time, I peel and slice the apples a day ahead and refrigerate them in a tightly covered container. The apple slices do turn a bit brown but the apple crisp tastes just as good.

3 pounds cooking apples (Cortland, Rome Beauty, etc.)	½ cup flour
	¾ cup oats
	½ cup brown sugar
¼ cup water	1½ teaspoons cinnamon
	5 tablespoons corn oil

1. Peel and slice the apples and put them into a greased 9×13-inch baking dish. Add the water.
2. Stir together the flour, oats, sugar, and cinnamon. Mix in the oil with a fork or pastry blender until the mixture is crumbly. Sprinkle the topping over the apples.
3. Bake uncovered at 350° for about 40 minutes or until the apples are tender. Serve warm.

8-10 servings

If you don't like oatmeal topping, try this one instead:

¾ cup flour	1½ teaspoons cinnamon
½ cup brown sugar	4 tablespoons oil

Stir the flour, sugar and cinnamon together and blend in the oil with a fork or pastry blender. Sprinkle over the apples and bake as above.

SHERRY-CHERRY COMPOTE

An exceedingly easy way to add interest to the end of a summer meal.

¾ pound fresh Bing cherries	2 tablespoons brown sugar
½ cup orange juice	½ cup sherry

1. Combine all ingredients in a saucepan. Bring to a boil and simmer covered for 10-15 minutes until the cherries are soft. Chill.

3-4 servings

SPEEDY PEACH CRISP

A dessert you can put together in just a few minutes with ingredients from the shelf.

1 No. 2½ can sliced peaches, well drained	1 teaspoon cinnamon
½ cup flour	¼ teaspoon nutmeg
½ cup brown sugar	¼ cup corn oil

1. Arrange the peaches in a greased 9-inch pie plate or a greased 8-inch square pan.
2. Stir together the flour, sugar and spices. Blend in the oil with a fork or pastry blender. Sprinkle the topping over the peaches.
3. Bake at 350° for 20-25 minutes or until the topping is browned. Serve warm.

6 servings

FRESH PEACHES AND GRAPES IN WHITE WINE

Festive but not fattening. Perfect for a warm summer day.

2 medium-sized ripe peaches (preferably Freestone)
½ cup halved seedless green grapes

1 tablespoon sugar
⅓ cup white wine

1. Drop the peaches into boiling water for about 30 seconds. Remove with a slotted spoon.
2. Rub off the peach skins and cut the peaches into thin slices. Place in an attractive bowl with the grapes. Sprinkle the sugar on the fruit and let stand for 20-30 minutes.
3. Add the wine to the fruit and marinate several hours or overnight in the refrigerator. Stir once or twice.

2-3 servings

APRICOT-FLAVORED PEARS

6 medium pears, peeled and cut into thick slices
¼ cup apricot preserves

¼ cup dry white wine or white vermouth
½ cup granola

1. Arrange the pear slices in an 8-inch or 9-inch greased pie plate.
2. Beat together the apricot preserves and white wine or vermouth with a fork or small wisk. Pour over the pears.
3. Sprinkle the granola over the pears and bake at 350° for

about 30 minutes or until the pears are tender but not mushy. Delicious served warm.

6 servings

PEAR CRISP

You may also want to try this with the oatmeal topping described under Apple Crisp.

6 medium pears, peeled and cut in thick slices
2 tablespoons water
1 tablespoon lemon juice
½ cup flour
½ cup brown sugar
1 teaspoon cinnamon
¼ cup oil
½ cup chopped walnuts (optional)

1. Arrange the pears in a greased 9-inch Pyrex pie plate. Add the water and lemon juice.
2. Stir together the flour, sugar, and cinnamon. Blend in the oil until crumbly. Add the walnuts if desired. Sprinkle over the pears.
3. Bake at 350° for 30 minutes or until the pears are tender but not mushy. Serve warm.

6 servings

about 30 minutes or until the pears are tender but not
mushy. Delicious served warm.

6 servings

POACHED PEARS WITH
OR WITHOUT MELBA SAUCE

A superb dessert that is as delightful to look at as it is to eat.

6 pears, preferably Anjou
3 cups water
¾ cup sugar

½ teaspoon vanilla (optional)

Melba Sauce

10-ounce package frozen
raspberries
2 teaspoons sugar (optional)

2 tablespoons kirsch (optional)

1. Peel the pears without removing the stems.
2. Bring the water, sugar and vanilla (if desired) to a boil
   and simmer covered for 5 minutes. Add the pears. Bring
   to a boil, lower the heat and simmer covered for about
   25-30 minutes or until the pears can be easily pierced with
   the tip of a sharp knife. Let cool in the syrup. Remove the
   pears from the syrup with a slotted spoon.
3. If the melba sauce is not desired, boil down the syrup to
   about one-half its volume. Cool, chill, and serve with the
   pears.
4. To prepare the melba sauce, drain the berries. Save the
   syrup. Press the berries through a fine strainer with a
   wooden spoon. Discard the seeds.
5. Flavor the raspberry purée with sugar or kirsch if desired.
   For a slightly thinner sauce stir in a few tablespoons of
   the reserved syrup. Yield is about ½ cup sauce.

6 servings

PINEAPPLE AND RASPBERRIES

An especially attractive and delicious dessert. Serve it from a clear glass bowl for your guests to admire.

1 medium or large fresh pineapple

2 10-ounce packages frozen raspberries, thawed

1. Cut off and discard the leafy part of the pineapple. Using a large knife, cut the pineapple lengthwise into 4 wedges. Trim the core from each wedge. Separate the pineapple meat from the shell with a grapefruit knife. Cut the pineapple meat into bite-sized chunks. This can be done by cutting it right in its shell.
2. Combine the pineapple and the thawed berries in a large bowl and chill.

8-10 servings

BRANDIED PLUMS

Since this keeps well in the refrigerator, I usually make it in large batches to enjoy for a few weeks. A jar of these plums in their beautiful pink syrup is a fine gift to take when visiting friends and I even freeze some for this purpose. (Santa Rosa plums are good—allow about 6-7 plums per pound.)

1 cup water
½ cup sugar

1 pound red plums
2-3 tablespoons brandy

1. Bring the water and sugar to a boil and simmer covered for 5 minutes.

2. Cut the plums in half and remove the pits. Add half of the plums to the hot syrup. Simmer until the plums are tender, about 5-10 minutes. Remove with a slotted spoon. Repeat with the rest of the plums.
3. Cool the syrup and stir in the brandy. Pour over the plums and chill.

4-6 servings

RHUBARB AND APPLESAUCE

This is one of the simplest and best rhubarb recipes I've seen. I enjoy the tartness of the rhubarb and add no sugar at all.

4 cups of diced rhubarb
⅓ cup water

2 cups applesauce
sugar to taste

1. Put the rhubarb and water in a saucepan, bring to a boil, and simmer covered over low heat until the rhubarb is tender, about 10-15 minutes.
2. Mix the rhubarb with the applesauce. Sweeten with sugar, if desired.

6 ¾-cup servings

MIXED DRIED FRUIT COMPOTE

An incredibly easy, elegant dessert with ingredients which can be stocked for use at a moment's notice. Equally good hot or cold.

1 11-ounce box dried mixed fruit
1 6-ounce can frozen juice concentrate (orange, pine-apple, or orange-pine-apple)
2 cans water

1. Mix the fruit, juice concentrate and water together in a pan. Bring to a boil and simmer covered for 20 minutes or until the fruit is soft. Serve warm or cold.

6 servings

CHERRY AND RAISIN COMPOTE

I first tried this because my husband's grandmother used to make it every Passover. Health-food stores usually have the dried cherries.

½ pound (1½ cups) dried cherries
½ cup raisins
2 cups water
1½ teaspoons potato starch or cornstarch mixed with 2 tablespoons water

1. Combine the cherries, raisins and water in a pot. Bring to a boil and simmer covered for 20-30 minutes or until the cherries are soft.
2. Stir the cornstarch or potato-starch mixture into the hot

cherries and simmer a few minutes until the liquid is
thickened and clear.

4 servings

SHERRIED APPLESAUCE JELLO

1 3-ounce package red Jello   1½ cups applesauce
1 cup boiling water   2 tablespoons sherry

1. Dissolve the gelatin in the boiling water. Stir in the applesauce and the sherry. Pour into 4 dessert dishes. Refrigerate until firm.

4 servings

ORANGE-RHUBARB GELATIN

In the springtime one can never have too many rhubarb recipes. Here's one of my favorites.

1 pound fresh rhubarb, cut   2 tablespoons grated orange
  in 1-inch pieces   rind
¼ cup water   1 orange, peeled and cut
1 cup orange juice   into sections
1 3-ounce package red gela-
  tin

1. Put the rhubarb and water into a saucepan, bring to a
   boil, lower the heat and cook covered until the rhubarb is
   tender, about 10-15 minutes.
2. Bring the orange juice to the boiling point and dissolve the
   gelatin in it. Stir together the rhubarb and the orange juice
   mixture. Stir in the grated orange rind.

3. Cool and refrigerate until slightly thickened. Stir in the orange sections and refrigerate until firm.

4 servings

APPLE CIDER JELLY

A very simple jelly with an intriguing flavor. Low-calorie too.

1 tablespoon unflavored gelatin
2 cups apple cider

½ teaspoon dried mint (optional)

1. Sprinkle the gelatin over ½ cup of the cider in a small saucepan and let stand 5 minutes.
2. Bring the cider to a boil, stirring to dissolve the gelatin. Stir in the remaining cider.
3. Powder the mint as finely as possible by rubbing it between 2 fingers. Stir the crushed mint into the gelatin mixture.
4. Pour into 4 dessert dishes and refrigerate until firm.

4 servings

ORANGE TAPIOCA PUDDING

Tapioca desserts are quick, healthy, and good. I like being able to control their sugar content which can't be done with prepared puddings. The basic pudding can be be varied by adding diced fruit or a few tablespoons of liqueur.

¼ cup quick-cooking tapioca
2½ cups orange juice
2 tablespoons sugar or to taste

1 teaspoon grated orange rind

1. Stir the tapioca, orange juice, and sugar together in a small saucepan and bring to a boil.
2. Stir in the grated orange rind and pour into dessert dishes.

5 ½-cup servings

BRANDIED CHERRY FLUFF

Whenever I serve this beautiful and rich-tasting dessert I get requests for the recipe. Here it is.

1 1-pound can or jar pitted sweet cherries in syrup (if you can find only the un-pitted cherries, remove the pits)
1 3-ounce package cherry gelatin

¼ cup brandy
½ cup skimmed evaporated milk, or ⅓ cup dry powdered milk plus enough water to make ½ cup milk, chilled

1. For faster whipping, pour milk into a medium bowl and chill it in the freezer until crystals begin to form.
2. Drain the cherries and save the syrup. If necessary, add water to the syrup to make 1 cup of liquid.
3. Bring the syrup to a boil and dissolve the cherry gelatin in it. Let cool and stir in the brandy. Refrigerate until slightly thickened. Stir in the cherries.
4. Whip the chilled skimmed milk with an electric beater until it is very thick and stands in peaks.
5. Fold ⅓ of the whipped milk into the gelatin mixture. Then fold in the remaining whipped milk. Pour into a 5-cup mold or individual dessert dishes. Refrigerate until firm.

For a slightly stronger brandy flavor, soak the drained cherries in ⅓ cup brandy for at least an hour, or overnight. Drain and use the brandy in the gelatin as above.

6 servings

LEMON-PINEAPPLE CHIFFON

This light, refreshing dessert is a favorite with my family and friends. If you want to serve it as filling for a pre-baked pie shell, use 2 envelopes of unflavored gelatin.

3 egg whites
1 No. 2 can crushed pineapple, unsweetened
1 envelope unflavored gelatin

1 teaspoon grated lemon rind
3 tablespoons fresh lemon juice
6 tablespoons sugar

1. Separate the egg whites and set them aside in a medium bowl to come to room temperature.
2. Drain the crushed pineapple and save the juice. If necessary, add water to the juice to give 1 cup of liquid.
3. Pour the juice into a small saucepan. Sprinkle the gelatin over the juice and allow to soften for about 5 minutes. Slowly bring the mixture to a boil and stir to dissolve the gelatin.
4. Pour the gelatin mixture into a large bowl. Stir in the lemon rind, lemon juice and 3 tablespoons of sugar. Refrigerate until slightly jelled. Stir in the crushed pineapple.
5. Beat the egg whites until frothy. Gradually add the remaining 3 tablespoons sugar and continue beating until the egg whites are very thick and glossy. Fold ⅓ of the egg whites into the pineapple mixture. Then fold in the remaining egg whites. Pour into a serving bowl or 6 dessert dishes. Refrigerate until firm.

6 servings

RASPBERRY SNOW

Few people will guess that the tartness in this dish comes from cranberry juice and the richness from skimmed milk. I have Rebecca Maciel, dessert chef at a New Hampshire country inn, to thank for the original recipe, from which this is a low-cholesterol adaptation.

1 3-ounce package raspberry Jello	¾ cup ice-cold evaporated skimmed milk or ½ cup
1½ cups cranberry juice	powdered skimmed milk plus enough water to give ¾ cup milk

1. Dissolve the raspberry jello in 1½ cups boiling cranberry juice in a very large bowl. Let cool and refrigerate until partially jelled. Beat at high speed with an electric mixer until fluffy and about double in volume.
2. Chill the skimmed milk until crystals begin to form around the edges. Beat it at high speed with an electric mixer until it is very thick and stands in peaks when the beater is removed. The skimmed milk increases about 5-6 times in volume with beating, so be sure to start with an adequate-sized bowl.
3. Fold the whipped skimmed milk into the whipped jello with a very large spoon. Refrigerate until firm, or spoon into individual dessert dishes and then refrigerate.

8-10 servings

COFFEE WHIP

In case you've ever wondered what to do with leftover coffee, try this recipe. It might even seduce you into purposely making too much coffee. Dieters can replace the sugar with artificial sweetener.

1½ cups strong coffee	¼ teaspoon vanilla
1 tablespoon unflavored gelatin	¼ teaspoon almond extract
¼ cup sugar	⅓ cup dry powdered milk
	⅓ cup ice water

1. Sprinkle the gelatin on ½ cup coffee in a small saucepan. Allow to soften about 5 minutes. Slowly bring to a boil and stir to dissolve the gelatin.
2. Add the remaining coffee, sugar, vanilla and almond extract. Stir well until the sugar is dissolved. Refrigerate in a medium-large bowl until the mixture just starts to jell.
3. For somewhat faster whipping, chill the blended powdered milk and ice water in a bowl in the freezer until crystals form at edges. Whip with an electric beater until the mixture is very thick and stands in peaks. Fold ⅓ of the whipped milk into the gelatin mixture. Then fold in the remaining ⅔. Refrigerate until firm.

6 servings

COFFEE PUDDING

Hardly anyone will guess that this rich, creamy and unusual-tasting dessert is basically cottage cheese. Start out with the smaller amount of instant coffee and add more to taste.

8 ounces dry or low-fat cottage cheese
3 tablespoons sugar
2 tablespoons Sabra or coffee liqueur

2 tablespoons skimmed milk
½-1 teaspoon instant coffee granola or toasted slivered almonds for garnish (optional)

1. Put all the ingredients into a blender container. Blend until very smooth and no trace of the grainy texture of the cottage cheese remains. Add more milk if necessary.
2. Pour into dessert dishes and chill. Garnish with granola or toasted slivered almonds, if desired.

2-4 servings

HOT FUDGE PUDDING

Variations of this recipe keep cropping up in magazines, newspapers, and friends' recipe files. Its popularity is well deserved. The batter rises to form a cake with a fudge sauce underneath. Try this version some winter evening for chocolate-lovers you know.

1 cup flour
3 tablespoons cocoa
2 teaspoons baking powder
¾ teaspoon salt
½ cup sugar
½ cup skimmed milk or water
2 tablespoons oil

1 teaspoon vanilla
½ cup chopped walnuts (optional)
½ cup firmly packed brown sugar
¼ cup cocoa
1⅔ cups boiling water

1. Stir the flour, cocoa, baking powder, salt, and sugar together. Stir in the milk or water, oil, vanilla, and nuts. Spoon the batter into an 8- or 9-inch oiled baking pan.
2. Sprinkle the brown sugar and ¼ cup cocoa over the batter. Pour the boiling water on top of everything. Bake at 350° for 40 minutes.

6-8 servings

BUTTERSCOTCH-BROWNIE PUDDING

Rebecca Maciel was kind enough to suggest proportions for this recipe which should please people with a sweet tooth.

1 cup flour
1 tablespoon baking powder
½ teaspoon salt
1¼-1½ cups brown sugar, firmly packed

2 tablespoons oil or melted margarine
½ cup milk or water
1 teaspoon vanilla
¼ cup chopped walnuts
1⅓ cups boiling water

1. Stir the flour, baking powder, salt, and ½ cup brown sugar together. Add the oil or margarine, milk or water, and vanilla, and mix until thoroughly blended.
2. Spread the batter in a greased 8-inch square pan. Sprinkle with nuts and the remaining ¾-1 cup brown sugar. Pour boiling water over all.
3. Bake at 375° for ½ hour. Serve hot or warm.

6-8 servings

MERINGUES

Meringues readily absorb moisture from the air and lose their crispness so they should be eaten soon after they're made. Some food stores carry prepared meringues which you might also want to try. Since meringues are basically egg whites and sugar, you don't have to worry about their saturated-fat or cholesterol content.

4 egg whites at room temperature	⅔ cup sugar
¼ teaspoon cream of tartar	½ teaspoon almond extract or vanilla

1. Beat the egg whites to soft peaks with the salt and cream of tartar. Add the sugar gradually and continue beating until stiff peaks form. Beat in the almond extract or vanilla.
2. Form 8 meringues on baking sheets lined with brown paper. Use a pastry bag if you have one or just the back of a large spoon to shape 4-inch meringue shells with walls about 1-inch high and a depression in the center for filling.
3. Bake at 275° for 1½ hours or until the meringues are crisp and dry. Turn the oven off and let the meringues cool in the closed oven for 1-2 hours.

8 meringues

Serve with:

hot or cold Fresh Blueberry Sauce
Cherries Jubilee
sliced fresh fruit topped with Melba Sauce (see Poached Pears)
hot or cold Cranberry-Sherry Relish
canned pie filling flavored with brandy

DESSERT CRÊPES

Just because this has the reputation of being the queen of all desserts, don't let it frighten you. Approached casually, it can be fun to prepare as well as to eat. A special crêpe pan would certainly be useful, but I don't have one and get perfectly good results in a 9-inch Teflon frying pan. I use the same batter for crêpes as for blintzes. The crêpes can be stored wrapped in foil or plastic wrap in the refrigerator or freezer. I don't bother putting waxed paper or some other material in between the crêpes and I've never had difficulty separating them.

Batter

1 cup flour
2 tablespoons sugar
½ teaspoon salt
1 teaspoon grated orange rind (optional but very good)

3 egg whites
1¼ cups milk
2 tablespoons oil

1. Stir the flour, sugar, and salt together. Beat the orange rind, egg whites, milk, and oil together lightly and stir into the flour mixture. Beat with an electric beater at low or medium speed until smooth.
2. Brush a Teflon frying pan or crêpe pan with 1 tablespoon of oil. Warm over medium heat. Pour in 2-3 tablespoons of batter. Quickly tilt the pan to spread the batter thinly in all directions. Cook until the top surface of the pancake is set and the underside is light brown around the edges. Turn and cook briefly on the other side. Add a very small amount of oil to the pan after each crêpe is removed. Cook the remaining batter the same way. Stack the completed crêpes on top of each other. The first crêpe rarely comes out satisfactorily. Don't be discouraged. Persevere.

12-14 crêpes

CRÊPES WITH ORANGE SAUCE

½ cup margarine
½ cup sugar
2-4 teaspoons grated orange rind

2 tablespoons Cointreau or Triple Sec
2-3 tablespoons chopped almonds (optional)
⅓ cup orange juice

1. Cream the margarine, sugar and orange rind. Blend in the liqueur and chopped almonds if desired. Spread about 1 teaspoon of this mixture onto the side of each crêpe that was browned last. Roll up each crêpe into a cylinder.
2. Place the rolled crêpes in a greased baking dish.
3. Heat the remaining margarine mixture with the orange juice in a small saucepan. Spoon the sauce over the crêpes.
4. Warm the crêpes in a 350° oven for about 7-10 minutes. Serve 2 crêpes to each person, spooning the sauce over the crêpes.

6-7 servings

Variations
Spread the crêpes with your favorite jelly or preserves. Roll up the crêpes or fold in quarters. Place in a greased baking dish or chafing dish and heat through with any of the following sauces:
Fresh Blueberry Sauce
Cherries Jubilee
applesauce flavored with rum
canned cherry pie filling flavored with brandy
defrosted frozen strawberries and sliced bananas
            (my 11-year-old's favorite)
Cranberry-Sherry Relish

FRESH BLUEBERRY SAUCE

This sauce is delicious hot or cold over meringues, crêpes, angel food cake, ices, or fruit.

2 cups berries
½ cup water
6 tablespoons sugar
4 teaspoons cornstarch

1-1½ teaspoons grated lemon rind
3-4 teaspoons fresh lemon juice

1. Stir the berries, water, sugar and cornstarch together in a small pot. Slowly bring to a boil, stirring. Simmer a few minutes until thick and clear.
2. Remove from the heat and stir in the lemon rind and lemon juice.

About 1½ cups

CHERRIES JUBILEE

This festive and showy dessert sauce is much easier to prepare than one might expect. Serve it on meringues, crêpes, ices or plain cake.

1 1-pound jar or can dark sweet pitted cherries (if you can find only unpitted sweet cherries, remove the pits)
1½ tablespoons cornstarch

1 tablespoons sugar or 2 tablespoons currant jelly
½ teaspoon grated lemon rind
¼ cup brandy

1. Drain the juice from the cherries into an attractive pan or chafing dish. Stir in the cornstarch and sugar or currant jelly. Slowly bring to a boil, stirring. Simmer a few minutes until clear and thickened. Add the cherries and heat through.
2. Warm the brandy in a small pot and add it to the cherries all in one spot. Ignite the brandy. (For absolutely foolproof ignition, light the brandy while it's still in the small pot and pour it immediately over the cherries.) Stir the sauce around gently until the flames die out. Serve hot.

About 2 cups

BANANA ICE

A delicious ice with a strong fruit flavor. The egg whites are beaten before beating the partially frozen banana mixture, to avoid having to wash the beaters twice.

¾ cup sugar
1¾ cups warm water
3 very ripe medium-sized bananas, mashed

¼ cup fresh lemon juice
2 egg whites at room temperature

1. Add ½ cup plus 2 tablespoons of sugar to the water and stir to dissolve.
2. Mix together the sugar mixture, mashed bananas and lemon juice. Pour into a 9-inch square metal pan or 2 metal ice cube trays. Freeze until a ½-inch periphery is firm. Transfer to a large bowl and refrigerate while doing Step 3.
3. Beat the egg whites until frothy. Gradually add the remaining 2 tablespoons of sugar and continue beating until thick and glossy.
4. Beat the partially frozen banana mixture until fluffy.
5. Fold ⅓ of the beaten egg whites into the banana mixture. Then fold in the remaining egg whites. Return to the

metal pan or ice cube trays and freeze until firm. Remove from freezer about 5 minutes before serving.

6-8 servings

CANTELOUPE ICE

This natural-tasting fruit ice is a favorite of my family. It was suggested to me by my friend, Shirley Roth. Weight watchers can omit the sugar for a very low-calorie dessert. One medium canteloupe has only 120 calories.

1 small or medium-sized ripe   2 tablespoons sugar or to
  canteloupe   taste

1. Cut the canteloupe in half and remove the seeds. Cut into slices. Remove the peel.
2. Dice the canteloupe pulp and purée in a blender or food mill.
3. Stir in sugar and freeze in a small shallow metal pan such as an 8-inch pie plate. Allow to soften briefly before serving.

4 servings

ORANGE-YOGURT SHERBET

This tart sherbet is a perfect summer dessert and is very easy to make. Allow it to soften briefly at room temperature before serving.

2 egg whites
1 cup yogurt
1 6-ounce can frozen orange or pineapple-orange juice concentrate, partially defrosted

2 teaspoons grated orange rind
2 tablespoons sugar or to taste

1. Separate the egg whites and set them aside.
2. Stir the yogurt, juice and orange rind together until well blended. Pour into a shallow metal pan (8-inch square is fine) and freeze until about a ½-inch periphery is firm. Refrigerate while doing step 3.
3. Beat the egg whites until thick. Gradually add the sugar and continue beating until the egg whites are thick and glossy.
4. Turn the partially frozen sherbet out into a large bowl and beat until thick and smooth. Fold in ⅓ of the beaten egg whites and then fold in the remaining egg whites. Return to the metal pan and freeze until firm.

6-8 servings

PINEAPPLE-ORANGE ICE

No one will guess that the creaminess in this tart ice comes from Cream of Rice. Vary the kinds of juices to get different flavors.

1 6-ounce can frozen orange juice concentrate
1½ cans water
2 cups pineapple juice
¼ cup sugar or to taste

¼ cup quick-cooking Cream of Rice
1 teaspoon grated orange rind

1. Mix the orange juice, water, pineapple juice, and sugar in a pot. Bring to a boil and slowly add the Cream of Rice, constantly stirring. Cook another minute and continue stir-

ring. Remove from the heat; cover and let stand 3 minutes. Stir in the orange rind.

2. Whirl in a blender until completely smooth and no trace of graininess remains. Pour into a 9-inch square metal pan or 2 metal ice cube trays. Freeze until firm around the edges.

4. Turn out into a large bowl and beat until thick and fluffy. Return to the pan or ice cube trays and freeze until firm. Remove from the freezer at least 5 minutes before serving.

6-8 servings

WHIPPED TOPPING

For best results, prepare this topping just before using. It will need rewhipping if allowed to stand too long.

Either:
⅓ cup skimmed-milk powder and
⅓ cup ice water or fruit juice
Or
½ cup evaporated skimmed milk

1½-2 tablespoons sugar
½ teaspoon vanilla
½ teaspoon lemon juice (optional)

1. Mix the skimmed-milk powder and water or juice in a bowl. Chill the mixture, or the evaporated milk, in the freezer until crystals just begin to form around the edges.
2. Whip with an electric beater on high speed until stiff. Beat in the sugar, vanilla, and lemon juice if desired.

About 1½ cups

PASSOVER DISHES

Passover may seem an unsurmountable challenge to low-cholesterol cooking when one thinks of those 9- or 12-egg sponge cakes and other egg-laden Passover dishes. This chapter, however, is the product of much experimentation and should get you through Passover with compliments.

When approaching Passover cooking, the first thing to remember is that many year-round dishes are acceptable during Passover, i.e., Orange-Honey Chicken, most salads, most gelatin desserts when made with gelatin certified for Passover use. Walnut or Pecan Macaroons and Almond Kisses do not have to be modified for Passover. Second, many recipes can easily be adapted for Passover by substituting peanut oil for corn oil, potato starch for cornstarch (Veal Tzimmes, for example), and matzo meal for bread crumbs (e.g., Sautéed Chicken Breasts).

While peanut oil doesn't have as high a concentration of polyunsaturated fatty acids as corn oil or safflower oil, I use it without qualms during Passover.

	saturated	mono-unsaturated	polyunsaturated
Peanut	18	47	29
corn	10	28	53
safflower	8	15	72

MATZO-MEAL PANCAKES

My sons pays these pancakes the ultimate compliment of saying that they taste just like "regular" pancakes. Served sprinkled with sugar or spread with preserves, they make a Passover breakfast you'll want to have again next year.

1 cup matzo meal	3 egg whites
2 tablespoons sugar	1 cup milk
½ teaspoon salt	oil for frying

1. Stir the matzo meal, sugar and salt together. Beat in the egg whites and milk until thoroughly mixed.
2. Heat 2 tablespoons oil in a 9-inch frying pan. Drop the batter by heaping tablespoonfuls into the oil. Fry until golden brown. Turn and fry the other side until golden brown, adding more oil as needed. If the batter thickens with standing, stir in a little more milk.

16 3-inch pancakes

MATZO-MEAL MUFFINS

These muffins are an excellent choice for lunches or snacks outside the home since they don't crumble like matzo. I always prepare at least several batches during the holiday.

1½ cups matzo meal	1 cup milk or water
¾ teaspoon salt	¼ cup melted margarine or
3 tablespoons sugar	oil
3 egg whites	

1. Stir the matzo meal, salt and sugar together.
2. Beat the egg whites and milk or water together. Beat in the melted margarine or oil.
3. Pour the egg mixture into the matzo-meal mixture and mix thoroughly. Spoon into greased muffin tins or ungreased foil cups.
4. Bake at 350° for 30 minutes.

12 muffins

MATZO BRIE

Just because you're on a low-cholestrol diet doesn't mean that you can't enjoy a matzo brie for Passover. The onion adds an important zesty flavor to this dish.

4 egg whites
4 tablespoons skimmed milk
¾ teaspoon salt
dash pepper

1 tablespoon grated onion
2 matzos broken into 3-inch pieces
2 tablespoons margarine

1. Beat the egg whites, milk, salt, pepper and onion together.
2. Soak the matzo pieces in water for a few minutes. Drain and press dry. (I use an 8-inch square baking dish for the soaking.) Add the matzo to the beaten eggs.
3. Melt the margarine over medium heat in a 9-inch frying pan. Add the egg and matzo mixture. Fry until eggs are set on underside and then turn. Fry until egg mixture is completely set.

2-4 servings

ORANGE MATZO BRIE

Orange matzo brie has the color but not the saturated fat of matzo brie made with whole eggs. Its fruity taste is a delightful surprise to the uninitiated.

4 egg whites
3 tablespoons skimmed milk
4 teaspoons frozen orange juice concentrate
1 tablespoon grated orange rind
⅛ teaspoon salt
2 matzos broken into 3-inch pieces
2 tablespoons margarine

1. Beat the egg whites, milk, orange juice concentrate, orange rind and salt together.
2. Soak the matzo pieces in water for a few minutes. Drain and press dry. Add to the beaten eggs.
3. Melt the margarine over medium heat in a 9-inch frying pan. Add the egg and matzo mixture. Fry until the underside of the egg mixture is set and then turn. Fry until the egg mixture is completely set.

2-4 servings

MATZO BALLS (PESACH)

Our grandmothers would probably smile at the idea of putting seltzer in matzo balls but it gives the desired effect of lightness without cholesterol.

½ cup matzo meal
½ teaspoon salt
¾ teaspoon powdered instant chicken soup
dash onion powder

3 egg whites
3 tablespoons club soda (preferably cold)
2 tablespoons chopped parsley (optional)

1. Stir the dry ingredients together.
2. Very lightly stir the egg whites, club soda, and parsley (if desired) with a fork and pour over the dry ingredients. Mix well and refrigerate at least one hour.
3. Form into 8 1½-inch balls and drop into a large pot of boiling salted water.
4. Reduce heat and simmer covered for 30 minutes. Do not remove the lid during the cooking period. Remove with a slotted spoon and serve in soup.

8 matzo balls

SHARON'S CHAROSES

My sister's charoses is so good that you'll probably want to double or triple the recipe.

1 large or 2 small apples, peeled, cored and coarsely diced (about 1¼ cups)
½ cup chopped walnuts or ⅔ cup walnut pieces

4 teaspoons sugar
½ teaspoon cinnamon
1 tablespoon sweet Kosher wine

Put the apple and nuts in a wooden chopping bowl and chop until fine. Stir in the sugar, cinnamon and wine.

PASSOVER KNISHES (VERENIKES)

Although this recipe does involve a fair number of pans and bowls, I'm sure you'll find these tasty potato morsels worth the effort. Serve verenikes as a hot hors d'oeuvre, a side dish, or a main dish with green vegetables.

Filling

¾ cup diced cooked chicken
½ cup diced onion
1 tablespoon oil

½ teaspoon salt
1-2 tablespoons egg white

Potato Shell

1 pound potatoes
½ teaspoon salt
dash pepper

1 egg white
2 tablespoons matzo meal

1. Sauté the diced onion in oil until soft, about 10 minutes. Transfer to a chopping bowl, add the chicken and chop until fine. Stir in the salt and enough egg white to bind the mixture. Set aside.
2. Peel, boil and mash the potatoes. Mix in the salt, pepper, egg white and matzo meal.
3. Place about 3 tablespoonfuls of the potato mixture into the palm of your hand. Make a depression in the center and fill with about one teaspoonful of filling. Bring the edges of the potato up and around the filling to completely cover the filling. Flatten into a patty.
4. Brown the patties on both sides in hot oil. Drain on paper towels. Serve hot.

9 3-inch knishes

APPLE MATZO-FARFEL PUDDING

A perfect side dish for any Passover meal. Tastes very much like a noodle kugel.

3 cups matzo farfel
⅓ cup sugar
¾ teaspoon salt
1 teaspoon cinnamon
1½ cups finely diced apples

4 egg whites
1½ tablespoons oil
¾ cup raisins (optional)
¾ cup chopped walnuts (optional)

1. Cover the matzo farfel with water and soak for a few minutes. Drain well in a colander and transfer to a large bowl.
2. Stir the sugar, salt and cinnamon together and sprinkle over the farfel. Mix in the remaining ingredients.
3. Pour into a well-oiled 8-inch square baking dish, cover, and bake at 350° for 30 minutes.

6 servings

MUSHROOM MATZO-FARFEL PUDDING

A very tasty side dish which can also be used as a poultry stuffing.

½ pound mushrooms, sliced
1 celery stalk, chopped
1 medium onion, chopped
3 tablespoons oil

4 cups matzo farfel
1½ teaspoons salt
2 egg whites

1. Sauté the mushrooms, celery and onion in the oil over medium heat until soft, about 10-15 minutes.
2. Cover the matzo farfel with water, soak for a few minutes and drain well in a colander.
3. Mix the farfel, sautéed vegetables, salt and egg whites.
4. Bake in a well-greased 8-inch square baking dish, covered, at 350° for 30 minutes.

8 servings

COTTAGE CHEESE-MATZO PUDDING

This pudding has a blintz-type filling between layers of matzo and makes an excellent Passover lunch or supper.

1 pound dry or low-fat cottage cheese
4 egg whites
¼ cup sugar
½ teaspoon cinnamon
1 cup skimmed milk
3 matzos
1 tablespoon margarine

1. Mix the cottage cheese, egg whites, sugar and cinnamon together and set aside.
2. Pour the skimmed milk into an 8-inch square baking dish. Soak each matzo separately in the milk for about 2 minutes. Lift out the matzo and set aside. Save the leftover milk for addition to the pudding before baking.
3. Place one matzo in a greased 8-inch square baking dish. Pour half of the cheese mixture over it. Repeat the layering with another matzo and the rest of the cheese mixture. Top with the third matzo. Dot with small pieces of margarine.
4. Pour the milk saved from the matzo-soaking into the dish. Bake uncovered at 350° for 35-40 minutes or until the pudding is set (firm) and the top matzo is golden.

3-4 servings

COTTAGE CHEESE MATZO-FARFEL PUDDING

This Passover version of Cottage Cheese-Noodle Pudding is a favorite Passover meal for our family.

3 cups matzo farfel
2 cups water
2 cups finely chopped apples
1 teaspoon cinnamon
½ teaspoon salt
½ cup sugar

1 pound low-fat cottage cheese
3 egg whites
raisins, chopped dates chopped walnuts (optional)

1. Mix the matzo farfel and water together. Let sit for a few minutes and drain well in a colander.
2. Add the remaining ingredients to the matzo farfel and mix well.
3. Bake in a well-oiled 8-inch square baking dish, covered, at 350° for 30 minutes.

4-6 servings

PASSOVER CHICKEN À LA KING

An easy main dish casserole to lend variety to mid-week Passover meals.

3 cups matzo farfel
2 cups water
2 sprigs parsley, chopped
1 small onion, chopped
1 stalk celery, finely chopped
½ teaspoon salt

2 cups (½ pound) diced cooked chicken
2 tablespoons potato starch
2½ cups chicken broth, or 2½ cups water plus 2½ teaspoons powdered chicken soup mix

1. Mix the matzo farfel and water and let stand for a few minutes. Drain well in a colander.
2. Mix the farfel with the vegetables, salt and chicken.
3. Mix the potato starch and ¼ cup broth together in a small saucepan. Add the remaining broth. Bring to a boil, stirring, and simmer a minute or two until thickened. Stir into the farfel mixture.
4. Bake in a well-oiled 8-inch square baking dish, covered, at 350° for 30 minutes.

3-4 servings

EASY PASSOVER ORANGE CAKE

This cake takes to little time to prepare and tastes so good that you'll want to make it a Passover perennial for your family.

½ cup matzo cake meal
¼ cup potato starch
½ teaspoon salt
2 egg whites
½ cup oil

⅔ cup sugar
3-4 teaspoons grated orange rind
½ cup chopped walnuts (optional)

1. Stir the matzo cake meal, potato starch and salt together.
2. Beat the egg whites, oil, sugar and orange rind together with an electric mixer for 3 minutes. Stir in the dry ingredients until thoroughly blended. Stir in the nuts if desired.
3. Bake in a greased 8-inch square pan at 350° for 25 minutes.

8 servings

PASSOVER APPLE CRISP

Topping
6 tablespoons matzo cake meal
6 tablespoons sugar

¾ teaspoon cinnamon
2 tablespoons + 1 teaspoon oil

Filling
5 medium apples, peeled and sliced (not McIntosh)

2 tablespoons sugar

1. Stir the matzo-cake meal, 6 tablespoons sugar and cinnamon together. Stir in the oil and mix until crumbly.
2. Place the apple slices in an oiled 9-inch pie plate. Sprinkle with 2 tablespoons sugar. Sprinkle topping over the apples.
3. Bake at 350° for 40 minutes or until the apples are tender.

6 servings

PASSOVER APPLE PIE

This dessert has swirls of golden dough on top of sweetened sliced apples.

½ cup matzo cake meal
2 tablespoons potato starch
½ teaspoon salt
4 egg whites
¼ cup sugar
4 tablespoons oil

4 tablespoons orange juice
5 cups very thinly sliced apples (not McIntosh)
¼ cup sugar
1 teaspoon cinnamon

1. Stir the cake meal, potato starch and salt together.
2. Beat the egg whites, ¼ cup sugar, oil and orange juice together until thoroughly mixed. Stir in the cake-meal mixture to form a smooth batter.
3. Put the apples into a well-greased 9-inch pie pan. Stir the sugar and cinnamon together and sprinkle over the apples.
4. Spoon the batter over the apples (not all of the apples will be covered).
5. Bake at 350° on the lowest shelf of the oven for 30-35 minutes. If the topping browns before the apples are tender, cover with aluminum foil for the remainder of the baking.

6-8 servings

PASSOVER APPLE CAKE

This cake is so light and delicious that you'll forget that it's made with matzo meal. No one will miss those egg-rich sponge cakes when this dessert is served.

1 cup matzo meal
½ teaspoon salt
5 egg whites (3 in one bowl,
  2 in another)
½ cup oil

¼ cup orange juice
1 cup sugar
½ teaspoon cinnamon
4 cups thinly sliced apples
  (3-4 apples)

1. Stir the matzo meal and salt together and set aside.
2. Beat 3 egg whites until stiff and set aside.
3. Beat the remaining 2 egg whites, oil, orange juice, and ¾ cup sugar together for 5 minutes. Stir in the matzo meal until thoroughly blended. Fold in the stiffly beaten egg whites.
4. Spoon half of the batter into a greased 8-inch square pan or a greased 9-inch pan. Arrange the apples over the batter. Mix the remaining ¼ cup sugar with the cinnamon and sprinkle over the apples. Spoon the rest of the batter over the apples.
5. Bake at 375° for 35-40 minutes.

8 servings

ORANGE-NUT COOKIES

The fresh orange taste of these cookies is very tempting.

1 cup cake meal
½ teaspoon salt
6 egg whites
¾ cup sugar

⅔ cup oil
1 tablespoon grated orange
  rind
¾ cup chopped walnuts

1. Stir the cake meal and salt together and set aside.
2. Beat the egg whites, sugar, oil and rind together until thoroughly mixed. Blend in the cake meal. Stir in the nuts.
3. Drop by teaspoonfuls onto greased cookie sheets. Bake at 375° for 15 minutes. If crisper, flatter cookies are desired, flatten the teaspoonfuls of batter with the bottom of a glass dipped in sugar and bake for about 12 minutes.

50 cookies

MOCK OATMEAL COOKIES

A very good, very easy cookie which will not last very long in any household.

1 cup matzo meal
1 cup matzo farfel
⅔ cup sugar
¾ teaspoon cinnamon

¾ teaspoon salt
3 egg whites
⅓ cup oil

1. Stir all the dry ingredients together. Add the egg whites and oil and mix until thoroughly blended.
2. Drop by teaspoonfuls onto well-greased cookie sheets. Bake in the top of the oven at 350° for 20 minutes. Remove at once from cookie sheet.

36 cookies

PASSOVER BROWNIES

Chocolate lovers will appreciate this Passover treat.

½ cup matzo cake meal
¼ teaspoon salt
6 tablespoons cocoa
2 egg whites

⅔ cup sugar
½ cup oil
½ cup chopped walnuts

1. Stir the cake meal, salt, and cocoa together.
2. Beat the egg whites, sugar and oil together lightly. Stir the

cocoa mixture into the egg white mixture and mix until thoroughly blended. Stir in the nuts.
3. Bake in a greased 8-inch square pan at 350° for 20-25 minutes.

16 2-inch brownies

COMPANY MENUS

Entertaining

One of my great pleasures is having people come to visit, chat, and eat. Since I like to entertain frequently and I have a busy life otherwise, I try to make entertaining as simple and easy as possible.

It's not necessary to prepare elaborate, time-consuming dishes for company. In fact, guests may enjoy themselves more if they don't feel that you've spent days in the kitchen on their behalf. An uncomplicated but delicious cake will be enjoyed as much as the most involved torte. And you'll probably want to have company more often if it doesn't mean a great deal of work.

Advance planning and organization are the keys to successful entertaining. (I'm studying city planning and a motto in our kitchen is: "If you can plan a seder, you can plan a city.") Planning can help avoid a frantic last-minute rush and can give your entertaining the smoothness which makes you and your guests feel comfortable. I advise making a list of all the tasks involved in having company, such as food shopping, food preparation, checking silver, table linens, sugar bowls, etc., even filling the coffee pot. Then decide what can be done when, and leave as little for the last minute as possible. Take advantage of the fact that many foods can be frozen or prepared a day or two ahead and refrigerated.

I always keep tomato juice and low-calorie drinks on hand since dieters may prefer them to cocktails. In my experience, guests appreciate being directed to specific seats at the dinner table, so I usually have a seating arrangement in mind.

Just because company is coming is no reason to drop one's low-cholesterol eating pattern. Most people, in fact, won't even be aware that the food is low-cholesterol unless the topic is brought up in conversation. Our friends show no reluctance to accept our dinner invitations because low-cholesterol food will be served.

Whatever your favorite style of entertaining—brunch, coffee and cake, cocktail party, buffet, barbecue, sit-down dinner, holiday celebration—it can be carried out with great success with low-cholesterol food. Go ahead and see for yourself.

Menu Planning

Menu planning is a skill which involves many different considerations. First, we want our meals to provide all of the required nutrients. To assure this, foods should be carefully selected from the four basic food groups: the Meat Group which includes meat, poultry, fish, eggs, dry beans, dry peas, and nuts; the Vegetable-Fruit Group; the Milk Group; and the Bread-Cereal Group. Very briefly, our daily diet should include at least two servings from the Meat Group, four servings from the Vegetable-Fruit Group, with one dark green or yellow vegetable and one citrus fruit or tomato, two or more glasses of milk for adults, and four servings from the Bread-Cereal Group.*

Wise menu planning uses foods which are in season when they are most flavorful and cheapest. A seasonal awareness of food can greatly heighten one's eating pleasure. For example, there is simply no comparison between fresh and canned asparagus or between tomatoes in January and in August.

Successful menu planning achieves a balance between contrasting flavors and textures. Try to combine strong-tasting dishes with mild ones, crunchy dishes with smooth ones. With a substantial main dish, serve a light dessert. With a hearty soup, serve a light main course. Try to avoid similarities be-

* For a clear discussion of food nutrients and recommended amounts for inclusion in the diet, I suggest a booklet, *Family Fare, A Guide To Good Nutrition*, Home and Garden Bulletin No. 1, U.S. Department of Agriculture. It can be purchased for 45¢ from the Superintendent of Documents, U.S. Government Printing Office, Washington, D.C. 20402.

tween courses such as "cream" soup with a "creamed" main dish.

Despite the extra dishes, I like to include a number of separate courses in dinners I prepare. Even if the appetizer and dessert are just fresh fruit in season (which is what I generally serve for my family meals), I think that they help to make a meal more of a special event to be leisurely enjoyed. I always include a salad with my dinners and frequently pass around a plate of crunchy raw vegetables.

The physical presentation of food should not be neglected when planning menus. Food should be appealing to the eye as well as to the palate. Often a simple garnish such as a few parsley sprigs or slices of tomato can make a dish much more visually attractive.

For company menus, I think it's wise to plan the meal to suit the guest. Dieters will appreciate a low-calorie meal. People who are not adventurous in their choice of foods will appreciate a simple meal. Guests who enjoy different or unusual foods may appreciate sampling foods from foreign cuisines.

Following are some simple menus which I have enjoyed. These are intended mainly as suggestions to stimulate your own imagination. I've included a large number of recipes in this book in order to provide a wide selection of acceptable foods. I hope that you will experiment and choose the flavor and texture combinations which you find most appealing.

HOLIDAY MENUS

Rosh Hashanah I

Challah
Apple Slices and Honey
Gefilte Fish or Sweet and Sour Fish
Chicken Soup With Kreplach
Chicken Jubilee or Cranberry Veal Roast
Spiced Orange Rice or Apricot Kugel
Green Salad
Honey Cake   Taglach

Rosh Hashanah II

Challah
Apple Slices and Honey
Celery Stalks filled with either Curried-Chicken Spread or
      Chopped Chicken with Pineapple
Chicken Soup
Orange-Honey Chicken
Potato Kugel
Carrot Tzimmes
Green Salad or Spinach Salad
Pineapple & Raspberry Macédoine
Mandel Brot   Almond Macaroons

Succot or Rosh Hashanah Open House

Sliced Apples and Honey
Honey Cake
Taiglach
Mandel Brot
Holiday Sugar Cookies

Almond Macaroons
Walnut or Pecan Macaroons
Cottage Cheese Rugelach
Sweet Kosher Wine

Chanukah

Tahini, Baba Ganoush, or Hummus
Pita Bread
Potato Latkes
Cottage Cheese Pancakes or Cottage Cheese-Applesauce Pancakes
Applesauce
Three-Bean Salad or Grapefruit-Gelatin Salad
Holiday Sugar Cookies
Honey Cake or Cupcakes decorated with Blue and White Frosting

Purim Seudah

Chopped Chicken with Pineapple
Celery Stalks
Challah
Chicken with Orange Stuffing
Herbed Green Beans
Mixed Green Salad or Haman Salad
Hamantaschen   Mohn Cookies

Passover Seder Dinner

Charoses
Gefilte Fish or Sweet and Sour Salmon or Halibut
Chicken Soup with Matzo Balls
Veal Roast or Roast Turkey or Roast Chicken
Apple or Mushroom Matzo-Farfel Pudding or Verenikes
Carrot Tzimmes
Spinach and Orange Salad
Passover Apple Cake or Fresh Fruit Cup and Almond Kisses

Passover Dairy Family Dinner

Fruit Cup

Cottage Cheese-Matzo Pudding or Cottage Cheese-Matzo-
 Farfel Pudding
Matzo-Meal Muffins
Asparagus Vinaigrette (if in season) or Broccoli and Onion
 Salad
Baked Apples and Mock Oatmeal Cookies

Shavuot

Challah
Cold Borscht or Strawberry-Pineapple Soup
Sweet-and-Sour Fish or Herring-Cranberry Surprise
Blintzes with sweetened berries and yogurt
Green Salad with Honey-Lemon Dressing
Cheesecake

Thanksgiving

Roasted Chestnuts
Fruit Cup
Roast Turkey
Sweet Potatoes and Apples or Sweet Potatoes and Pineapple
Spinach with Garlic
Pumpkin or Cranberry Bread
Cranberry-Pineapple Salad or one of the cranberry relishes
Basic Apple Cake or Pumpkin Spice Cake

COMPANY MENUS

Hot Weather Luncheon

Melon
Tuna or Salmon Mousse with lettuce and tomatoes, or Se-
 viche, or Mimi's Tuna-Chick Pea Salad
Baking Powder Biscuits
Fresh Strawberry Pie or Strawberry-Rhubarb Chiffon Pie

Cold Weather Luncheon

Cream of Cauliflower Soup
Spinach-Cottage Cheese Pie
Herbed-Carrots Salad
Peach Crisp or Baked Apple

Company Fish Dinner (Hot Weather)

Cottage Cheese Pastries
Blueberry or Plum Soup
Fish Fillets Véronique
Bulgur Pilaf
Sautéed Zucchini
Cucumbers with Dill
Brandied-Cherry Fluff or Lemon-Pineapple Chiffon

Company Fish Dinner (Cold Weather)

Filo Pastry Hors D'Oeuvres
Carrot Soup
Scrod with Walnut Sauce
Oriental Broccoli
Orange-Nut Bread
Green Salad
Apricot-Flavored Pears or Apple Crisp

FAMILY MENUS

Family Shabbat Dinner

Challah
Chicken Soup with Kreplach or Matzo Balls
Crispy Baked Chicken
Carrot Kugel
Green Beans with Garlic

Green Salad
Apple Crisp with Oatmeal Topping

Family Fish Dinner

Split-Pea Soup
Oven-Fried Fish
Cous Cous
Sautéed Green Peppers or Italian Roast Peppers
Cole Slaw
Raspberry Snow

Family Dairy Dinner

Fresh Fruit Cup
Applesauce-Cottage Cheese-Noodle Pudding or Lasagne, or
  "American Chop Suey"
Green Salad
Sliced Raw Vegetables
Brownies or Peanut Butter Cookies

Breakfast

Fresh Fruit Salad
Granola and Milk
Pancakes, or French Toast, or Puffy Orange Omelet and
    Muffins
Coffee   Milk

FOREIGN MENUS

Oriental-Style Dinner

Chicken-Watercress Soup
Teriyaki Chicken
Oriental Cauliflower or Bean Curd with Mushroom and Scal-
    lions

Rice
Bean-Sprout Salad
Mandarin-Orange Cake

Middle Eastern-Style Dinner

Tahini, or Baba Ganoush, or Hummus
Pita Bread
Lentil Soup II
Middle Eastern-Style Veal Stew or Chicken with Middle
    Eastern Spices
Rice with Turmeric
Green Salad
Mixed-Dried-Fruit Compote
Date Bars

Indian-Style Dinner

Indian Potato Fritters
Curried Tuna
Rice
Green Salad
Orange Tapioca Pudding
Walnut-Brandy Cookies

Italian-Style Dinner

Marinated Mushrooms
Zucchini Soup
Italian-Style Veal Stew
Spaghetti or Baked Eggplant Slices
Italian Bread
Green Salad with Italian Dressing or White-Kidney-Bean
    Salad
Banana or Canteloupe Ice
Mandel Brot or Almond Kisses

SUGGESTIONS FOR BUFFET DINNERS

All of the following dishes can be easily eaten without a knife, balanced on a person's lap.

Chicken or Turkey Tetrazzini
Chicken à la King
Veal Tzimmes or any of the veal-stew dishes
Spinach-Veal Meat Loaf
Sweet and Sour Meatballs
Veal Meatballs
Mushroom Cutlets
Mushroom- or Spinach-Soy Grits Loaf
Any of the soy bean dishes
Any of the cottage cheese-noodle casseroles
Fish in "Egg" Lemon Sauce
Smoked Cod in Cream Sauce
Curried Tuna

SUGGESTIONS FOR LEFTOVERS

Vegetables

Russian Salad
Additions to "Cream" Sauce for Poached Fish
Canned corn in Corn Fritters

Chicken

Curried-Chicken Spread
Chopped Chicken with Pineapple
Chicken à La King

Chicken Tetrazzini
Chicken Salad

Fish

Mock Shrimp Salad
Mock Lobster Salad
With "Cream" Sauce for Poached Fish

Macaroni

Tuna-Tomato-Macaroni Salad
Chicken-Macaroni Salad
Macaroni and Cheese

Applesauce

Applesauce Cake
Cottage-Cheese-Applesauce Pancakes
Sherried Applesauce Gel

Coffee

Coffee Whip

Appendix

Fatty Acid Composition of Selected Foods

Food	Serving Size	Saturated	Oleic (mono-unsaturated)	Linoleic (poly-unsaturated)
Whole milk, 3.5% fat	1 cup	5	3	trace
Cottage cheese, creamed	1 cup	6	3	trace
Cottage cheese, uncreamed	1 cup	trace	trace	trace
Cream cheese	3 ounces	18	11	1
Pasteurized process American cheese	1 ounce	5	3	trace
Ice milk	1 cup	4	2	trace
Eggs	1 large	2	3	trace
Lean beef steak, broiled, lean only	2.4 ounces	2	2	trace
Chicken, broiled, flesh only	3 ounces	1	1	1
Lamb chop, broiled, lean only	2.6 ounces	3	2	trace
Salmon, pink, canned	3 ounces	1	1	trace
Almonds, shelled, whole kernels	1 cup	6	52	15
Coconut, shredded or grated	1 cup	39	3	trace
Peanuts, roasted, salted, halves	1 cup	16	31	36
Walnuts, black or native, chopped	1 cup	4	26	21

Fatty Acid Composition of Selected Foods (Cont.)

| Food | Serving Size | Saturated | Fatty Acids (in grams) Unsaturated | |
			Oleic (mono-unsaturated)	Linoleic (poly-unsaturated)
Avocado, California, 3⅛-inch diameter	1 avocado	7	17	5
White bread, enriched, firm crumb type	1 pound loaf	4	10	2
Whole wheat bread, firm crumb type	1 pound loaf	3	6	3
Butter	1 cup (½-pound)	102	60	6
Corn oil	1 cup	22	62	117
Cottonseed oil	1 cup	55	46	110
Olive oil	1 cup	24	167	15
Peanut oil	1 cup	40	103	64
Safflower oil	1 cup	18	37	165
Soybean oil	1 cup	33	44	114
Mayonnaise	1 tablespoon	2	2	6

Obtained from the Home and Garden Bulletin No. 72, U.S. Department of Agriculture, *Nutritive Value of Foods.*

EQUIVALENTS

Apples
2 pounds unpared=3 cups pared, sliced

Bananas
2 medium or 2 small=1 cup mashed

Chocolate
1 square unsweetened chocolate=3 tablespoons cocoa plus 1
    tablespoon margarine

Chicken
2 cups diced cooked=one-half pound
2 raw, boned breasts from a 1-pound chicken=one-half pound

Cottage Cheese
1 pound=2 cups

Cornstarch (for thickening)
1 tablespoon=2 tablespoons flour

Egg Whites
8 large=1 cup

Flour
1 cup cake flour=⅞ cup all-purpose

Garlic
1 clove=⅛ teaspoon garlic powder

Herbs
1 tablespoon chopped fresh = ½-1 teaspoon dried

Lemon
1 medium = 3 tablespoons juice

Milk
1 cup sour milk or buttermilk = 1 cup minus 1 tablespoon milk
    plus 1 tablespoon lemon juice or vinegar

Margarine
1 pound = 2 cups

Onion
1 medium-large = 1 cup chopped

Orange
1 medium = 6-8 tablespoons juice

Salt
1 teaspoon regular = 2½ teaspoons Kosher

Sugar
1 pound brown = 2½ cups, packed
1 pound confectioner's = 3½ cups, packed
1 pound granulated = 2 cups

Yeast
1 cake compressed = 1 package dried, reconstituted in 2 table-
    spoons water

KITCHEN EQUIPMENT

I find a brisk toothbrush very useful for cleaning strainers, colanders, graters, garlic presses, etc. My husband first suggested this piece of kitchen equipment and now I wouldn't be without it.

Wooden cutting board.

Sharp knives and a knife sharpener.

Electric blender.

Wooden chopping bowl and hand chopper—very handy for chopping cooked chicken and meat, raw mushrooms, herring, string beans, etc.

Several wire wisks of different sizes. I find a very small wisk, about 5 inches high, especially useful for mixing ingredients right in the measuring cup.

Several sets of measuring cups and spoons, conveniently located.

Hand grater with different sized cutting edges for grating onions, beets, orange or lemon rinds, etc.

Wok, if you do a lot of oriental-style cooking.

Electric mixer.

Index